VISUAL DESIGN
SOLUTIONS

VISUAL DESIGN SOLUTIONS

Principles and Creative Inspiration for Learning Professionals

CONNIE MALAMED

WILEY

Cover design and typography: Michael J. Freeland

This book is printed on acid-free paper.

Published by John Wiley & Sons, Inc., Hoboken, New Jersey

Published simultaneously in Canada

For general information about our other products and services, please contact our Customer Care Department within the United States at (800) 762-2974, outside the United States at (317) 572-3993 or fax (317) 572-4002.

Wiley publishes in a variety of print and electronic formats and by print-on-demand. Some material included with standard print versions of this book may not be included in e-books or in print-on-demand. If this book refers to media such as a CD or DVD that is not included in the version you purchased, you may download this material at http://booksupport.wiley.com. For more information about Wiley products, visit www.wiley.com.

Library of Congress Cataloging-in-Publication Data has been applied for and is on file with the Library of Congress.

ISBN 978-1-118-86356-5 (pbk)
ISBN 978-1-118-86348-0 (ebk)
ISBN 978-1-118-86404-3 (ebk)

Printed in the United States of America

SKY10077837_061824

CONTENTS

PART 4 Practicing Design

LIST OF FIGURES AND TABLES

FIGURES

TABLES

This book is dedicated
to the hard-working creative learning professionals
who want to make a difference.

PREFACE

Unlike most graphic and visual design books, this one is intended to serve learning professionals. Conventional graphic design books are brimming with insights and examples, but their lessons are focused on designing ads, brochures, logos, and posters. There are excellent principles in these books and I highly recommend starting a design book collection. But the application of commercial graphic design knowledge to learning materials only goes so far. After that, you may feel that you are on your own, flying solo.

The visual design of learning materials has a unique set of requirements compared to that of most other designed products. Although we all share the goal of content clarity, designers of learning experiences are overly concerned that their content be understood, retained, and applied to new situations while also being motivating and engaging.

Furthermore, the materials we design may be quite extensive, such as for a substantial eLearning course, an online learning portal, or a slide set for a full day of training. Our materials might also be interactive, which presents a new set of design issues. Unlike many graphic design studios involved in branding and advertising, we may not have the latitude to innovate as much as we would like. We must ensure that we are true to our highest priority, which is clear communication.

If you are like most learning designers, you have little to no background in visual design. Yet you wear many hats and are often responsible for the visual communication aspect of your materials—whether you create them yourself or collaborate with others. Without the appropriate foundation knowledge, it can be difficult to make the best visual design choices. This book presents a rationale for why you should intensely care about visual design. It presents core principles that will give your work the greatest impact in the least amount of time and provides practical ideas and inspiration for solving visual design challenges.

This book does not teach you how to produce graphics, nor does it promote a particular software package. Many of the suggestions and approaches can be performed with the graphics or slide creation program of your choice. Start with one that is easy to learn and move on to a program with advanced functionality when you need more power. You can make great improvements by applying the foundation principles of visual design, regardless of what program you use.

INTRODUCTION

If I could be anything right at this moment, it would be a good fairy whispering encouraging thoughts in your ear. I'd be hovering over your shoulder every time you embarked on a visual design task. "You'll find a good solution," I would whisper. "Play with your design and see what you discover."

I would snuff out that little discouraging voice in your head. You know the one. It's the voice that replays the disparaging comment from an insensitive adult long ago, "Is that a tree or a person?" It's the voice of that relative who proclaimed that no one in the family is creative. It's the story you tell yourself as you compare your talents to those of accomplished artists.

Now is the time to reject those defeating ideas. Why let them follow you through adulthood like an anchor around your neck? When you toss away those negative thoughts, you make room for the pure creativity that pulsed through you as a child. It's still there—somewhere inside.

Don't make the mistake of confusing drawing skills for design skills. The truth is, visual design has little to do with the ability to render. To improve at design, you need to know some basic principles of visual communication. You need to make a commitment to explore and practice so you will develop competence. And you need a heightened sensitivity to seeing design in the world around you—to fine-tune your perceptions.

The fact that you are reading this book is a statement about yourself. You are hoping to gain proficiency in visual design and you have started on the path. Even if you are reading this for a required course, you will appreciate gaining competence in this realm. Who wouldn't? In today's multimedia world, the ability to visually communicate is a necessary and powerful skill.

Think of reading this book as one step in the right direction. This is only a part of your remarkable journey. You will need to continue to learn, practice, and discover. Improving your design skills and abilities is a lifelong endeavor.

May you find enjoyment and success on your path.

Connie Malamed

THE BIG IDEAS

Growing into the role of a designer means seeing, thinking, and working like one. This section describes the impact of visual design and how to embrace the role of the designer.

Like a Hand in Glove

"The need for clear and imaginative communication has never been greater."
— Phillip B. Meggs

THE FRAMEWORK

THIS CHAPTER answers these questions:

- Why do visuals benefit learning?
- How can I use visuals to improve learning?
- What is the impact of visual design on learning?

Learning design and visual design go together like a hand in glove. They are a perfect fit for each other, yet it's rare to hear the terms spoken in the same breath. Even those who acknowledge that graphics are essential for learning may not be aware of the reverberations that visual design has throughout a learning experience. Visual design affects the quality of learning, the value of the communication, and the motivation of the audience members. It leverages the brain's innate capabilities, improves engagement, and satisfies the audience's aesthetic sensibilities.

In this chapter, you'll gain a better understanding of why graphics benefit learning and how design affects the overall user experience.

THE VISUAL BRAIN

There's something special about vision. Together the eye and brain work in ways that are no less than wondrous. Consider this. Our eyes are in nearly constant movement, but we rarely notice it. We rapidly recognize objects in complex scenes regardless of their size, color, position, and rotation.

We perceive depth precisely because a different image is registered with each eye. In normal vision, we see six million different colors and lots of detail, both close up and at a distance. We see with different acuity levels depending on the task we are performing (Kosslyn, 1994). We adapt to a wide range of light intensities, so we can see at dusk and also in bright light. And all of this occurs with little to no conscious awareness.

Scientists estimate that over 50 percent of the brain's cortex (the outside layer) is involved in visual processing (Snowden & Thompson, 2012), whereas auditory processing uses around 10 percent and the other senses use even less. Thus, our brains devote more resources to vision than to any other sense.

The pure physiological power of our visual system is a compelling argument for ensuring that you take advantage of the audience's visual intelligence as you design learning experiences.

BENEFITS TO LEARNING

What happens when you look at a picture? (See Figure 1.1.) The process starts when your eyes pick up sensory data and send signals to a sensory register (also known as sensory or iconic memory). The information lasts here for less than a second and is sent to working memory. Through perceptual processes you select what to pay attention to, based on the features that catch your eye (during pre-attentive processing) and the visual patterns that are meaningful to your goals (during attentive processing).

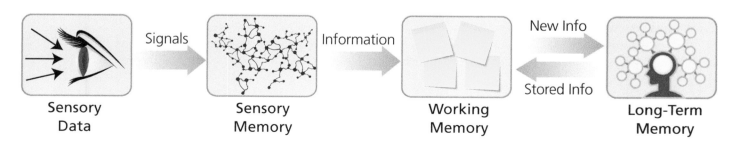

FIGURE 1.1. *How we process visual information.*

As you scan the picture, visual chunks are held in working memory for a few seconds. With help from your past experience and knowledge stored in long-term memory, you decode these marks on the screen or page. If the picture is easy to understand, this process happens rapidly. *Visual perception is faster than thinking.*

Research shows that text accompanied by relevant visuals is better for learning than text alone in many situations and under many conditions (Mayer, 2009). Pictures can strengthen visual discrimination by emphasizing important details. Visuals improve retention and aid in problem solving. Abstract visuals help people comprehend complex information and assist in building mental models. In fact, if you break the learning process down into smaller cognitive actions, you'll see that visuals can be valuable nearly every step of the way.

Pictures Capture Attention

Pictures are magnets for attention regardless of the medium. People usually look at the graphics of a web page before they read the text (Lin, Yeh, & Wei, 2013). The same is true for newspaper advertisements. Consumer research shows that pictorial ads are better at capturing attention than text ads, and this is true regardless of picture size (Goodrich, 2010; Pieters & Wedel, 2004).

In learning and information dissemination, pictures also draw attention. For example, in a study that explored the best way to convey messages about health risks, pictures attracted and held attention for a longer period of time than the same information produced in text alone (Smerecnik, Mesters, Kessels, Ruiter, De Vries, & De Vries, 2010).

Pictures of people and particularly pictures of faces summon our visual attention. Also, certain attributes capture attention without conscious awareness. Vivid colors, striking shapes, and motion capture pre-attentive attention.

Visuals Aid Recall

Encoding information in long-term memory is an essential activity of learning, and this is one more place where visuals shine. Relevant pictures help people remember corresponding text. By relevant, psychologists mean pictures that represent the objects or concepts presented in the text (Levie, 1987).

This may be due to the fact that our memory is typically better for concrete things than for abstractions. Pictures provide a concreteness—an association with a sensory experience—that has advantages over words, which are more symbolic.

Visuals Improve Comprehension

Pictures help learners understand complex text or narration because they convey information about spatial structure. We rely on the spatial structure of visuals to provide meaning. In a diagram or chart, designers use techniques that show relationships, such as placing related elements together in a group. This quickly communicates what is associated in a way that may be more difficult through text alone. The structural organization of a picture is thought to have a scaffolding effect that helps in the construction of new mental models (Eitel, 2013).

Because graphics hold attention for a longer period of time than text, researchers believe the additional attention plus the ease with which graphical information is extracted is another benefit to comprehension (Smerecnik, Mesters, Kessels, Ruiter, De Vries, & De Vries, 2010). Also, pictures can be rendered with extreme specificity. They can emphasize or exaggerate details to reduce ambiguity. This precision improves understanding.

Making Inferences

Certain types of graphics, such as information graphics, facilitate making inferences and solving problems. They function as an external memory aid by using arrangements that organize information in meaningful ways (Larkin & Simon, 1987). It is easier to make use of massive data when it is expressed as a graph. It is easier to work with a complex network of ideas when they are illustrated in a diagram.

Acquiring Skills

In terms of learning procedures, the combination of pictures and text is ideal. One study showed that line drawings and text were as effective as video when the drawings used arrows to show the actions involved in performing a simple medical procedure (Michas & Berry, 2000).

Looking at the range of cognitive tasks that adults perform, it becomes obvious that graphics support and facilitate thinking, problem solving, and learning. Regardless of whether the graphic is a simple icon, an elaborate illustration, or a complex data visualization, visuals provide a rich and textured language for expressing ideas.

THE PICTURE SUPERIORITY EFFECT

The value of visual design becomes clear when you consider the *picture superiority effect*. Several decades of research have established that in most recall and recognition memory tasks, concepts that are learned by viewing pictures are remembered better than their counterparts in words (Hockley & Bancroft, 2011). This phenomenon is known as the *picture superiority effect*.

Possible Reasons for Picture Superiority

Dual coding. Why do visuals add an element of memorability to information? One theory, known as *dual coding*, states that people process information through two distinct systems, one for verbal information (written and spoken words) and one for non-verbal information (images). According to this theory, pictures have an advantage over words by being encoded into long-term memory through both the visual and verbal channels. That is, pictures are encoded as an image as well as spontaneously given a verbal label. In contrast, words are encoded with just one verbal code (Paivio, 2006). Two codes written to memory increases the chance of retrieving the information compared to information that is coded in only one way (Paivio, 1986).

This theory would also explain why the picture superiority effect improves with chronological age. If a person does not have the inner language available to formulate a name for a picture, then dual coding does not seem to occur (Whitehouse et al., 2006).

Perceptual distinctiveness. Another theory explains picture superiority as a result of the distinctive visual appearance that images have when compared to text. The drawing of an object, such as a tree, can have infinite variations. Compare this to text, which must be visually homogenous to facilitate reading. The varied features of pictures could be encoded more distinctively in memory than words and be responsible for their memorability.

Leveraging Picture Superiority

The use of both pictures and text or narration is often the most effective choice in learning design. When pictures can convey the same or additional information as words in a meaningful way, they will augment the learning experience. Here are some of the many ways to use visuals to enhance learning:

- Use relevant visuals to represent concrete objects explained in text or narration.
- Use visual analogies to relate unfamiliar concepts to previously learned information.
- Show two or more things that need to be remembered in association with each other.
- Leverage the features of spatial layout to bring order and structure to information.
- Focus on the aesthetics of visuals to increase motivation.
- Use visuals for low literacy audiences or for those who speak a native language that differs from the materials.

VISUAL DESIGN IMPACTS EMOTIONS

One aspect of instructional science that is growing in importance is the consideration of a learner's emotional state. This is another area where visual design has impact. Consider your own experience with a well-designed product. Have you ever been delighted by a new app that feels intuitive or a device that works without having to look at the manual? The experience creates a positive emotional state that carries over to your judgment of the product. People use feelings as information, just as they use facts.

Likewise, learners make subjective judgments about their experiences based on how easy materials are to use and process. A well-thought-out visual design contributes to a favorable experience that influences a learner's attitude and motivation toward learning tasks. A learner will be more attentive and engaged with highly usable materials, compared with those that are frustrating or unappealing. Effective visual design impacts learning success.

AESTHETIC PLEASURE AND MOTIVATION

Aesthetics may not be the first thing practitioners consider when designing learning experiences, but the pleasure derived from an elegant design can't be ignored. Aesthetic pleasure—the pure appreciation of beauty—produces an enjoyable experience that is yet another demonstration of the value of visual design. Like a usable design, one that is aesthetically appealing has the potential to keep learners feeling positive, interested, and motivated.

We are attuned to aesthetics at a very basic level. In his book, *The Design of Everyday Things*, Donald Norman (2013) points out that we are affected on a visceral level by our immediate perception of an object, causing it to attract or repel us. The rapidity of feelings people experience upon immediate exposure to a design trumps the slower nature of cognition and frames subsequent thoughts (Pham, Cohen, Pracejus, & Hughes, 2001).

The importance of aesthetics in the design of websites, software applications, and mobile apps has grown to the point at which a beautiful design and elegant interface are considered part of effective implementation. Yet this trend has been slower to affect the world of learning design, even though there is research to support the importance of aesthetics.

For example, early research into how aesthetics can affect multimedia learning shows that the use of certain colors and shapes can induce positive emotions that people maintain while viewing instructional materials (Um, Plass, Hayward, & Homer, 2012).

Just as marketers seek ways to provide enjoyable experiences to gain and retain consumers, learning professionals can design materials to delight their audience. We can learn from consumer products and design learning materials with the same aesthetic sensibility of a product going to market.

THE TAKEAWAYS

- Our brains devote more resources to vision than to any other sense.

- Visuals capture attention, aid recall, improve comprehension and interpretation, and help with skill acquisition.

- The picture superiority effect demonstrates that pictures are remembered better than their counterparts in words in most recall and recognition memory tasks.

- An effective design can create a positive feeling in users, influencing their judgment and evaluation of a learning experience.

- Appealing designs can increase positive emotions and motivation because they speak to our appreciation of beauty.

Think Like a Designer; You Are One

"Design is a messy endeavor."
— Ellen Lupton

THE FRAMEWORK

THIS CHAPTER answers these questions:

- Can I design if I don't draw well?
- What is the purpose of design?
- How do I start designing?
- When can I break the rules?

Look around your room. Every manufactured or hand-made item you see was designed by someone. Every object began life as an idea—a spark in someone's imagination. Perhaps this was followed by a sketch, a diagram, or a blueprint. Somehow the idea was planned and produced in a tangible form.

What do you have in common with those who transform ideas and bring them into the world? If you create something from nothing, if you conceive of solutions or help implement them, you are a designer. Designers solve problems. They gather information to understand the issues, work through an analytical and creative process, and overcome challenges to produce a solution. Successful designers improve our world.

In this chapter, you will find out about the many reasons people design. You will learn about a design methodology you can use to create effective solutions. And just in case you weren't certain, this chapter will validate that you are a designer. Isn't it time to start thinking like one?

VISUAL DESIGN VERSUS FINE ART

You may be surprised to learn that you do not need drawing talent to work as a visual designer. Although drawing is a useful skill to have for sketching ideas, it is not a requirement for design. In fact, anyone who can sketch geometric shapes and stick figures can express many ideas. Rendering is not a requirement for design work because design is different from fine art.

It is easy to see why many people confuse visual design with art. Both visual design and art are creative endeavors. Visual design and fine art rely on many of the same visual principles to communicate. Yet, the nature of each craft is quite different. As Saul Bass, influential designer of the last century, stated, "What distinguishes design from art is the person doing the work. An artist is internally centered, bringing work out of an inner reservoir. The designer is other centered; finding a dynamic relationship with a client brings the work to its fullest potential" (Laufer, 2012, p. 216). Here are some of the differences between visual design and fine art.

The purpose is different. Whereas design has a utilitarian purpose, art is created as an end in itself. Design is concerned with an object's purpose, so that form follows function. Fine art is concerned with form first. The form may express a concept or an aesthetic principle, but it is rarely utilitarian.

The initial stimulus is different. Practicing designers create solutions that fulfill someone else's requirements. In contrast, an artist uses his or her talents to manifest ideas and feelings and to share the work with others. Art comes from an inner motivation; it is personal.

The resources are different. Designers typically start with assets provided by a project's sponsor. They may be given branding guidelines, photographs, or content to work with. Artists typically start with a blank sheet of paper, an empty canvas, or a lump of clay.

The skills are different. Designers study visual principles and learn to use graphic applications to create solutions. Artists study composition and develop talents in the fine arts, such as painting and sculpture.

Success looks different. Design is effective if it achieves the objective. Success means that the design works—it was understood as intended and fulfilled its purpose. On the other hand, audiences are encouraged to interpret art however they wish. The artist may not explain his or her work in words, hoping to leave the experience open-ended.

THE PURPOSE OF DESIGN

It is worth taking a deeper look at the purpose of design to better understand what it's about and where you fit in. Here are some ways to look at the many different objectives of design.

Design Creates Solutions

The primary purpose of design is to devise the best solution to a problem while meeting all of the requirements. Every problem has its own set of constraints, such as the media to use, the size of the budget, or the schedule you must meet. The design process uses constraints as a springboard for building creative solutions.

Design Communicates and Informs

The goal of visual communication is to transmit ideas and information in a purposeful way, taking the sponsor's message and translating it for an audience. The communication has two parts—content (the information) and form (how it is designed). No matter how relevant and meaningful the content, if the form fails, the information will not be conveyed. Effective designs convey an accurate message in both form and content.

Design Instructs

When training or education is the objective of a design, the visual form must enhance the potential for comprehension and retention of the material. The challenge is to make a straightforward presentation that is visually appealing. A design that instructs provides a logical organization and structure, draws attention to key points, and clarifies complex content. Through images and words, this type of design enables learners to construct knowledge.

Design Persuades

Sometimes the purpose of design is to persuade. In learning design, the intent of persuasion is to transform attitudes, values, and beliefs in order to change behaviors. Both the visual form and the content must be motivational to grab attention and elicit emotions. A persuasive design must be deeply meaningful to the audience.

THE ROLE OF THE VISUAL DESIGNER

Visual design sits at the convergence of many fields and domains of knowledge. It requires competence in visual thinking to conceive of graphic solutions and to express ideas visually. An understanding of visual communication is also a necessity. This helps you translate information into a visual form that audiences understand.

It is fundamental to know and apply the principles of graphic design, which help you create effective compositions that serve your purpose. Also, a knowledge of what makes an effective photograph or illustration will help you select the best images. This knowledge is also helpful when working with or hiring photographers and illustrators.

A foundation in psychology is necessary to get a sense of how people apprehend and assimilate visual information. Technical know-how is valuable for creating and modifying images. It's also useful for estimating time to completion, as well as for predicting what can be achieved in different mediums. Some might say that an understanding of business is essential to align visuals to an organization's objectives. Finally, some awareness of cultural trends is needed. Staying abreast of current design directions may help you understand the look and feel that clients expect.

As you can see, the role of the visual designer is broad and complex. You are not expected to immediately become an expert in all of these skills and areas of knowledge. But with motivation and practice, you will begin to synthesize the varied aspects of visual design.

A VISUAL DESIGN PROCESS

Just as in learning design, there are many methodologies that systemize the visual design process. What are the advantages of using a structured design method? First, it brings order to a creative process that may seem chaotic. Second, using a proven system may give you confidence that you will find a workable solution. But don't be deceived into thinking that following a method is like going from point A to point B. Design usually puts you on a meandering path, with fitful starts and surprise endings. If you embrace the process, though, you will find unexpected rewards.

A Design Methodology

What follows is a five-step design methodology for the visual design of learning and informational materials. Figure 2.1 shows the steps, which include:

1. Define the Visual Problem

2. Research and Discovery

3. Ideate

4. Conceptualize and Visualize

5. Implement and Refine

The level of effort you invest in the method should make sense for the size of the project. For smaller projects, find ways to shortcut the process or enter the process at a step that makes sense in your workflow.

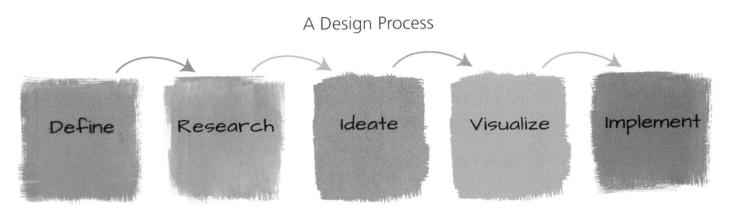

FIGURE 2.1. *A design process that takes you from idea to implementation.*

Step 1: Define the Visual Problem

Before embarking on a design, it is best to step back and define the problem. The visual problem encompasses the entire set of requirements that affect the appearance of the materials you are designing and the underlying message that they convey. By clearly defining the problem, you are more likely to come up with an effective solution.

Here are some examples of visual problem statements that a learning designer might start with and then continue to clarify with specific criteria and constraints:

- Create the visual design for a course that teaches international business travelers the most important customs in highly visited countries.

- Create the visual design for a set of short simulations teaching the most important functionality of a new time management application.

- Create the visual design for a mobile performance support tool that repair personnel can use to troubleshoot equipment while out in the field.

- Create the visual design for a web-based self-directed learning portal that teaches project management skills.

- Create the visual design for a poster-sized chart for healthcare workers that lists the most effective pharmaceuticals for pain management.

Step 2: Research and Discovery

During the Research and Discovery phase, collect enough background information to gain a big-picture view of the visual problem that needs to be solved. If you use a standard learning design method, you can integrate this into your normal work flow by focusing on the visual aspect of the problem as well. Gather what you can about the audience, organization, and content. Some specific ways to do this are listed below:

- Interview the client or sponsor to understand the mission and goals of the organization or department (this is important, even if it is an internal department).

- Interview members of the audience, identifying their characteristics and needs.

- Discover the visual preferences of both the audience and the client.

- Gather visual assets from the organization, such as their logo, branding colors, photos, and other graphics.

- Review visual communications from the sponsor, such as the website, brochures, and instructional materials.

- Review how others have solved a similar visual challenge for inspiration.

Step 3: Ideate

The third step is to take what you've learned during Research and Discovery and use it to formulate ideas for solutions. Ideation is about generating and recording numerous ideas without judging them. During this phase, every idea is considered valuable—so be bold. Here are some activities for ideation.

Brainstorming. This may be the first approach that comes to mind when you think of generating ideas. It can be done individually (good for people who don't like to speak up) or with a group (good for capturing different perspectives). State the problem and come up with as many design solutions as possible. Let the stream of creative solutions flow.

Mind-mapping. Use hand-drawn or digital mind maps to make free associations. Write down a central concept in the center, such as something that describes a theme or a characteristic of the audience or content. Then draw associated words in bubbles that connect to the original concept. Continue in this fashion until you have a network of associated words. Use it to look for patterns and new relationships and as a source for generating more ideas.

Sticky notes on a whiteboard. If your ideation involves logical ordering or categorizing, use sticky notes on a whiteboard— one per idea. This can also work with group brainstorming, in which the group stands around the whiteboard and adds a sticky note with an idea as each thought emerges.

Adapting proven designs. Another approach is to play with visual design solutions that you know have worked in the past and modify them to see whether they can work for the present problem.

When you feel that you have exhausted your supply of ideas, begin to review them and select the most usable options. You will be considering what will work with the content and audience, as well as the time it will take to execute, cost estimates, and the human resources you have available. Select one or a few ideas that will feed into the next step.

Step 4: Conceptualize and Visualize

If the idea passes the viability test, start to apply a tangible vision to the design problem. To visualize the ideas, get away from the computer and make rough sketches with paper and pencil or pen. Remember, you do not need to be a skilled artist to express yourself. Use simple lines and shapes to represent objects and people, and use words, too.

There is a special magic that happens from sketching. It seems to open creative pathways and encourages playful exploration. Designer and professor Jessica Helfand said this about the exploration process: "Draw and write and don't think about the end result. Just free yourself to explore. After a thorough exploration, pull elements you want to move forward with and start forming them into a layout" (Beard, 2013, p. 24).

Your visualizations can be thumbnail sketches to start. Thumbnails are small drawings for conveying ideas, like those shown in Figure 2.2. Use thumbnails to find ways to organize images and text. Later in this process, you may want to make larger versions of a few designs and add more detail. When you are satisfied that you have conceptualized enough options, use your best judgment to select the ones that have the most potential for success. Always remember the people for whom you are designing.

Step 5: Implement and Refine

During the Implementation phase, you will transform your sketches into designed compositions. Use the best solutions from the previous step and execute them in a graphics program. Take advantage of the computer's power to experiment with color, typography, and layout. You will learn about these aspects of design throughout this book.

In this final step, you will decide on the visual direction. Refine your ideas to so that they capture what you want to communicate. Ensure the designs have a cohesive and professional appearance, so that you are comfortable sharing them with your team or client for discussion and further revisions.

During discussions, others may want to know your rationale for making certain design decisions. With a solid foundation in visual design, it will be easy to explain the principles on which your work is based. This is one of the benefits of studying intentional design.

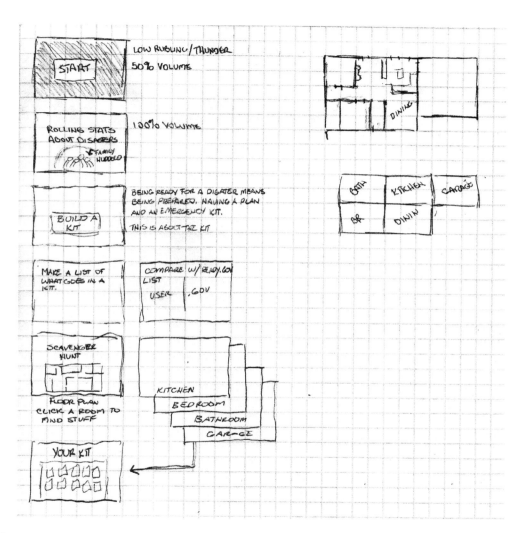

FIGURE 2.2. *Small thumbnail sketches help you visualize ideas. Illustration by Kevin Thorn, NuggetHead Studioz.*

THE MINDSET OF THE VISUAL DESIGNER

What are the rewards and challenges of being a designer? Working as a designer means you will develop ways to understand the problems of others, conceive of solutions, express and clarify ideas, collaborate with stakeholders, and make your ideas tangible. On the other hand, designers must deal with uncomfortable pressures and demands to produce. Let's look at some of the issues you may face.

Creativity Concerns

Designers are often expected to be spontaneously creative on demand. It is important to remember that creativity does not necessarily equate to originality. The likelihood of generating original ideas day after day is small. Instead, ideas usually build collectively—often concurrently—on the ideas of others. Creativity is more likely to happen by making new connections between existing ideas.

Also, there is no guarantee that the most original or innovative solution will be the best one to meet the objectives of the design problem. It takes equanimity and foresight to prepare yourself for the demands of a creative job. It's helpful to remember that creativity won't disappear, but it may need to be nourished.

You can nourish it by discovering what keeps you motivated, by keeping sources of inspiration nearby, and by connecting with other practitioners to share ideas and perspectives on design practices.

Self-Doubt

Self-doubt is often part of the creative process. The sooner you accept the fact that you may always have doubts about your design work, the less it will interfere with your progress. Part of managing self-doubt is acceptance of your current level of proficiency:

- Accept the current level of your skills and knowledge.
- Be determined to continue improving. Design is a lifelong learning endeavor.
- Compare your work with your previous work. See how you've developed.
- When you see good design work, use it as motivational fuel. Life isn't a competition.

Breaking the Rules

The principles you study in design books are guidelines for building a solid foundation in design theory. These guidelines are the light that will lead you out of the darkness of making random design choices. Visual design principles emerge from many disciplines: graphic art and fine art; cognitive science and psychology; cultural traditions and global conventions. Yet the principles cannot apply to every situation. As your confidence, skills, and knowledge grow, you will know when it is appropriate to break the rules. When you do so, do it with thoughtful intention. Sometimes you have to forge your own path. That's part of the power of being a designer.

How to Be an Effective Designer

To get the most out of being a designer, it takes a certain combination of flexibility, openness to new ideas, and empathy for the audience. Here are ten tips that can help you develop into a more effective designer:

1. Learn to really see.
2. Continually expand your visual language.
3. Share ideas freely.
4. Seek out thoughtful criticism.
5. Trust your intuition.
6. Find inspiration in the world around you.
7. Start with paper and pencil or pen.
8. Practice visualizing your ideas.
9. Strive to learn and improve your skills.
10. Rise to the occasion.

THE TAKEAWAYS

- Design is utilitarian, creating solutions that convey someone else's message. In contrast, art is typically an end in itself, expressing the artist's inner life.

- Design solves problems, communicates ideas and concepts, educates and instructs, and persuades.

- The visual designer benefits from skills and knowledge in visual thinking, visual communication, graphic design principles, psychology, cultural awareness, and technical know-how.

- A process you can use for design includes: (1) Define the Visual Problem, (2) Research and Discovery, (3) Ideate, (4) Conceptualize and Visualize, and (5) Implement and Refine.

CHAPTER

3

Work Like a Designer

"The fewer design decisions that seem arbitrary, the better."
— Bob Gill

THE FRAMEWORK

THIS CHAPTER answers these questions:

- What tools do I need to practice visual design?
- How can I design with a team?
- How can I speed up the design process?
- Where can I find ideas and inspiration?
- What graphic format should I use?

It's one thing to make a commitment to becoming a better designer and another to practice it in a work environment. The work environment introduces the pressures of meeting deadlines and staying within a budget. Team work introduces diverse viewpoints, which can add new ideas to the mix as well as miscommunications that result in design inconsistencies. Being creative on demand can exhaust the imagination.

In this chapter, you will learn ways to overcome these challenges. You will also discover some best practices for fulfilling the visual design role at work.

■ ■ ■

BUILD A GRAPHIC DESIGN TOOLBOX

If you marvel over the brilliant graphics you see in design books and magazines, there is something you may not realize. Most of the talented designers who create these graphics are using professional tools, whereas most amateur designers are not. Professionals often have a high-end monitor to display accurate colors, they may use a digital tablet and pen to work with precision, and they are using professional graphics software that is loaded with functionality.

Professional designers use professional tools, and if there is any way you can do this, you should, too. Although a quality toolset will not magically transform you into an expert designer (only wearing all black will do that), your skills improve and your tasks become easier when you use software and hardware intended for design work. Fortunately, there are now a few free alternatives to the more expensive software applications. Here are some of the tools to consider for building a professional visual design toolbox.

Tools for Sketching

Sketching ideas is a standard practice of visual designers, and it only takes the ability to draw simple shapes and simplistic people to convey your thoughts. Anyone who has to solve visual problems should consider purchasing two sketchbooks. A large sketchbook is ideal for the desk, and a smaller one is good for carrying around to capture ideas when they strike. Sketching tools are not expensive, so this is a good place to start and a good habit to develop.

Sketching is another way to think. It helps you generate solutions. You can lay out a screen from a rough sketch, draw mind maps to brainstorm, and create diagrams to organize content. Sketching helps you play with ideas, communicate with team members, and discuss concepts with clients and stakeholders.

All you need is a standard pencil to sketch, but if you really want to explore this medium, you can use artists' pens and pencils. These come in varied levels of darkness and thickness. You may find that a variety of pens and pencils helps you to better express your ideas.

Graphic Tablets

It's possible that nothing will improve your graphic abilities more than ditching the mouse for a graphic tablet and stylus. A digital tablet, shown in Figure 3.1, provides a flat drawing surface for drawing with a digital pen. Attempting to draw freehand to trace an object or to cut out backgrounds with a mouse is similar to drawing with a bar of soap. Creating graphics with a digital tablet feels like you are using a pencil. The exception is when drawing certain types of digital illustrations, which are made by **setting points on a path.** For this type of drawing, many illustrators prefer using a mouse to create each point with a click.

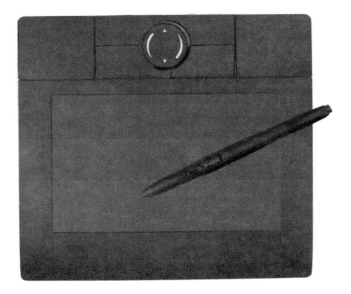

FIGURE 3.1. *In most cases, a digital tablet provides more control and greater accuracy than a mouse when working with graphics.*

If budget is a problem, start out with a less expensive tablet and get used to doing graphic tasks without a mouse. Over time, you may be delighted with the results. The more expensive tablets will have additional functionality, including more levels of pressure sensitivity that replicate drawing with a pencil.

Image Editing Software

Bitmap graphics, such as photographs, are made up of pixels. Vector graphics, such as illustrations drawn on the computer, are created by mathematical descriptions. To work with these different formats, designers typically use different types of software, although technically there are some overlaps in functionality. To learn more about graphic formats, see Know the Technical Terms later in this chapter.

Image editing software has functionality for modifying and manipulating bitmap graphics. You can also use an image editor as a paint program for creating visuals. Here are some recommended image editors:

- **Adobe Photoshop.** Photoshop is the premiere graphic editing tool for professional designers because of its powerful features and capabilities. You may find it is worth the effort to learn at least the basics of this software. The drawback is its price. Students and teachers do receive an educational discount on Adobe products.

- **Adobe Photoshop Elements.** Elements is a reduced and lower-priced version of Photoshop with a limited but reasonable set of image enhancement and editing capabilities. Elements is one way to start learning some of the functionality of Photoshop.

- **GIMP (download at** gimp.org**).** Possibly the most popular free graphic editor at the time of this writing, GIMP has a lot of power for the price—free. It has capabilities for retouching photos and composing images, a paint program, and converts files to various image formats.

- **Microsoft PowerPoint.** Over the years, PowerPoint has grown in graphic capabilities that are easy to learn and use. If you are using PowerPoint as the basis for online learning, presentations, storyboards, or any type of sketching to communicate ideas, this software will fulfill some of your graphic needs.

Illustration Software

Illustration software is designed to create and modify vector graphics, which are scalable to any size. Icons, computer-illustrated people, and objects are often created as vector graphics. The most well-used of these programs include:

- **Adobe Illustrator.** Illustrator allows you to draw with points, lines, and curves to create paths that become objects. Individual points that make up an object are easy to select and modify, every element can be re-sized, and text renders smoothly. Being a professional design tool, Illustrator is pricey and the learning curve is a bit steep.

- **Corel Draw.** Many consider Corel Draw to be the best alternative to Illustrator. If budget is an issue, the Home and Student Suite may meet your needs.

- **Inkscape (download from** inkscape.org**).** Inkscape comes recommended as a solid alternative to the pricier applications and it is free. It is both Windows and Mac compatible. Although Inkscape doesn't have all the capabilities and features of Illustrator or Corel Draw, you can probably complete most of the drawing tasks you need with Inkscape.

WRITE A VISUAL STYLE GUIDE

Just as professional design tools make graphic tasks easier, writing a visual style guide makes the effort of designing easier. A style guide offloads some of the cognitive demands that the design process imposes. It allows you to make style decisions once, document them, and then refer to them throughout a project. Style guides define attributes like the color palette, typography, and image format for a particular design solution. Whether you work alone or with a team, a style guide helps ensure that the design is consistent. It creates one standard for an entire course or project.

Writing a guide is also helpful for thinking through the details of a project. It clarifies your thoughts and removes the temptation to make random or ambiguous decisions in a moment of pressure. If there is a hiatus on a project, you can depend on your trusty style guide when you jump back in. And down the road, you may be able to modify and reuse the style guide for future projects.

What to Specify

In your visual style guide, you can add more than a list of design specifications. Consider adding the objectives of the design, a description of the content and sample screens to exemplify the standards. Table 3.1 is a sample of the types of standards to include in a guide for an eLearning course. Adjust it for your purposes. For print-based materials, for example, you might include the style of page headers and footers; placement of page numbers; and type, size, and weight of paper. A style guide doesn't tell you how to make design decisions; it specifies the decisions you make.

DESIGN WITH TEMPLATES

So far you have seen how professional tools and a style guide can make design work more efficient. Templates are another way to optimize the design and production process. A template is a master design that you can use repeatedly in an eLearning course, slide presentation, web page, or job aid. It consists of a layout with designated placeholders for visuals and text that you fill in according to need. Figure 3.2 shows a sample template.

Benefits of Using Templates

You have probably seen the advantages of using templates in your own work. When you make a change to one template, it makes a change to all the screens that use it (although you may have to reapply the layout again). Here are some additional benefits:

- **Promotes consistency.** Templates provide consistency so that users know how things work and where to find information.

TABLE 3.1.   **Sample of what to specify in a visual style guide for an eLearning course.**

Visual Element	What to Specify
Screen Layout	Identify the types of templates in the course, describe their organization, show screen shots, and include as separate files when appropriate.
Color Palette	Main colors: identify the key colors in your palette. Specify colors in an RGB (122 127 130 for medium gray) or hexadecimal (#7A7F82 for medium gray) format Accent colors: identify one or two accent colors Hyperlinks: specify the color of hyperlinks
Typography	Titles or large text: specify typeface, style, color, size, and alignment Subtitles or second largest text: specify typeface, style, color, size, and alignment Body text: typeface, style, color, size, and alignment Captions; typeface, style, color, size, and alignment Labels: typeface, style, color size, and alignment
Readability	Linespacing: identify how much space to allow between lines of text within a paragraph Paragraph spacing: identify how much space to allow before and after paragraphs
Images	Image style: identify types of images to use, such as color photos, black and white photos, illustrations, or clip art Image sizes: specify standard sizes of images for each type of screen (example: split screen photos will be 512x768) Image borders: identify whether images will have borders and the color, style and line thickness of the border Captions: Identify where they will be placed and whether they will be numbered
Logo	Note which style of logo to use on the title screen. It won't be needed on other screens
Showing Emphasis	Specify the pictorial technique for pointing out information, such as an arrow, circle, or highlight Specify the properties of each pictorial device, such as the type of arrow and the colors of each technique
User Interface	Identify the color and style of any user interface elements you control Icons: style and size of icons for navigation or other UI purposes

FIGURE 3.2. *Design title screen templates to grab attention. Templates designed by the eLearning Brothers.*

- **Improves efficiency.** When you use templates, you do not have to redesign every screen from scratch. Simply create a template for each type of screen you will need.

- **Reduces overwhelm.** Similar to writing a style guide, when visual design decisions are made ahead of time, you have more mental space to focus on getting the instructional or information content right.

- **Leaves room for creativity.** Although some people find templates restrictive, they do not need to be. Not only can you design creative templates, but you can always have one blank template so that when you have a real purpose, you are free to create a one-off design. If you create too many unique screens, however, you will defeat the purpose of using a template.

Starting with Templates

To create templates, first categorize the types of screens or slides that you might need. For example, you might need one template for interactive activities and another to show tables and graphs. Then, for each type of template, create a layout or framework. For example, designate the size of the margins and where to place all of the visual elements (images, shapes, and text). You will learn how to design layouts in Chapter 4, Organizing Graphic Space.

If you want to keep things flexible, you can use multipurpose placeholders that may hold many types of images or blocks of text. If you need to keep the design more stringent, specify what type of element to insert in each placeholder.

Here are some examples of templates you may want to design if you are working on an eLearning course, training slides, or presentation. The templates you need will vary according to your specific project.

Sample Templates

Title screen template. The title screen is the first look that viewers have at your visual communication. Give it impact and appeal so that it grabs attention and motivates viewers to continue. Set the title in large text so it has prominence. Try to convey the message through one large graphic or a well-designed set of smaller graphics. The title screen is a good place to be bold. Figure 3.2 shows two title screen layouts.

Content templates. You can design different types of content templates for varied instructional purposes, such as one for making comparisons and another for diagrams with call-outs. The template shown in Figure 3.3 helps viewers understand varied perspectives on a topic by creating regions of space to place different characters who will speak their viewpoints.

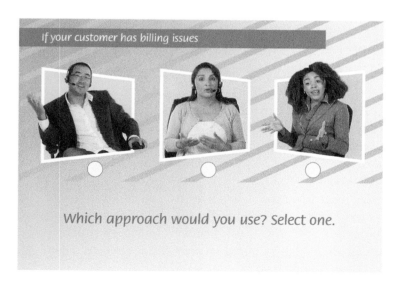

FIGURE 3.3. *Content template for providing expert opinions in text or audio. Cutout people from the eLearning Brothers.*

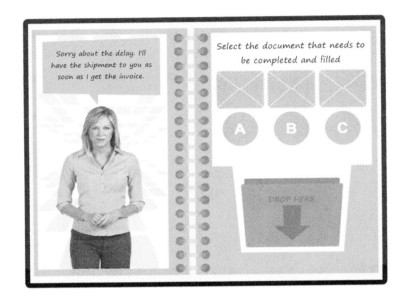

FIGURE 3.4. *Example of a template for a drag-and-drop interaction. Template design by the eLearning Brothers.*

Interaction templates. The effective use of interactivity in eLearning and on websites provides a way to simulate real-world situations in a safe environment. It also allows learners to play games and to choose which information to access. By designing a few interactive templates, the audience will not have to relearn the user interface with every new interaction. Although the interaction can be complex, the design should be easy to use and understand. Figure 3.4 shows an example of a template that can be used for a drag-and-drop interaction.

Text-only template. There are times when you simply must have an all-text template, such as for a critical definition or a brilliant quote that you want to stand apart from everything else. An all-text template does not mean that the screen or slide will be completely filled with text or bullet points. We are past that point in our visual design evolution. Rather, it will just have a few lines or a paragraph at most, set off through a simple design that brings it focus. Figure 3.5 is an example.

WHERE TO FIND VISUAL INSPIRATION

Design doesn't happen in a vacuum. "Design ideas are more apt to flow from a mind that has been imprinted with rich and varied visual experience than one that has had limited exposure," write the authors of *Design Dialogue* (Stoops & Samuelson, 1990,

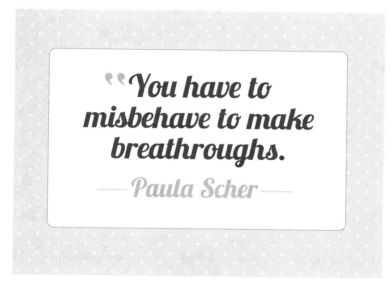

FIGURE 3.5. *Sample template for a quote screen.*

p. 16). Make it a habit to study existing designs to trigger new ways of thinking. Find inspiration in the world around you and reinterpret what you see to solve your design problems.

When looking for innovative ideas, keep the project's objectives in the forefront of your search. Don't try to copy someone else's design pixel-for-pixel. Rather, borrow some of the most compelling aspects of an inspiring design and thoughtfully apply them to meet your own objectives. Here are some ways to enrich your design imagination.

Analyze Other Designs

When you see a design that moves you, deconstruct the designer's approach to increase your awareness. You might ask yourself questions like these:

- What makes this design effective?

- What message does the visual convey?

- How did the designer handle the layout?

- What element first attracted my attention and why?

- How does the color palette affect me?

Over time, this type of analysis will happen automatically, whenever you see an intriguing design.

Collect Compelling Designs

Make the best use of your time by collecting the designs you find most appealing to browse later when you need inspiration. Gather brochures, catalogs, mailers, pages from magazines, and printouts that have compelling design ideas and keep them in a folder or paste them into a sketchbook. Use an online bookmarking or web clipping tool to keep track of impressive website designs as well as graphic design and typography websites that show examples.

Use Design Resources

There are countless resources online and offline for finding design ideas and inspiration. Here are places where you can learn about design and find creative nourishment.

Graphic design portfolios. There are many online platforms for artists and graphic designers to show their portfolios. Look through these collections to study how others are using space, form, color, and typography to communicate a message. Some well-known portfolio platforms are *Behance, Dribble, DeviantArt,* and *CarbonMade*.

Magazines. Browse online and print magazines to examine their layouts. Notice where images are placed and how elements are aligned. See how the designer shows what is of primary importance and what is subordinate. Are there any creative treatments that could work for your projects?

Design museums. If you live in or happen to be traveling to a major city, check whether there is a design museum nearby. Alternatively, there are many design museums online, such as Cooper-Hewitt National Design Museum, Design Museums of London, Design Museum of Denmark, and the Museum of Arts and Design in New York.

Advertising. Do you typically ignore advertisements? Instead, study them for creative ideas. Many advertising studios have large budgets to write persuasive copy and produce captivating visuals. There just might be the seed of an idea there that you can use. Online you can view the *Webby Awards, Ads of the World,* and the *Clio Awards*.

Information and interactive graphics. You may find novel ways to explain or represent information by studying the designs of professionally made information and interactive graphics. Look for the "real" infographics created by visual journalists and data visualization experts. Genuine infographics compress information to make it manageable, providing insights for understanding and problem solving.

Image collections and search engines. If you are stumped for a way to visualize a concept, see how others have taken on this challenge. Perhaps you can improve on what they've done. Search stock photo sites, search engines, and online photo galleries for the concept. You may find it visualized in a way you hadn't imagined.

PowerPoint and Keynote slide decks. Browse through websites that provide examples of slide design to spark your imagination. One site that attempts to show the best slide designs is *Note and Point*.

Visual design and photography books. Consider starting a collection of visual design and photography books that are bursting with examples. Also, graphic novels can provide ideas for visualizing stories.

There are an abundance of resources and ways to replenish your creative powers. Let these approaches become a standard practice of your role as a visual designer.

KNOW THE TECHNICAL TERMS

As a designer, your job will be easier and you will make smarter choices when you understand the technical side of graphic creation and graphic file formats. Regardless of the graphics program you use, you need to know a few important basics about digital graphics. Some of these terms are discussed throughout the book, so this primer is important.

Width First, Then Height

The size or dimensions of a computer graphic are referred to with two numbers, such as 720 x 540 or 1024 x 768. The first number always refers to the width and the second always refers to the height. For pictures viewed online, the unit of measurement is the pixel, which is the smallest element of a computer image.

A graphic that is 720 x 540 pixels is 720 pixels wide and 540 pixels tall. When the first number of the two is larger, you know the graphic has a horizontal orientation. When the second number is larger, the graphic has a vertical orientation. When the dimensions are equal, the graphic is square.

Size and Resolution Are Different

The *size* of a graphic refers to its width and height in pixels, inches, or whatever unit you are using. In contrast, the *resolution* of a digital graphic refers to either: dots per inch (dpi) or pixels per inch (ppi) (pixels per centimeter (is also used). These are measurements of dot or pixel density.

Dots per inch (dpi). This measurement refers to the number of dots in a linear inch. Dots per inch is typically used for printing. Up to a point, as the dots per inch increase, the clarity of the printed image improves.

Pixels per inch (ppi). This measurement refers to the number of pixels in a linear inch. A higher resolution has more pixels per inch, providing a better quality image but a larger file size.

Both image size and resolution affect the file size of an image. Larger dimensions and a higher resolution increase the size of a file. When creating images to display online, you must find a balance between image quality and size of the file so the images will look good, yet display quickly.

Bitmap Versus Vector Images

Have you ever been frustrated by the blurry and pixelated appearance of a small photograph that was enlarged? When you understand the difference between bitmap and vector images, you will understand why this happens and you will never have to face a blurry image again.

Image technology is easier to grasp when you know that images are displayed in two main formats: bitmap and vector. As explained earlier, bitmaps are made up of pixels, and vectors are created by mathematical descriptions. Bitmap and vector images use different file formats. There are also hybrid graphic file formats that contain both vector and bitmap graphics.

Bitmap Images

Bitmap graphics are made from a blend of pixels—each one contains color information that comprises the image. Photographs and scanned pictures are bitmap graphics. Bitmaps (sometimes called raster images) have a fixed resolution, which means they can't be made larger without losing quality. This is why a small photograph becomes blurry or has jagged edges when you enlarge it. You can't add information that wasn't there originally. The lesson? Use bitmap images at the size they were created or smaller. If you want the image to display in a large size, you must start with a large image.

Advantages of bitmap images:

- Can be created with a digital camera, scanner, or in a paint program
- Have subtle tones of gradation
- Can have a transparent background (in the PNG file format)
- Wide selection available at stock photo sites

Disadvantages of bitmap images:

- Can't be enlarged without distortion or jagged edges
- File size is typically larger than for vector images

Bitmap Image Formats

The two most common image formats for online display are JPG and PNG. The key difference between the two formats is that the PNG format allows for a transparent background.

All bitmap images are actually rectangles. When you see an image with a background that is cut out, the area outside the shape is transparent so that only the non-rectangular portion of the graphic displays. PNG files achieve this by storing transparency data in what is known as an *alpha channel*, which indicates whether a pixel should be displayed as opaque or transparent. See Figure 3.6 for a visual explanation.

The JPG format does not have an *alpha channel*, so you cannot display a transparent background in a JPG file. Table 3.2 shows the most common bitmap file formats you'll come across.

GEEK SPEAK: TRANSPARENCY

In formats that specify transparency information, like the PNG format, each pixel has a transparency value. A pixel that is fully transparent has a value of 0 percent in the alpha channel. A pixel that is completely opaque has a value of 100 percent in the alpha channel. A partially transparent pixel will have an intermediate value. Partial transparency allows some of the background to show through.

Vector Images

Vector graphics display via a set of instructions described through mathematical expressions. The instructions tell the software how to draw the points, lines, curves, and paths. Because the graphics are created from instructions rather than pixels, they can be made any size without losing image quality. This means that vector images are scalable. You can create vector images with vector drawing tools like Adobe Illustrator, Corel Draw, and Inkscape. Many digital illustrations and icons are created as vector graphics.

Advantages of vector images:

- Scalable—the image maintains quality when enlarged

- File size is usually smaller

- Can have a transparent background

- Ideal for work that needs to be displayed in both small and large sizes

Transparent Area   Transparent Area

FIGURE 3.6. *Transparency information stored in an alpha channel allows graphics to appear non-rectangular.*

TABLE 3.2. **Common bitmap image formats.**

File Format	About	Best Uses
JPEG/JPG (.jpeg/jpg)	Created for displaying photographs in a compressed format, making the file size smaller. JPG files can display millions of colors. They can usually be saved at different levels of quality. The higher the quality, the more image information is included. JPG does not support transparency.	Photographs Graphics with many colors Images with lots of detail Large graphics, because the file size is smaller than PNG
PNG (.png)	A full-color replacement for the GIF format that supports transparent backgrounds. PNG files can display millions of colors. They use a different type of compression than JPG, making their file size larger.	Graphics with flat areas of color Photographs (but the file size will typically be larger than JPG) Line drawings Transparent backgrounds High-quality graphics for the web
GIF (.gif)	The GIF format only supports 256 colors, which can cause unsightly bands of color in photographs. GIF images can have a transparent background. A GIF file can hold multiple images for creating very simple animations. The file size is small.	Low bandwidth environments requiring a small file size Graphics with flat areas of color, like buttons Simple line drawings Clip art Very simple animations
TIFF (.tiff/.tif)	Supports high-quality images with millions of colors, layers, and transparency. TIFF is typically used for importing graphics into professional publishing and layout programs. Images saved in this format usually have a large file size.	High-quality images for print documents
BMP (.bmp)	The BMP format supports high-quality images, although the file size is typically too large for web graphics.	High-quality image output is required When TIFF format is not available
PDF (.pdf)	A hybrid format that supports both bitmap and vector graphics.	High-quality documents with text and images for print
PSD (.psd)	The native format for Photoshop and Photoshop Elements.	When you need to retain layers, styles, masks, and other features of the program for future editing.

TABLE 3.3. **Common vector image formats.**

File Format	About	Best Uses
EPS (.eps)	A hybrid format that supports vector and bitmap graphics. EPS files are created with drawing programs. This format is commonly used when sending out vector graphics for print. Stock vector graphics are usually in this format.	Illustrations and scaleable graphics When a small file size is required For importing into publishing or layout programs for print
WMF (.wmf)	A hybrid format that supports vector and bitmap graphics. This format is used for Microsoft Office Clip Art.	When you want to modify clip art and exchange parts with other WMF files When PowerPoint is your graphics editor
SVG (.svg)	A newer vector format for web graphics that supports interactivity and animation. Images and behaviors are defined in an XML text file. SVG files are created in drawing programs like Inkscape and are not supported in older browsers.	Illustration graphics For web interactivity in modern web browsers
AI (.ai)	Native Adobe Illustrator format	When you need to retain layers, styles, masks, and other features of the program for future editing For importing a scalable graphic into a publishing or layout program

Disadvantages of vector images:

■ Typically requires drawing software to create or edit

■ Usually requires more skill to create

■ Selection of stock artwork is smaller than that of bitmap graphics

Table 3.3 above shows the common vector file formats.

THE **TAKEAWAYS**

- Acquire and learn to use professional design tools to improve the quality of your work.

- Prior to starting extensive design work, write a visual style guide to keep track of your design decisions.

- Create design templates for different types of screens to save time and to guarantee consistency.

- You can find design ideas and inspiration by analyzing expert designs, creating a personal collection of appealing designs, and using the many online and offline resources around you.

- Bitmap graphics, such as photographs, store color information in pixels. They lose quality when they are enlarged.

- Vector graphics, such as digital illustrations, are created from mathematical descriptions. This allows them to be resized without losing quality.

2

BUILDING BLOCKS
OF DESIGN

Visual design involves the arrangement of visuals and type in two-dimensional space. This section describes ways to manipulate these building blocks so that you can design with intention.

Organizing Graphic Space

"White space is like air. It is necessary for a design to breathe."
— Alex White

THE FRAMEWORK

THIS CHAPTER answers these questions:

- What is graphic space?
- How should I use white space?
- How do I know where to put the text and images?
- How can I create a professional looking layout?

Graphic space is more than the container that holds your design. It is the area where you organize and manipulate images and text to communicate visually. Although you may think of this area as "just a background" to hold visual elements, graphic space is a design element in its own right. Space communicates information when you use it intentionally.

In this chapter, you will learn how graphic space informs a design. You will see how you can shift your perspective so that the background becomes as important as the foreground. Most important, you will see how becoming aware of space will help you to become a better designer.

GRAPHIC SPACE

Graphic space is the two-dimensional area you work with in visual design. It is a tangible element, similar to images and type. This two-dimensional space has certain properties that you should consider when you design, as shown in Figure 4.1. These properties help define space and create the conditions for designing with it.

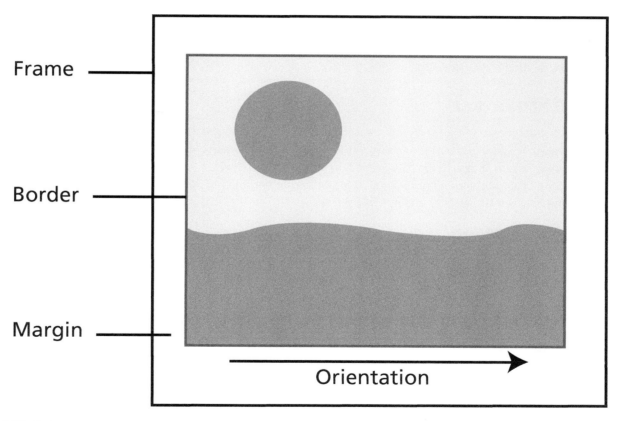

FIGURE 4.1. *Properties of graphic space.*

Properties of Graphic Space

- **Orientation** is the direction of the space. Slides and eLearning courses are typically horizontal in orientation. Print materials often have a vertical orientation. The rectangular shape of the graphic space is a product of its orientation.

- A **frame** encloses the space and gives it definition. Images, shapes, and text have a dynamic relationship with the frame.

- A **border** is a visual element placed around graphic objects. It creates its own window of space.

- The **margin** is the area in-between the frame and the visual elements. The size of the margins can have a powerful effect on how people perceive the visuals and text.

The purpose of defining these characteristics is to help you see that graphic space is an object itself with its own qualities. Keep the properties in mind as you design.

POSITIVE AND NEGATIVE SPACE

When we look at a graphic, we often perceive it as having two layers: a foreground and a background. We see the forms as the foreground or positive space and everything else as the background or negative space. Negative space is often referred to as white space in graphic design, although the background does not need to be white.

White or negative space includes all of the unused areas that are not filled with an image, shape, or text. Effective designs create a relationship between white space and non-white space.

Why Is White Space Important?

There is a reason you should care about white space. It sets off the forms and text through contrast. White space also gives the eyes a place to rest. When a screen or slide uses white space successfully, viewers get a sense of ease that you cannot have when white space is ignored as a design element.

In addition, ample white space makes it easy to perceive and mentally process information, a crucial formula for effective learning design. When a screen, slide, or page is complex or confusing, learners become frustrated and lose interest.

White Space Conveys Meaning

White space is part of the vocabulary of visual language that carries meaning, depending on the context. For example, suppose you were creating graphics for a presentation about neglect of the elderly population. To convey this concept, you have two options. In one, you can use a photograph of an elderly woman alone in a room surrounded with books, photographs, and a piano. In the second, you can use a cut out photograph of an elderly woman alone in a sea of dark negative space, like that shown in Figure 4.2. In this context, the white space in the second option amplifies the feeling of loneliness and is a better choice for conveying the message.

FIGURE 4.2. *Space conveys meaning. In this graphic, it creates a sense of loneliness.*

Now think about the print advertisements you've seen for high-priced furniture. Did you ever notice that these ads use lavish amounts of white space? In this context, white space creates a sense of sophistication and elegance. The reader's eyes flow easily around the objects. Plentiful space can also create a light and open feeling. Depending on the context, you can use white space in the same way that you use words—to communicate meaning.

HOW TO ACTIVATE WHITE SPACE

If you find it difficult to "see" white space, it is because the nature of human perception pushes it to the background. The trick is to start to see white space as a form of its own. Notice the shapes of white space that are created between all of the elements on the screen, the space from the elements to the frame and the space in between the letterforms, as shown in Figure 4.3.

Techniques to Activate White Space

Successful designs create a relationship between positive and negative space. This is known as *activating* the white space. Here are some approaches for giving white space a more prominent role in your designs:

1. **Design with generous margins.** This simple technique is a good way to start thinking about and seeing the effects of white space.

2. **Create functional areas.** Combine or group similar types of content. Then arrange them so there is sufficient white space surrounding each group. It's easier to lay out a few groups with sufficient white space than to deal with many small elements.

3. **Make templates for consistency.** You probably do not have time to design all the slides in a one-hour course from scratch. If you design several templates that use white space successfully, you can ensure the screen won't be too crowded.

4. **Seek balance.** Compare the proportion of white space to the proportion of non-white space. Proportion refers to the relationship of the size of the elements to each other and to the overall design. Adjust the scale of visuals and text to find a balance in these proportions. You can find balance in asymmetry as well as in symmetry.

5. **Use a grid.** A grid can help you plan a layout that uses white space effectively. See more about grids later in this chapter.

6. **Resist the urge.** White space is not a blank area that must be filled up. It is a design element in its own right. If you feel the urge to fill it up or if your clients request this—resist. Resist!

During the design process, work with the layout to create a relationship between foreground and background so that it looks and feels harmonious.

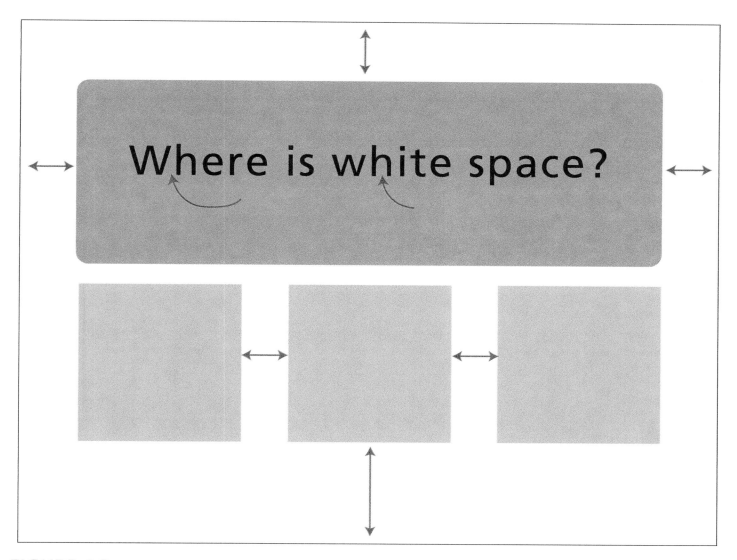

FIGURE 4.3. *Notice the shape of the white space between elements.*

LAYOUT

When you arrange a room, you make sure that the flow of movement and the furniture are conducive to the room's purpose. Similarly, graphic designers arrange images and words in a layout so they are conducive to the design's purpose. A layout creates structure in space through the considered placement of elements in order to solve a problem.

Visual design focuses on constructing layouts that are organized to create meaning. This is especially important in the learning domain, where the audience is not only required to recognize and comprehend information, but to retain it and apply it later. Layout is also essential for any design where a user needs information quickly and clearly.

One of the big challenges you face, then, is how to create a composition that's attractive and also easy for viewers to perceive and process. There are effective layout techniques to achieve this, which include:

- Establishing a visual hierarchy,

- Working with a grid, and

- Using the rule of thirds.

Paying attention to alignment and balance will also help. These topics are explored next.

Visual Hierarchy

Look at the sample title slide layout shown in Figure 4.4. What element first catches your eye? For most people, the large picture is the most dominant element because of its size and placement. The next element that probably attracts your eye is the title. The subtitle is subordinate to the title.

These levels—from dominant to subordinate—refer to the visual hierarchy or sequence in which viewers see the components of a design. In your layout, make the most important content the most dominant feature. You can control this through many techniques, including varying the size of the elements (the largest will usually attract attention) and using intentional placement (upper left is usually the visual entry point).

A successful visual hierarchy provides a focal point and presents a clear message. An ineffective hierarchy makes it difficult for viewers to know where to look first. In a poor layout, no single element stands out well enough to grab attention, creating a muddled message. There is a lot more to learn about visual hierarchies, so be sure to read Chapter 8, Establish a Visual Hierarchy.

Layout Issues to Avoid

Producing a pleasing and useful layout is a core design skill. It will be helpful to know about a few common layout issues to avoid.

BUSINESS TRAVEL
An Introduction to Global Etiquette

FIGURE 4.4. *What catches your eye first? A three-level visual hierarchy.*

Avoid the extremes. Unless it helps with your message, stay away from graphic space extremes. Too many visual elements can make a layout look and feel cluttered. If this is your problem, remove unnecessary elements or group smaller elements together. If a visual is not adding to the message, it is probably detracting from it. A less common issue is an extreme amount of white space, which at times can feel bare and empty. If this is your problem, enlarge the image or text.

Avoid holes in the layout. You may discover areas of white space that are accidentally trapped by the surrounding elements, like that shown on the left in Figure 4.5. This type of unplanned space creates static regions of white space that don't serve a purpose. If this is the issue, try to move that space to the outside of the layout, as shown on the right.

Avoid inconsistent spacing. You will want some level of consistency in the spacing of your elements. Seek a balance, but don't be boring. For example, the image on the right in Figure 4.5 uses consistent spacing, but the varied poses and bright colors prevent it from being dull.

Avoid being too clever with the layout. Clever ideas are great, but some can go awry and confuse the communication. If your ingenious visual concept is making the layout difficult to read or understand, discard it. Have the courage to destroy what doesn't work.

FIGURE 4.5. *Random small areas of white space look unplanned (left). Try to move the space to the outside (right).*

USING GRIDS FOR LAYOUT

One proven way to gain competence in layout design is to use a grid. It provides a structure for positioning images and text. A grid is not a guaranteed solution to every design problem, but it provides a solid framework and potentially speeds up the design process. Although you may think a grid will constrain your designs, in practice, a grid presents an underlying order on which you can place a multitude of layouts.

What Is a Grid?

A typical grid separates a surface into horizontal and vertical sections. Some common grid options for eLearning courses and slides include a 3x3 and a 4x4 grid, although you can create as many sections as you like. These sections of space become the structure for placing visual elements in a purposeful way.

Applying a Grid

Most applications that provide design features allow you to display a grid. If your authoring tool does not include grid functionality, you can create your own in a graphics program and then bring it into the authoring tool. In this case, place the grid in a slide master, use it to design, and then remove it at the end. Or import the grid and place it on every screen where it is needed, move it to the background, arrange the elements, and then remove the grid.

The method you use for working with a grid should help you design within a structure, but not be so intrusive that you can't see what you're doing. It may take some time to get used to this approach to design.

Parts of a Grid

In order to think about and work with a grid, you should know its parts. The elements of a grid include the margins, columns (from vertical lines), flowlines (horizontal lines), modules (cells in a matrix), and zones (multiple modules). See the parts in Figure 4.6.

Types of Grids

Several types of grids are helpful for learning and information designs, including the column, modular, and hierarchical grids. These are shown in Figure 4.7.

Column grid. Use a column grid when designing pages with large blocks of text, like manuals and web pages, and when working with split-screen slides. To create a column grid, place vertical lines at the desired intervals, leaving sufficient white space for margins and space in between columns. Do not feel compelled to make the columns the same width. For example, in a two-column (split-screen) design for an eLearning course, the column for pictures might require a greater width than the column for text.

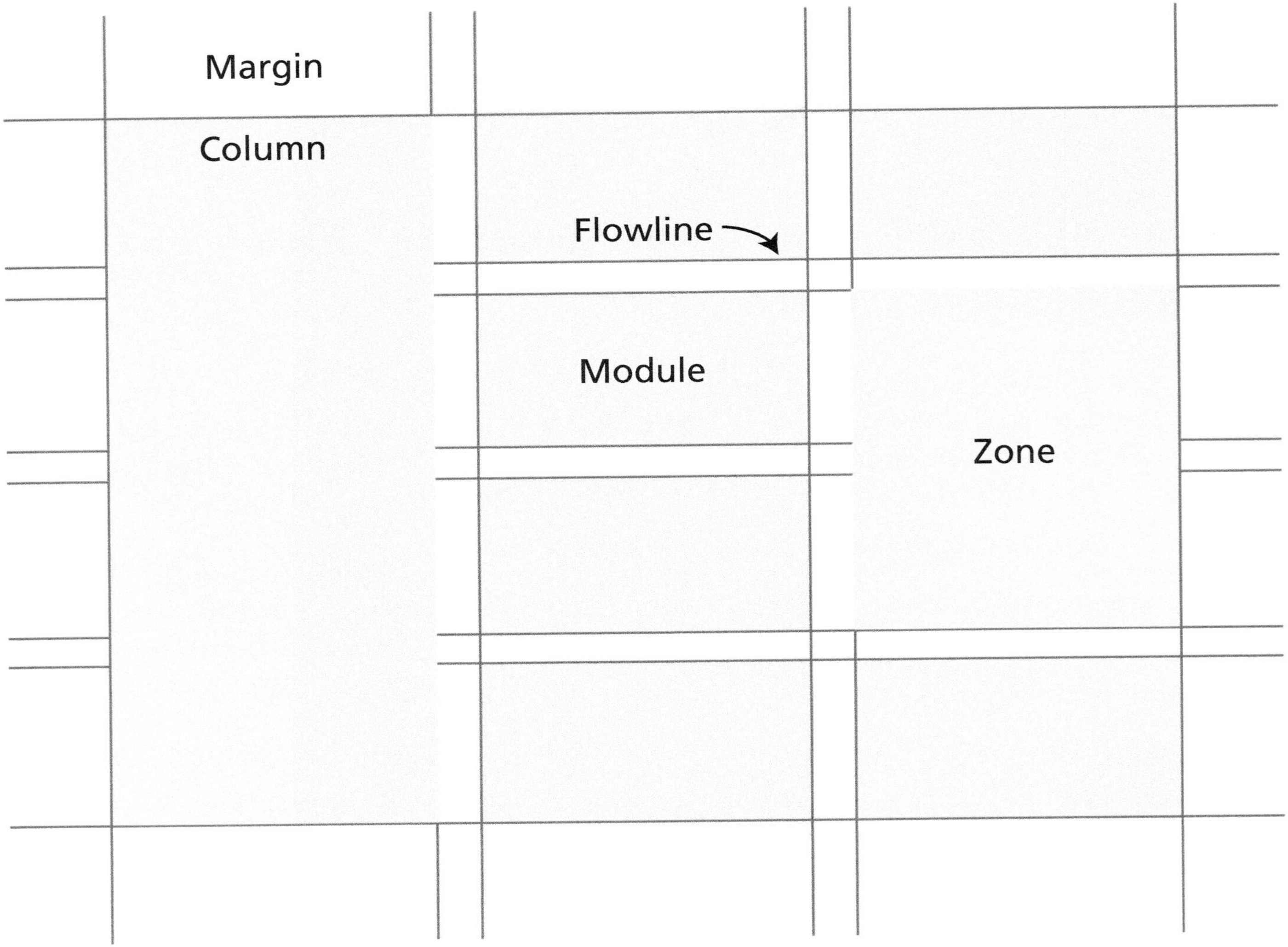

Margin

Column

Flowline

Module

Zone

FIGURE 4.6. *Parts of a grid.*

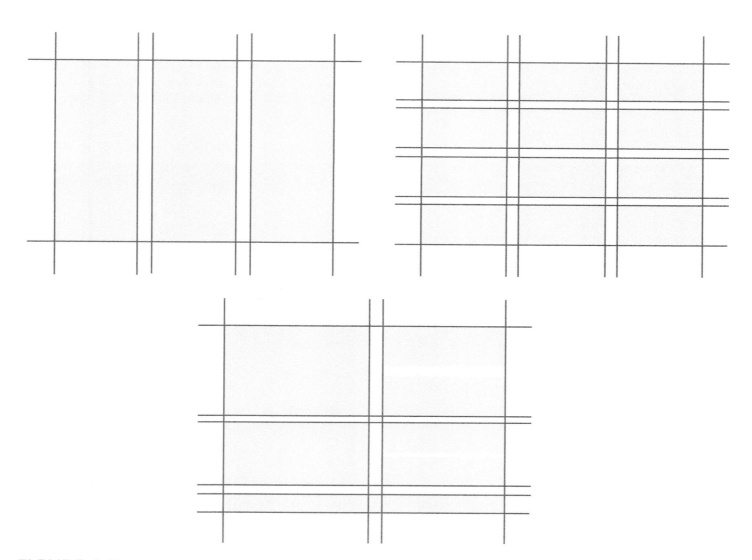

FIGURE 4.7. *Types of grids: columnar (upper left), modular (upper right), and hierarchical (bottom).*

Modular grid. A modular grid uses horizontal lines, called flowlines, in addition to the vertical lines. The flowlines break up the space into individual units. You can place an image or a block of text across many modules creating zones. These work well for eLearning design, presentation slides, and any designs that require small units of information or consistent regions.

Hierarchical grid. If you take a modular grid and size it for the order of importance, you have a hierarchical grid. This type of structure uses unequal horizontal areas, with the largest zones reserved for the most prominent elements.

Breaking the Grid

In course design, we are always looking for ways to engage the learner. One way is through the element of surprise, which you can achieve through visual design. When it makes sense instructionally, such as to emphasize a key point or to show drama in a story, don't hesitate to break the grid and use a wildly different approach, like placing elements on a diagonal orientation.

THE RULE OF THIRDS

You may develop a preference for using the 3x3 modular grid, like that shown in Figure 4.8, for eLearning and presentation slides because it is based on the *rule of thirds*, a well-known compositional technique for creating an attractive layout in photography,

FIGURE 4.8. *Comparison of a photo using a central focal point, on the left, with one that uses the rule of thirds, on the right. Viewers typically find the off-center placement more interesting.*

film, and graphic design. A 3x3 grid divides the framed space into three sections vertically and horizontally, resulting in four intersection points and nine cells or modules. Apply the rule of thirds by positioning the most important element at one or more of the four intersection points (referred to as *power points*).

Another way to apply the rule of thirds is to place the dominant element along any one of the lines. For example, place a photo of a person so his or her eyes meet the top line. Whichever approach you use, the rationale for the rule of thirds is that it prevents photographers and designers from centering everything. Using the rule of thirds, a horizon line can never cut a picture in half and an important person will never be placed directly in the center. The rule of thirds will make your designs more dynamic, which will hold the viewer's attention for a longer time.

ALIGNMENT

Alignment is one of the keys to making your designs easy to understand because people benefit from organization and structure while their eyes scan a screen. Alignment refers to placing the edges or centers of elements in line with each other, rather than placing them randomly. Alignment provides visual order by creating implied vertical or horizontal lines along the edges. Viewers make visual connections between images and text that are aligned.

Alignment also gives a design a professional look because the layout appears to be thoughtfully designed. You will probably find it easier to notice when elements are out of alignment if you use a grid. Many authoring tools have functionality for aligning objects. Take advantage of this and use the alignment features.

Types of Alignment

Although you are familiar with the types of alignment that word processors provide, you have more options in visual design. There are several types of alignment and each provides a different effect.

Edge alignment. This refers to aligning elements to each other's edges. They can be aligned to the left or aligned to the right. This is good for blocks of body text (flush left is best for reading) and for forms with a rectangular shape. Edge alignment will order and refine your designs.

Center alignment. This involves arranging elements based on their center lines. Center alignment works well for irregular shapes, but can also work for rectangular shapes. Centering everything on a slide or page, however, can create a dull symmetry, although it is certainly appropriate for some designs.

Overlapping alignment. Overlapping refers to elements that are partially overlaid on top of each other. This is often used in photo layouts or to add realism in scenarios, such as when simulating strewn papers on a desk.

Non-linear alignment. Although alignment is usually based on a horizontal or vertical axis, there are some cases when you may want to follow a non-linear or irregular path. For example, you can place text on a curved path so it aligns to the edge of a circle.

Mixing many types of alignment can create disorder and make it more difficult to know where to look. If you're not sure where to place an image, title, or block of text, find a place to align it with another element on the screen or page.

BALANCE AND VISUAL WEIGHT

It's difficult to think about the design of graphic space without considering whether you want to achieve a symmetrical or asymmetrical balance. *Balance* refers to arranging elements so that their visual weight is distributed evenly.

Visual Weight

Are you wondering how a non-physical object can have visual weight? *Visual weight* refers to the degree that an object attracts or pulls the viewer's attention and sustains it.

Heavy properties. We perceive visual elements as heavier when they are large, dark, high contrast, and complex or dense, such as a group of small visuals in close proximity. Visual elements that are farther out toward the edge of the graphic space have more visual weight than centered elements. Also, placing objects according to the rule of thirds gives them more visual weight.

Light properties. We perceive visual elements that are light in color, small in size, simple in construction, or less dense as having a lighter visual weight.

SYMMETRY AND ASYMMETRY

Two ways to achieve balance in a layout are through symmetrical and asymmetrical designs. When you understand what each approach communicates, you can choose one or the other with purpose.

The Symmetrical Layout

When you center the elements along a vertical or horizontal axis so that they are evenly distributed on both sides, you create a symmetrical design. If you draw a line down the center of the page in a symmetrical design, the left side appears to be a mirror of the right side. This type of balance is appealing. It projects stability and harmony. See Figure 4.9 for a symmetrical design that conveys a state of rest or equilibrium. Symmetrical designs are a formal approach to layout that is aesthetically pleasing. There is a certain simplicity and familiarity in symmetry that makes it easy to decode and interpret.

With all these advantages, why not always use a symmetrical layout? The disadvantage is that when you use identical forms on both sides of the axis, a design can appear inert. The white space may look like leftover space rather than designed space. When white space is not intentionally designed as a shape, it is static. Furthermore, with symmetrical designs, you may find it more difficult to create emphasis or a focal point.

FIGURE 4.9. *A symmetrical design conveys equilibrium. Cutout person courtesy of eLearning Art.*

The bottom line is that symmetry works if you are seeking a harmonious, restful design. If you use this approach, remember to also activate the white space.

The Asymmetrical Layout

When you place the elements in an unequal arrangement with respect to the axes, you create an asymmetrical design. Asymmetry creates tension and instability, which adds interest. Because an asymmetrical layout uses the entire graphic space, there is more room to emphasize elements by making some larger than the others.

Asymmetry and white space. You may observe that asymmetrical designs are more likely to display dynamic white space than passive designs. Asymmetry almost forces the negative space to become part of the design. Still, manipulating and controlling the white space is key to a successful asymmetric layout.

Finding balance. Even though an asymmetrical layout is uneven, you can create balance by using elements on either side of the axis that create a counterpoint to each other. Figure 4.10 is an example of a title screen that is balanced through visual weight, even though it is asymmetrical. The large and dominant element with a heavy visual weight on the right is balanced by several smaller elements with a lighter visual weight on the left.

Purposeful imbalance. Achieving balance is not a requirement with asymmetry, however. Depending on what you want to convey, a layout can be intentionally unbalanced. This conveys a disturbing tension and causes discomfort. To achieve this effect, play with the placement and size of the elements until the design is purposefully out of balance.

Both symmetry and asymmetry inherently communicate meaning. Each one projects a different sensibility and evokes a different psychological state. A symmetrical design tends to be static, creating a peaceful and restful composition. An asymmetrical design tends to produce an active and dynamic composition. Choose the approach that best fulfills the objective of your design.

DEPICTING DEPTH IN GRAPHIC SPACE

A lesser-used method for manipulating graphic space in learning materials is creating the illusion of depth. Even if you are not confident in your drawing abilities, there are ways you can take advantage of the human ability to see three dimensions in a flat plane. Adding depth to your design opens up a whole new realm of visual possibilities that can enhance scenes in storytelling, improve the clarity of explanations, and add realism when needed.

Techniques for Depicting Depth

Here are some techniques for adding cues to create the illusion of depth.

FIGURE 4.10. *An asymmetrical design is dynamic. Cutout person courtesy of eLearning Art.*

FIGURE 4.11. *Use a stock photo with a linear perspective as a background to add realism to a story or scenario. Cutout people courtesy of eLearning Art.*

Linear perspective. An easy way to show depth is to find stock photos or illustrations that depict a linear perspective. The edges of a road or a row of buildings on both sides of a street will form two parallel lines that appear to converge in the distance. Use this perspective for a background and place cutout characters or objects in the foreground. Figure 4.11 demonstrates how this can add drama and realism to a story or scenario.

Occlusion. Objects that are closer to the viewer hide or occlude objects that are farther away. To create the illusion of depth, overlay objects that you want to appear in the foreground over the objects meant to be far away. Occlusion is the strongest pictorial cue for depicting depth (Ware, 2008).

Size of objects. You can create perspective through relative scale. Large objects appear closer, and smaller objects appear farther away.

Color. Warm colors, such as yellows and oranges, usually appear to be closer to the viewer than cool colors, such as blues and purples. Use color in this way to achieve depth.

Texture detail. The detail of an object's surface texture is more visible when the object is close to the viewer. As the object recedes in the distance, the texture gradient becomes denser and the surface appears smoother.

Shadows. Placing shadows behind objects and casting shadows on other objects is a visual cue that depicts depth.

THE **TAKEAWAYS**

- Visual design involves the arrangement of images and type in graphic space.

- Think of two-dimensional space as a design element that is as important as images and text.

- White space or negative space does not need to be filled up. Rather, it needs to be intentionally designed and considered as a shape.

- Design with a grid for consistency and unity.

- Align elements with each other by their left, right, or center axes. Or use an overlapping or non-linear alignment.

- Use a symmetrical layout to achieve a restful and static design; use an asymmetrical layout for one that is more dynamic.

CHAPTER

Selecting and Creating Images

"Listen to your eyes."
— Robin Williams

THE FRAMEWORK

THIS CHAPTER answers these questions:

- What types of images should I use?
- What graphics are best for learning?
- Should I use realistic or abstract graphics?
- How can I modify stock images?

Of the three components that make up design—visuals, type, and space—you are probably most accustomed to working with visuals. In this book, visuals refer to the photography, illustrations, graphs, diagrams, icons, and shapes in your design. The right visuals used in the right way are essential to many aspects of learning.

As a designer, think broadly at first and explore all of your options. Do you need a representational image or a conceptual depiction to improve comprehension? Consider the nuances of each image you use in terms of what it communicates and how it will be perceived and interpreted by the audience.

In this chapter, you will explore ways to expand the repertoire of visuals you select. You'll discover techniques for adding interest and emotional appeal to your visuals. You will learn how to select or create images with visual qualities that align with your intent.

SO MANY CHOICES

When you think about the images you might select in learning or presentation materials, do you envision the same types of graphics for every project? If so, take the time to consider all of your options and alternatives. The array of choices is nearly overwhelming.

As you consider what type of visual to select, remember that the learner or viewer will be *reading* the visual—decoding and interpreting it for meaning—along with the text. Therefore, seek out visuals that are high quality, appropriate for the communication, and effective for your purpose. Let's review your choices, which include photographs, illustrations, 3-D art, silhouettes, icons, dingbats, infographics, shapes, and found art.

Photographs

Photographs may be the first type of graphic that comes to mind—and for good reason. There are millions of photographs available at stock photo sites. Photos are dependable and versatile—they can represent something concrete, tell a story, or convey an abstract idea, as shown in Figure 5.1.

Most important, photographs are credible. Author Mark Galer describes the hidden power of photographs: "A photograph, whether it appears in an advertisement, a newspaper, or in a family album, is often regarded as an accurate and truthful record of real life. Sayings such as 'seeing is believing' and 'the camera never lies' reinforce these beliefs" (2007, p. 130).

To the contrary, you and I know that the content of a good photograph is intentionally framed by the photographer to include the most suitable visual information and to exclude anything extraneous. Furthermore, we know that the designer selects which part of the photograph to use. Yet an audience will see the photograph as "real," even though it is a two-dimensional representation.

There are some disadvantages to using photographs, however. Stock photos often present people in settings and poses that look artificial. In addition, it can be difficult to find stock photos that are inclusive—showing varied ages, genders, races, and ethnic groups involved in the activities you want to show. You may find that shooting your own photographs will more accurately represent what you want to express.

Color photos. Photographs in full color are appealing and add visual interest. Color provides a layer of information that is helpful for recognizing objects and scenes. You can use color to enhance the emotional content of a message because color conveys a mood. Color photographs are the default format of stock media and are what most clients and audiences expect. Choose color photographs when you want to:

- Meet client and audience expectations,

- Emphasize credibility,

- Depict an object or scene realistically,

- Use vivid imagery, or

- Create a striking abstract background.

Photographs can...

show something concrete

tell a story

convey
a concept

FIGURE 5.1. *Photographs are versatile. They can represent something concrete, tell a story, or convey an abstract concept.*

Black and white photos. Black and white photos (shades of gray) are more subdued than color. This makes them subordinate to stronger elements on the screen or slide. If you choose to go with black and white, you may want to use this image style throughout your project for consistency. One exception might be to use black and white photographs to represent times past, in contrast to color photographs that represent contemporary times. Choose black and white photographs when you want to:

- Provide a less conventional treatment,
- Make the photographs subordinate to other visual elements,
- Present serious content,
- Portray events in the past,
- Add artistic flair, or
- Design for print when color is too expensive.

Most graphic programs make it easy to convert a color photograph to shades of gray, but do so with care. Don't just accept the default settings of the program. You will often need to optimize the contrast and brightness of converted photographs to improve their quality.

Illustrations

Illustrations are hand-drawn representations of real or imagined people and objects. They can release you from the constraints of photographs, which are expected to be realistic. The magic of a drawing comes from the illustrator, who interprets and translates the subject. Illustrations are typically less complex than photographs and are often stylized. Photorealism is the exception. In this case, the artist is so precise that it is difficult to distinguish the illustration from a photograph.

In this book, I refer to illustrations as those created on a computer or rendered on paper with pen, pencil, or paint. Regardless of the tool used to create them, illustrations are compelling because of their variety and uniqueness, as shown in Figure 5.2. Use illustrations when you want to:

- Portray things that cannot be seen,
- Show imaginary people and objects,
- Use a simplified or technical depiction,

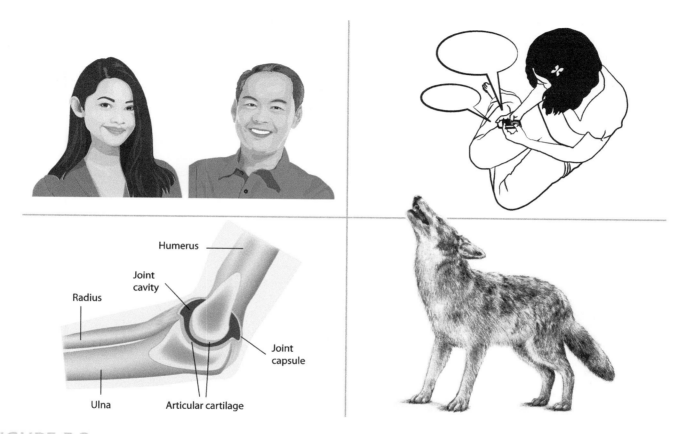

FIGURE 5.2. *Illustrations are compelling because they often have a unique and distinctive style.*

- Address sensitive subjects, or

- Create a unique style.

Here are some categories of illustrations.

Vector illustrations. These are drawn on the computer using a vector graphics program (these are explained in Chapter 3, Work Like a Designer). The result is an illustration that can be scaled to any size without losing quality.

Hand-drawn illustrations. Created with pencil or pen, hand-drawn illustrations are distinctive, often reflecting the artist's unique style. Even though they start as hand-drawn representations, they can be digitized in a variety of ways and used in eLearning courses, slides, websites, and other learning materials.

Line art. These illustrations are created with lines of varying thickness. Line illustrations may not have interior shading and are usually rendered in black and white.

Comic style illustrations. The comic style refers to an illustrated narrative that tells a story. You'll go deeper into this in Chapter 15, Tell Stories with Visuals.

Clip art illustrations. You've probably seen low-quality cartoon figures in slides and training manuals that people refer to as *clip art*. Clip art has a bad reputation because much of it looks cheap. But not all clip art is of the same caliber. If you are working with limited funds, you may need to rely on higher quality free clip art for your graphics. When speaking to clients or stakeholders, I recommend referring to clip art as "stock illustration" to minimize the negative perception others may have. You will be able to make it look high quality.

If you are looking for a good clip art resource, try the vector-based illustrations from the Microsoft Office® clip art collection. You can find the collection in PowerPoint or view the collection online.

RESOURCES: GETTING CREATIVE WITH CLIP ART

Find more ideas for working with clip art from these resources:

- The Rapid eLearning Blog by Tom Kuhlmann
- *Better Than Bullet Points: Creating Engaging e-Learning with PowerPoint* (2nd ed.), by Jane Bozarth

The vector-based illustrations are WMF files and are resizable (although not all WMF files are vector). Vector clip art in a WMF format provides the most flexibility when PowerPoint is your graphic editor, because you can break the graphics apart by ungrouping them. When an illustration is ungrouped, you can modify and manipulate its individual parts, as shown in Figure 5.3.

For example, you can re-color a character's hair or move the arms into different positions. You can take two or more clip art objects, remove their backgrounds, and place them together in one shape. With characters ungrouped, you can switch body parts with other characters to create the poses you need. By exploring the options you have with clip art, you may find that they can meet your graphic needs.

FIGURE 5.3. *You can break apart vector-based clip art and modify it to meet your requirements. Here, the business suit in the upper right is placed on the two characters in military garb. Illustrations from the Microsoft Office® clip art collection.*

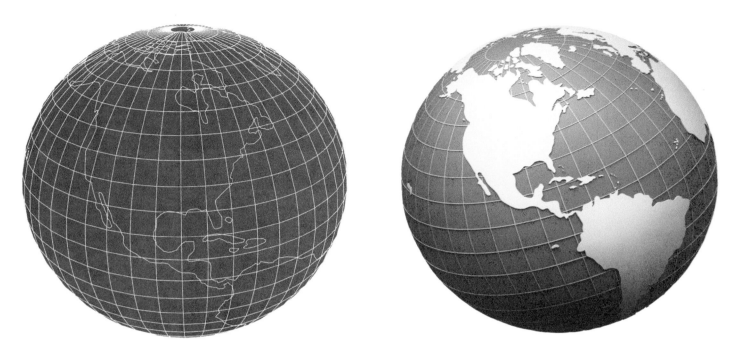

FIGURE 5.4. *3-D graphics are rendered from a wireframe model.*

3-D Computer Graphics

The graphics produced with 3-D modeling software appear three-dimensional because of their realistic shading, lighting, and textures. As shown in Figure 5.4, The artist creates a wireframe model of an object or person and then selects the desired light sources, surface textures, perspective, and depth. The computer renders the 3-D object, which exists as a mathematical model. It can then be rotated and viewed from all perspectives. Some 3-D graphics achieve photorealism, making them indistinguishable from photographs. Use 3-D computer graphics to:

- Show an object from many perspectives,

- Create an imaginary environment,

▓ Depict hidden parts in living systems or machinery, or

▓ Add appeal and interest to your work.

Silhouettes

A silhouette is a representation of a person or object that is filled in with a solid color or gradient (gradual blending together of two or more colors). Although silhouettes are usually black, they appear beautifully understated in tones of gray and become more dominant when filled in with a bright color. Regardless of the color, it is the lack of detail in the silhouette that makes it valuable. (See Figure 5.5 for some examples.) Use silhouettes to:

▓ Make a visual suggestion,

▓ Express an object or person in a subtle way,

▓ Avoid the distraction of showing a face,

▓ Be all-inclusive by showing people in a generic fashion,

▓ Create unique title and section screens, or

▓ Depict objects in graphs, charts, and diagrams.

Icons and Symbols

An icon is a highly abstracted and simplified graphic with very few details, although it is still recognizable. Icons are powerful because they convey a wide variation of meanings within a minimalist format. Because of their simplicity, easily recognizable icons are perceived and understood quickly. See whether you quickly grasp the meaning of the icons in Figure 5.6. From icons that represent objects, such as a bus stop icon, to icons that must be learned, like the "Do Not Enter" symbol, you can leverage icons to enhance the meaning of learning content. Use icons to:

▓ Communicate rapidly,

▓ Indicate categories of information,

▓ Represent the functionality of an application,

▓ Improve memory of a principle (as a mnemonic device), or

▓ Depict elements in a diagram or chart.

FIGURE 5.5. *Silhouettes are a subtle communication device. They are suggestive rather than literal.*

Dingbats

Dingbats are a category of typeface that consists of shapes, decorations, and symbols rather than letters and numbers. You can find several collections of dingbats in the Wingdings and Webdings typefaces, and many more collections can be found online. See the examples in Figure 5.7.

FIGURE 5.6. *Icons are a minimalist and powerful way to communicate.*

Sample of Webdings Symbols

Sample of Wingdings Symbols

Sample of Wingdings2 Symbols

FIGURE 5.7. *Dingbats are a source of icon-like drawings and symbols.*

Dingbat characters have several uses. They allow you to quickly create a small decoration as part of the content. You can also use dingbat symbols for a minimalist graphic or an icon, varying the scale by using a larger or smaller point size. Dingbats provide a free collection of icons and illustrations that are easy to access. Find out more about dingbats in Chapter 13, Add Some Excitement. Use dingbats when you want to:

- Add a flourish to a design,

- Depict objects as icons,

- Use a clean and simple illustration (use a large point size), or

- Create a minimalist version of an object.

Information Graphics

Information graphics refer to abstract representations, such as graphs, charts, diagrams, maps, and timelines. These types of graphics are essential for helping an audience understand quantitative information and complex ideas. They make statistics more real than "just numbers" and can be used to visualize concepts, as shown in Figure 5.8. Use information graphics to:

- Make abstract concepts concrete,

- Visualize statistics and data,

- Tell a story—using data, or

- Support a persuasive point.

Shapes

A shape refers to a two-dimensional closed outline that is a basic element of design. You can fill shapes with color, pattern, texture, or type. Shapes can be geometric (circle, rectangle, square, triangle) or organic (irregular).

You can use shapes to create a design, as a background for graphics and text, and to differentiate regions on the screen. Choose shapes so that they enhance the impression you want to project. Contoured shapes tend to be soft and inviting; rectangular shapes are more precise and structured. Organic shapes may be interpreted as ambiguous or vague or as a way to represent something that is natural. Figure 5.9 is an example of using shapes to structure the screen. Use shapes to:

- Define areas of a layout,

- Create an abstract background,

- Provide emphasis (when placed behind something),

- Organize and structure information, or

- Add visual interest to a design.

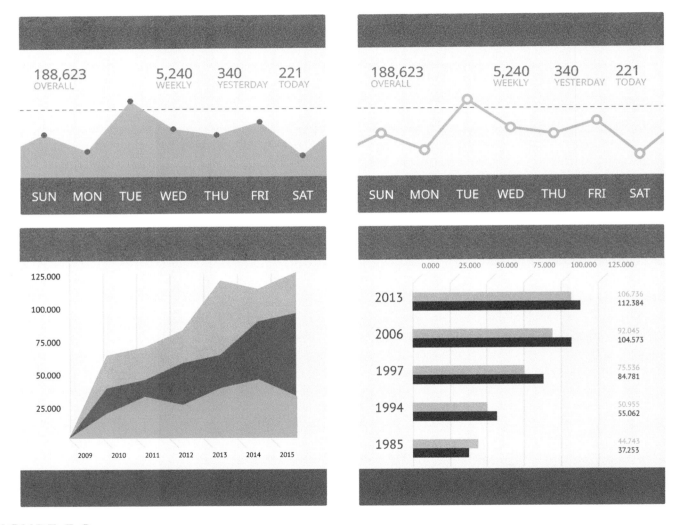

FIGURE 5.8. *Information graphics are a way to make abstract concepts concrete.*

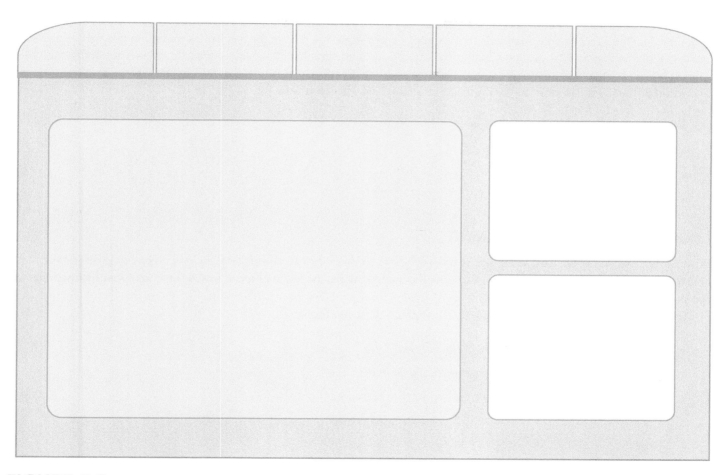

FIGURE 5.9. *One use of shapes is to structure a screen or slide.*

Found Art

Found art can add spice to your design. Find interesting patterns and unusual surfaces to scan for unique backgrounds and textures. Also, consider shooting photographs of the textures in a relevant environment and using these in your designs to bring a familiar look and feel to your materials. For example, the design of a course for mechanics might include metal surfaces of cars and tools. In Figure 5.10, scanned imagery of user manuals and graph paper enhance the title screen for a technical writing course. When you take the time to research the history associated with an organization or the content you are teaching, you may discover that found art can work in your project. Use found art when you want to:

- Enhance title and section graphics,

- Design unique backgrounds,

- Make a design relatable, or

- Create montages and collages.

CHOOSING IMAGES FOR LEARNING

With all of these image choices, what type is most effective for learning? Unfortunately, there is no one type of graphic that is best for all learning tasks. Choosing the most effective graphic depends on the purpose it will serve and your instructional and communication goals.

During the design process, it may help to ask yourself these questions:

- What is the purpose and function of the graphic?

- What type of graphic will add meaning to the content?

- What type of graphic will support the appropriate learning process?

- What type of graphic will project the tone I want to convey?

- How can the graphic be cohesive with the rest of the design?

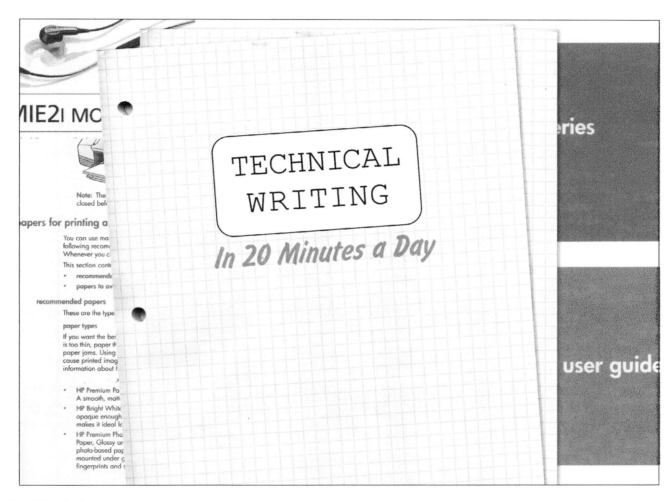

FIGURE 5.10. *Designing with found art can enhance your message.*

Complement Learning

As a general rule, use imagery that is complementary to the learning process and that supports the learning goal. When images are extraneous or distracting, they can interfere with learning (Mayer & Moreno, 2003). The aim is to have learners spend more time and cognitive effort on relevant graphics, rather than to waste it processing irrelevant visuals. Yet we can't forget that visuals have an aesthetic and motivational appeal. When you need to add a graphic for motivational purposes only, try to make the image subtle, such as using a silhouette, so that it does not distract.

Consider the Realism Continuum

One important aspect of working with images for learning is deciding whether they should be representational or abstract. If you think of imagery on a continuum of levels of abstraction, as shown in Figure 5.11, it can help to inform your graphic choices. At

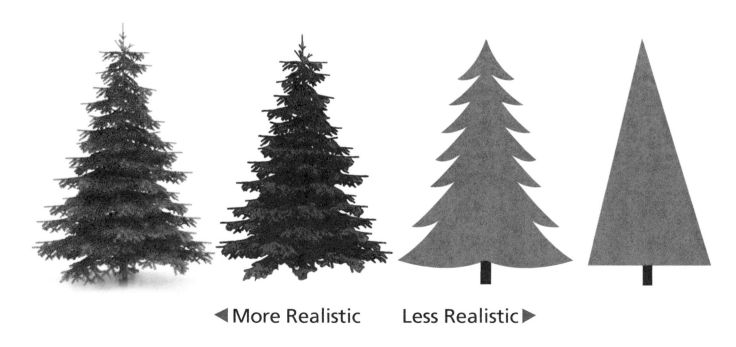

◀More Realistic   Less Realistic▶

FIGURE 5.11. *A tree seen on the continuum from realistic to more abstract.*

one end of the continuum are realistic or literal images. These demonstrate a high degree of likeness to an object. The details and shadows, the textures and color variances, replicate what you see in the physical environment. Photographs and photorealistic 3-D graphics are in this category.

Further along the continuum are graphics with some degree of abstraction, although they are still recognizable. These are distilled down to the essence of an object. There is no intent to make them appear realistic. Line art, silhouettes, and icons are in this category. At the far end of the continuum are conceptual or abstract graphics. These include diagrams, charts, graphs, maps, and timelines.

What Would You Choose?

Suppose you are designing instructions that explain how to operate a professional video camera to an audience with no previous experience. You can choose between the two styles shown in Figure 5.12. Assume each presentation points out the parts of the camera learners need to know and explains how to start. The only difference is that the first presentation consists of photographs and the second uses simple line drawings. Which approach do you think would be best?

FIGURE 5.12. *Simple visuals like the one on the right are often easier to understand than photographs, as shown on the left, because unnecessary information is filtered out.*

For novices, the line drawing approach is usually most effective. Even with a moderate or high level of competence with similar cameras, learners might still achieve better outcomes with simpler visuals (Scheiter, 2009). Photographs often include too much visual information that interferes with focusing on what is important.

Uses for Simple Illustrations

When a learner looks at a simple illustration, there is less information to examine and interpret, fewer visual distractions, and an increased chance of focusing on the right information when compared to a photograph. A general rule, based on research evidence, is to include only enough visual information needed for the task at hand (Hegarty & Canham, 2010).

Benefits of Distilled Graphics

In summary, some of the cognitive advantages of graphics that are distilled down to their important features include the following:

Quick visual scanning. When we read an image, we scan it to extract significant information. A graphic with a minimum of visual elements, such as a line drawing, will take less time to view and assimilate compared to one that is more complicated, such as a natural scene in a photograph.

Less information to process. Working memory has a limited capacity and is easily overloaded. Distilling a graphic down to its essential visual elements minimizes the amount of information that working memory has to process.

Fewer distractions. The presence of unnecessary elements can distract the viewer from focusing on the key message.

Fewer misunderstandings. Superfluous visual information has the potential to cause misunderstandings due to misinterpreted cues. A minimalist approach to visuals should avoid this problem.

Uses for Complex Imagery

This is not to say that you should only use simple illustrations for learning. Suppose you are teaching home inspectors to recognize safety hazards in residential housing. For this type of recognition task, you would want detailed photographs of common defects. The same is true for studying plant diseases. A true-to-life photograph would provide the best opportunity for identifying pathologies. In both of these cases, the learner needs to develop keen observation skills when visual complexity is required. In addition, experts can often manage the additional complexity of photographs and may prefer them.

Before selecting a style, then, consider the purpose of the graphic and what type of understanding it must support. Then select accordingly from the realism continuum.

Summary of Graphics for Learning

Table 5.1 has suggestions for specific graphic types to use for common instructional and communication goals.

TABLE 5.1. **Graphic types to use for varied goals.**

Instructional or Communication Purpose	Consider These Graphic Types
Depict concrete objects	Photograph 3-D graphic Illustration Clip art (particularly in diagrams and as game elements)
Tell a story or provide a scenario	Sequence of photographs Sequence of illustrations Timeline
Persuade an audience	Sequence of photos or illustrations to tell a story Photographs that evoke emotions Visualization of statistics and data
Explain unfamiliar or complex concepts and theories	Visual metaphor Diagram showing connections
Demonstrate a procedure	Show the steps in a sequence of photos or illustrations Flow chart Series of screen captures for software simulation
Explain a process	Diagram the stages or operations of the process Icons or simple illustrations to represent each component
Point out something specific	Arrow or pointed shape Highlight Outline of a circle
Depict components of a system	Illustrated object with labels Diagram of the structure
Make comparisons	Bar graph Pictograph Line graph with multiple lines Table (when specific values are important)

(continued)

TABLE 5.1. *(continued)*

Instructional or Communication Purpose	Consider These Graphic Types
Demonstrate trends in data	Line graph Scatter plot
Organization of information	Various chart types (hierarchical, radial, etc.) Concept map
Demonstrate motion without animation	Show object moving along a path Illustrations with motion lines Illustrations with arrows or dashed lines depicting movement
History or changes over time	Timeline (these don't have to be arrows) Sequence of photos or illustrations

CREATING IMAGES

Once you know the types of images you need for your project, you have three choices for obtaining them: select graphics from stock media sites, outsource the work to an illustrator or photographer, or create them yourself. Your skills, budget, and available time will help you make this decision. Before you skip the "create it yourself" option, give some thought to what you can create on your own. Here are some possibilities.

Combining Shapes into Simple Objects

If you only need simple objects, you can combine shapes in PowerPoint or a graphic application to create any number of things. Figure 5.13 shows how you can create buildings and an entire scene from geometric shapes. You can also use a gradient fill or texture for a more realistic surface.

Creating Illustrations

Sometimes a simple sketch may be compatible with the style of your design or fit in with the narrative of your story. For example, with a whiteboard for a background, hand-drawn diagrams are a natural fit. You can draw them on the computer or on paper and scan them. Illustration doesn't necessarily have to be complex or time-consuming for the message to be communicated successfully.

FIGURE 5.13. *This scene was formed from simple geometric shapes in PowerPoint.*

Taking Your Own Photographs

When you can't find the photos you need, when you're trying to tell a story, or when you need greater control of the image, take your own photographs or hire a photographer. Create a complete shot list of every photograph needed, including props and setting, ensure you have the appropriate equipment, and use professional image software for post-production enhancements.

Plan your own photo shoot when you want to:

- Visualize a scenario that takes place in a unique environment,

- Depict a person wearing clothing or a uniform specific to the scenario,

- Show specific equipment or machinery,

- Feature an expert, or

- Demonstrate steps of a process in photos.

MAKE EVERY GRAPHIC YOUR OWN

In the same way that you rework content to meet the needs of a particular learning experience, you should customize the images you select to improve their meaning and appeal. You don't have to accept stock images or even custom photos as they are. Make them your own. Find ways to take each image and maximize its potential by editing it, selecting its essential parts, or improving it. Here are some ways to do this.

Optimize Photos

Photographs typically need some type of visual optimization. They may have a slight blur or an unintended color cast or poor contrast. With graphics software, you can sharpen the image; adjust the brightness, contrast, and colors; and resize it in a way that meets your needs.

Crop Images

One of the most powerful image manipulation techniques is photo cropping. It refers to the practice of removing portions of an image to change the focal point. Cropping gives you control over the image's meaning, allowing you to create emphasis through better framing.

Crop images for dramatic impact by eliminating all of the extraneous and unimportant visual information. This makes it easier for the viewer to focus on what's important. In Figure 5.14, the cropped photo on the right captures the intensity of emergency work by focusing on the faces and movement of the medical personnel. You can crop with a hard line or feather the edges with graphic software.

When cropping a head, leave some extra room in front of the person so there is space in the direction the person is looking. When cropping portions of a body, many photographers recommend cutting at the 3/4 line—mid-forearm and shins.

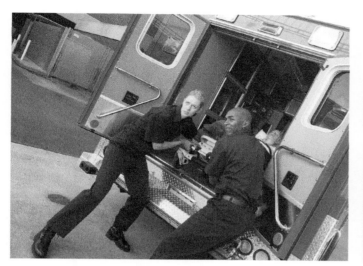 

FIGURE 5.14. *Before and after cropping. Notice how the cropped photo on the right is more dramatic and focused than the uncropped photo on the left.*

Use a Horizontal Slice

A unique cropping technique for wide photos is to use a narrow horizontal slice of the image. Prior to cropping, find a thin horizontal region of the image that will be recognized by the audience and will convey your point. When you crop a thin slice of a picture in this way, you capture a unique perspective of it. See Figure 5.15 for an example of several horizontal slices stacked on top of each other in a presentation slide about environmental responsibility.

Break It into Threes

You can create an interesting effect by taking one full-screen image and dividing it into three vertical pieces. Then separate the sections, placing some space between them. Although it is still easy to recognize the scene, this approach is eye-catching. With a graphic program, you can skew the outer sections for a perspective effect, as shown in Figure 5.16.

Add a Monochromatic Effect

Another way to make a graphic your own is to add a single color tone to a black and white photograph. A monochromatic tone creates a moody atmosphere. If your content is historical, for example, consider using photos with a sepia (reddish brown) effect

FIGURE 5.15. *Use a narrow but recognizable slice of several different photos to convey your message in an unusual way.*

FIGURE 5.16. *Break a full-screen image into three separate vertical pieces for an eye-catching effect.*

for an antique look. To avoid a monotonous palette, it may be best to use the monochromatic effect on one type of slide, such as for review screens or topic titles.

Add Borders

A common design practice is to add a very thin border around photos, particularly when you don't want the photo's edges to blend into the background. Borders are not always necessary, but when placed around a photo, they can add a finishing touch that makes the image stand out. Borders around pictures have their own conventions. For example, you can achieve a casual look by using a thick white border around photographs and skewing them on a slight angle.

Place People on New Backgrounds

Add your own touch to a photo by changing the background image. Using a graphics program, remove the background and place a person or object on a new one. You can play with this approach, incorporating unusual backgrounds in order to make a point.

As an example, in a presentation about the fear of public speaking, you might show the speaker presenting to an angry caveman, shown in Figure 5.17. Not only does this make the image unusual, but you are literally making the point that the fear of public speaking harkens back to something primal, as some research suggests. This is one way to enliven a conventional photograph and add meaning at the same time.

USE A CONSISTENT IMAGE STYLE

Do you ever wonder how experienced designers achieve a polished look in their products? One principle they follow is consistency in style. The style of an image includes its surface features and the personality it conveys. In a professional design, the visual styles are cohesive and the elements are well-coordinated. Here are some ideas for creating a consistent style.

First, Choose the Right Style

You, too, can apply a consistent approach to the images you select or create. The style you choose is an important part of the meaning you want to convey. Base your style choices on the audience research you accomplished early in the project. You don't want to use a skull and crossbones motif in a retirement course for seniors. Likewise, forget the flower petals and flourishes in a course teaching police how to reduce gang violence. Make sure the style you choose will:

- Appeal to audience members,
- Enhance the content, and
- Reflect the spirit or tone of the organization it represents.

FIGURE 5.17. *Change the background of conventional photographs to add meaning and a touch of surprise.*

On the other hand, you don't want your style to seem dull or repetitious. A surprise every so often is okay, too. Who said design was easy?

Select Consistently Unusual Images

You can create a unique style by consistently selecting compelling graphics. Rather than choosing the first image that shows up in your search results, look for something unusual that also contributes to the value of the content. Avoid selecting the most literal interpretation and avoid image clichés, such as groups of cheering people in business suits. *How often does that happen?* Tacky photos may ruin your credibility. See Figure 5.18 for a comparison of a cheesy image to represent teamwork with one that is more original. Here are some ways you can find novel images:

- Create a mind map to brainstorm imagery associated with your content.

- Use the terms "conceptual" or "abstract" in your search phrase at stock photo sites, such as "success concept."

FIGURE 5.18. *Comparison of an image cliché to represent teamwork on the left and a more original approach on the right.*

- Seek people in action doing real things, rather than people smiling at the camera.

- Use visual metaphors or humorous associations.

- At a stock photo site, start halfway through your search results, since most people start at the beginning.

- Find ideas by searching for images in search engines to see how others have visualized a topic.

Use One Format: Photos or Illustrations

An easy way to bring consistency to your design is to use either all photos or all illustrations for your *main images* or at least for the images that convey similar information. Otherwise, you are taking a chance that the lack of consistency will subtly disturb the audience. For example, don't switch from photographs of people to cartoons. On the other hand, you may need to switch from photographs of equipment to technical illustrations.

Use a Consistent Illustration Style

Illustrations can be highly variable, reflecting the nature of the content as well as the technique and tools of the illustrator. Try to use one consistent style of illustration, such as highly detailed line art or simplified, iconic graphics, as shown in Figure 5.19. This may be easier to do if you hire an illustrator.

Use a Similar Palette

To achieve a cohesive look, try to find photographs that have similar color schemes, such as a collection of photos with sunny, bright colors or a set of photos with a more muted palette. If you take your own photos, shoot them all in a similar environment and use the same lighting for consistency.

Use One Style of Clip Art

As mentioned previously, you may find usable vector-based illustrations in the Microsoft Office® online image collection. In this collection, the illustrations vary in style, from cartoon characters to fairly realistic drawings and everything in between. Much of the clip art is categorized by a style number, which you can find by inspecting the properties or details of each individual image, as shown in Figure 5.20. To find clip art with similar characteristics, search by this style number.

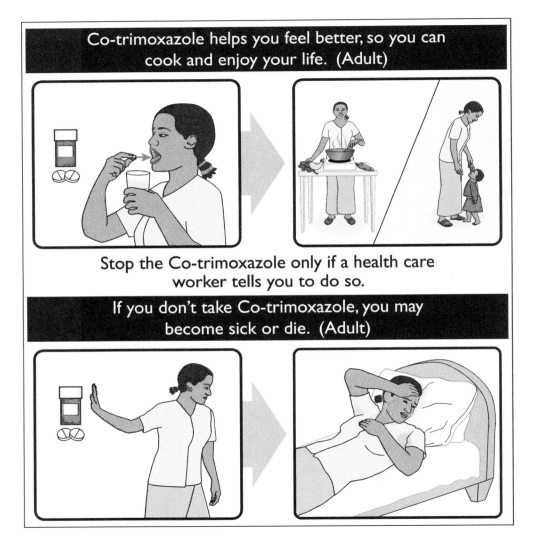

FIGURE 5.19. *Use one consistent style of illustration, as shown in this job aid teaching HIV/AIDS patients how to care for themselves. Illustrations by Alexey Terekov and Cris Wysong, Kwikpoint.*

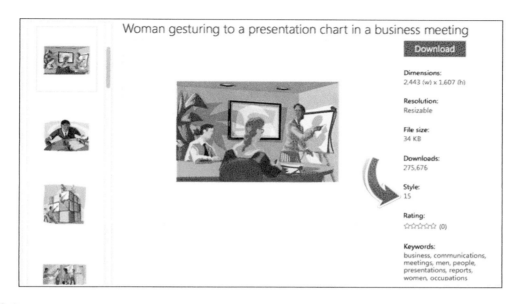

FIGURE 5.20. *Use the style number to find clip art with the same look.*

Make Varied Icons Consistent

If you find a variety of icons from different sources, there are ways to make them consistent. One approach is to remove the backgrounds and darken each icon to create a black silhouette. This makes it easier to recolor the icons to fit your needs. If you can't use silhouettes, take your dissimilar icons, remove their varied backgrounds, and place each one on a similar shape for consistency. See Figure 5.21 for this approach.

The Final Word on Consistency

To improve the consistency in a design, collect the images you select and examine them together as one set. Do they seem related? If not, see whether there is some way you can modify one visual quality across all of the images to increase their likeness.

FIGURE 5.21. *Placing varied icons (top) on a similar background (bottom) can improve the consistency of a design.*

THE TAKEAWAYS

- Consider the extensive variety of graphic types before selecting or creating visuals.

- Consider whether realistic, distilled, or abstract images will best meet your needs.

- When choosing an image type for learning materials, consider the graphic's purpose, the learning process you want to facilitate, and the communication goal.

- Optimize or customize images to better meet the needs of your project.

- Stick with a consistent image style for a cohesive look.

CHAPTER

Working with Type

"Typography exists to honor content."
— Robert Bringhurst

THE FRAMEWORK

THIS CHAPTER answers these questions:

- How can I tell typefaces apart?
- How do I select a typeface?
- How should I mix typefaces?
- How can I make text easy to read?

Typography is the art of designing with words and letters. The typeface you choose for learning and information content is a critical decision. Reading should be smooth and easy so it does not interfere with comprehension. Also, the design of type sends an impression, conveying what you want to communicate before the text is even read. The beautiful variety and range of typefaces provides a tremendous opportunity lo amplify your message.

Don't shy away from studying this building block of design. It is not difficult to grasp the basics of typography, and your eye will improve with practice. Like everything else in design, your choice of a typeface should be intentional rather than random.

In this chapter, you will learn to see letterforms in a new way. You will be given guidelines for making informed decisions about typography.

DIFFERENCE BETWEEN TYPEFACE AND FONT

Are designers snobs? Is there a reason they use the term *typeface* rather than *font*? Although some designers use these terms interchangeably, others would argue that this is incorrect usage. Here's the difference between the two. A typeface refers to the shared design of a collection of characters, including letters, numbers, punctuation marks, and symbols. Times New Roman, Garamond, Helvetica, and Arial are all typefaces. A typeface has a consistent visual appearance.

On the other hand, a font is a complete character set of a single style and some would say a single size of a typeface, such as Garamond bold 10pt or Garamond italic 12pt. A font is one variant of a typeface. A typeface is a family of fonts.

Another way these terms are differentiated is that the typeface is considered the design and the font is the physical embodiment of the design—a digital file or, at one time, metal letters. Nowadays, you may find knowledgeable people who interchange the terms *typeface* and *font*, using them as synonyms. But now you know the difference.

TYPE HAS PERSONALITY

A typeface communicates on several levels. On the surface, the design of the typeface informs how viewers perceive and recognize each letter. On a subtler plane, the style of the typeface affects the viewer as a result of its tone, mood, and attitude. It provides a subtle meaning beyond the text itself.

In *Elements of Typographic Style*, designer Robert Bringhurst writes: "The moment a text and a typeface are chosen, two streams of thought, two rhythmical systems, two sets of habits, or if you like, two personalities intersect" (2004, p. 22). This means that your selection of a typeface should work on every level—reflecting the content and evoking the desired audience response.

Typeface Personas

If you were designing a fire safety course for a workplace, you would not choose a typeface with flourishes designed for wedding invitations. You intuitively know that a typeface conveys a message and a mood. Your audience knows this, too. Research shows that people who are not trained in design pick up cues from a typeface and ascribe its characteristics to a personality.

There is remarkable consistency in the personalities that participants assign to a particular typeface. In one study, subjects viewed fifteen different typeface forms and were asked to describe the personality of each one by selecting from twenty adjectives. Participants were highly uniform in the personalities they associated with each typeface. For example, Arial had a *direct* persona, Comic Sans was considered *friendly*, and a showy script typeface, Counselor Script, was thought to be *elegant* by most participants. The study author concluded that readers are very aware when a typeface matches and mismatches the text (Brumberger, 2003).

HOW TO TELL TYPEFACES APART

One of the first steps in selecting a typeface is to look closely at your choices. No, even closer than that. Examining the anatomy of a typeface is the best way to understand typography. It trains your eyes to become attuned to the differences, similarities, and personalities of each letterform. This can help you make smart design choices and better understand type classification systems, which are based on form as well as typographic history.

Learning about the parts of letters also allows you to intelligently discuss your choices with designers, clients, sponsors, and stakeholders. Imagine the conversations you can have about serifs, ascenders, and x-heights!

Parts of Letters

There are many parts to a letter, but you don't need to remember them all. If you categorize the terms by attribute, such as "terms related to measuring height," they are easier to remember. Let's dissect the letterform and dive into anatomy.

Measuring Letter Height

The invisible lines. There are several implied horizontal lines that serve to measure the height of letter parts. Use these as a guide to help see the differences between typefaces. The important terms associated with height are shown in Figure 6.1.

- **Baseline.** The invisible line on which the letters sit.

- **Mean line.** The invisible line that marks the top of most lowercase letters that have no ascender (the line that extends upward).

- **Cap line.** The invisible line that marks the upper boundary of most uppercase letters.

Above and below the lines. Not all letterforms fit neatly within the invisible lines because they have ascenders and descenders. These parts vary by typeface and are another distinguishing characteristic.

- **Ascender.** The part of a lowercase letter that extends above the height of the letter x (x-height). These letters have ascenders: *b, d, f, h, k.* The height of ascenders varies among different typefaces.

- **Descender.** The part of a lowercase letter that extends below the baseline. Lowercase letters with descenders include: *g, j, p, q,* and *y.*

Prior to selecting a typeface, notice the shape and length of ascenders and descenders because they can interfere with a line of text above or below.

Terms referring to height. There are also a few terms that directly refer to the height of letterforms.

FIGURE 6.1. *Typographic terms associated with height.*

- **X-height.** The x-height is the distance from the baseline to the mean line of the lowercase letters without ascenders or descenders. It is determined by the letter x because this letter has no parts above or below the lines. Different typefaces of the same point size have different x-heights. A larger x-height is one of the qualities of type that makes text more readable at small sizes.

- **Cap height.** The cap height is the distance between the baseline to the top of the uppercase letters or the cap line.

Properties of Serifs

Most people are familiar with the serif. It is the small decorative projection placed on the end of the main strokes of the letters in some typefaces. These little feet distinguish serif typefaces from sans serif typefaces, which have no feet.

Two characteristics to notice about serifs are the thickness of the foot and how the serif is connected, displayed in Figure 6.2. Observe whether the foot is hairline (thinner than the main stroke), slab (thicker than hairline serifs), or wedge (triangular).

FIGURE 6.2. *Characteristics that distinguish serifs.*

Also notice whether the serif is bracketed, which means it is connected to the stroke of a letter with a smooth curve, or unbracketed, with no transition from the stroke to the serif.

Inside and Outside of the Letters

Here are some additional letter parts to pay attention to as you compare typefaces. They are shown in Figure 6.3.

- **Crossbar.** The horizontal bar that connects the middle of uppercase letters *H* and *A*.
- **Aperture.** The rounded negative space (white space) created by partially closed letters, such as the lower part of *e* and the top part of *a*.
- **Counter.** The empty space enclosed (or partially enclosed) in a letter form, such as in *p*, *o*, and *s*.
- **Bowl.** The round curves in a letterform that create a counter, such as in *b, d, P, Q,* and *R.* Bowls often extend beyond the mean line and baseline.

FIGURE 6.3. *Inside and outside of letterforms.*

Uniform or Contrasting Weight

One additional characteristic to look for in a typeface is the variance in the stroke of the letterforms. Notice whether the strokes are uniform or whether they transition from thick to thin within each letter. An easy way to train your eyes to see this is to draw a line through the thinnest parts of the letter *o*, as shown in Figure 6.4. Note the angle of the line, which can be diagonal, vertical, or horizontal. This is known as the *stress* of the typeface, and it shows the thick-to-thin transition in the stroke of a letter. Sans serif typefaces have less variation than those with a serif. Some, such as Verdana, have no stroke variation and, thus, no stress.

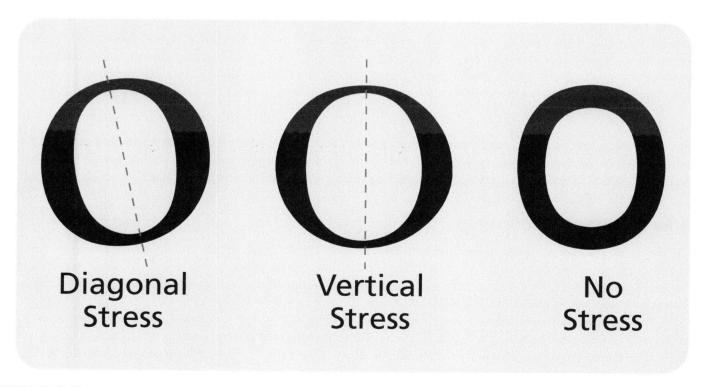

FIGURE 6.4. *Drawing a stress line through the thinnest parts of the letter o helps you see the stroke variation in letterforms.*

DISPLAY TYPE VERSUS BODY TEXT

The reason for using varied sizes and weights of text is to build a visual hierarchy. The hierarchy indicates importance and shows the viewer where to look first, second, and perhaps third. For example, in documents you probably build a visual hierarchy by using a larger point size or heavier weight for titles than you use for the text in paragraphs.

If you study the packaging of most products, you can deconstruct how the designer thought through the visual hierarchy. When you develop the habit of studying typographic hierarchies and design choices in packaging and magazine covers, you'll never be bored waiting in the checkout line of a supermarket again.

Display Type

Although many classic typefaces are readable at both large and small point sizes, some are designed specifically for headlines, titles, and subtitles. These are known as display type. Display typefaces are designed so that they quickly grab attention and look impressive at large point sizes. Often, display typefaces can be difficult to read at smaller sizes and in large blocks of text. Use display type to draw the eyes and to add emphasis, but use it judiciously. As a general rule, do not use display type for body text.

Body Text

Body type is designed to be easily read in a smaller point size. The letters should be recognizable with little effort. The most effective body type for extensive reading will have ample white space in the letter forms, a tall x-height and a medium weight. As a general rule, use the same body text with the same line spacing throughout a course, presentation, website, or job aid.

KNOW FOUR TYPE CATEGORIES

Typographic classification systems are based on both historical movements in typography and the characteristics of the letter-forms. For designing learning content, you probably only need to know four categories: serif, sans serif, script, and decorative. There are many more categories of type, and if you want to go deeper into this topic, see the Resources sidebar for a few books on typography that explain classification systems in detail.

Why do you need a classification system? As with any body of knowledge, categorizing the information is an act of sense-making. With a classification system in mind, you know where to start searching for the right typeface to fit your needs. Classification also helps you discuss typefaces with others and it trains your eyes to examine the important details that distinguish one typeface from another. Let's look at the characteristics of each class.

Serif Typefaces

Serif typefaces have small feet terminating the main strokes of the characters. The serifs vary in width by typeface, a distinguishing characteristic that adds personality to each form. Earlier in this chapter, Figure 6.2 showed how serifs vary in thickness (hairline, slab, or wedge) and vary in how they are connected to the stem of a letter (curved or at a right angle). In addition, serif typefaces are often designed with a graceful variation in the width of the stroke.

As a general rule, serif typefaces are considered easier to read for extended text in print (not online). This may be because it is easier to distinguish their letterforms, which have a thin to thick variation in each stroke, or perhaps because the feet move the eyes along. Although their superiority for print readability is debated by some, most books are printed in serif typefaces. See some examples of varied serif typefaces in Figure 6.5. Some are installed with your operating system or a graphics program, and others you can purchase or access for free online.

RESOURCES: TYPOGRAPHY BOOKS

- *Designing with Type: The Essential Guide to Typography* by James Craig and William Bevington
- *The Anatomy of Type* by Stephen Coles and Erik Spiekermann
- *The Elements of Typographic Style* by Robert Bringhurst
- *Thinking in Type: The Practical Philosophy of Typography* by Alex White
- *Thinking with Type: A Critical Guide for Designers, Writers, Editors, & Students* by Ellen Lupton

Sans Serif Typefaces

Sans serif typefaces do not have serifs. Another distinguishing factor is that they often have little to no variation in their strokes. The x-height of a sans serif typeface is often large. They are considered easier to read on monitors, possibly because of their clean and uniform lines. Figure 6.6 displays some well-known sans serif typefaces.

Script Typefaces

Script typefaces have varied strokes similar to handwriting, either cursive or print. They include everything from refined and graceful typefaces to casual letterforms you might use to simulate handwriting on a whiteboard. Some designers separate these into Formal Script and Casual Script.

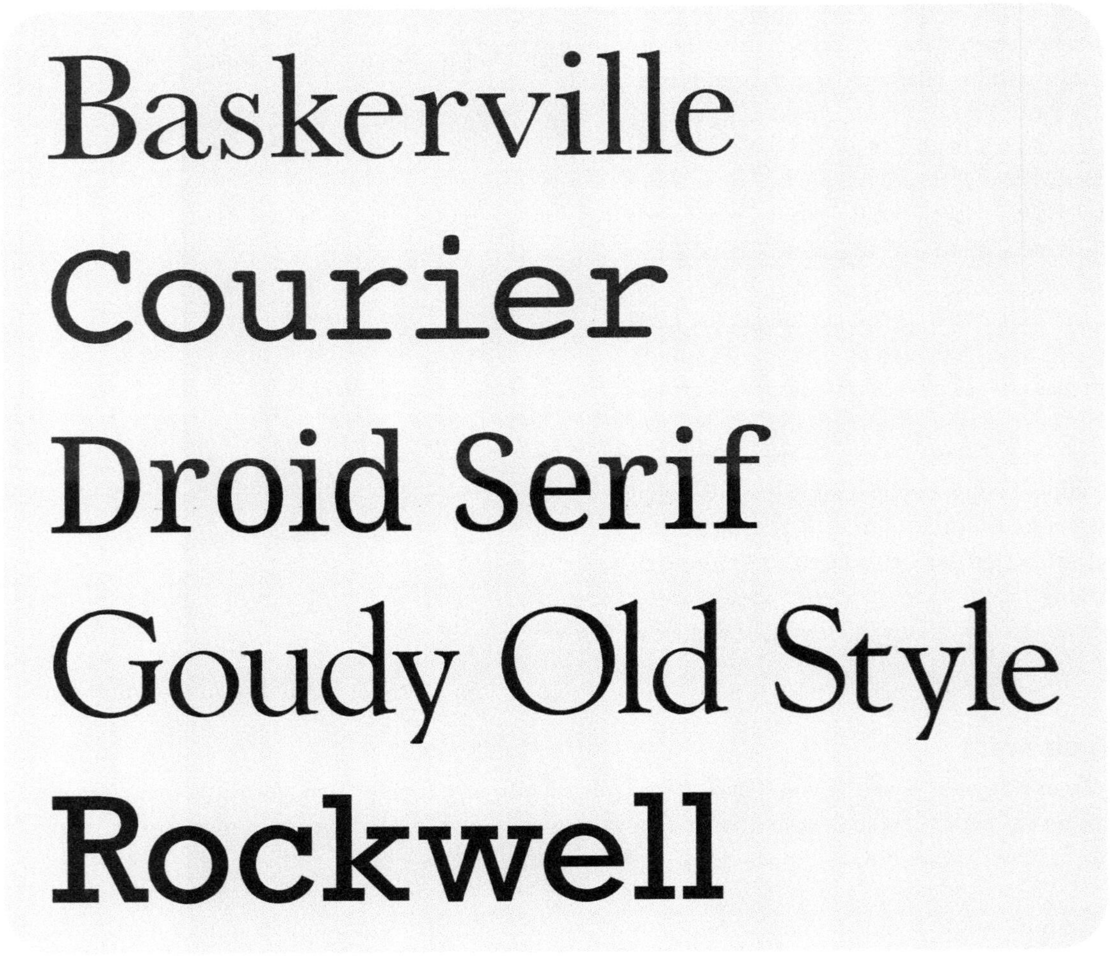

Baskerville
Courier
Droid Serif
Goudy Old Style
Rockwell

FIGURE 6.5. *A collection of serif typefaces, which have small feet at the end of the strokes.*

Franklin Gothic

Frutiger LT

Futura

Myriad Pro

Lucida Sans

FIGURE 6.6. *A collection of sans serif typefaces, which are without little feet.*

For learning and informational materials, avoid script typefaces with flourishes, connecting strokes, or distortions that make them difficult to read. Use highly readable script faces as secondary text to convey a message. One example might be the use of an elegant script typeface for titles in a sales course about a fashionable product line.

You can also use casual scripts that are easy to read for shorter bits of text when trying to project an informal ambience. For example, a casual typeface would work well in a graphic of a handwritten note or in speech balloons. The irregularity of handwritten letters conveys a personalized and appealing touch. For paragraphs of body text, however, rely on a clean serif or sans serif typeface.

When working with script typefaces, use both upper and lower case letters rather than all capitals, as this is easier to read. There are some exceptions, such as the cartoon and casual typefaces that are designed to be all caps. See the range of script typefaces in Figure 6.7.

Decorative Typefaces

The decorative category is a miscellaneous group of typefaces designers use in a large point size for display type (headlines and titles). This catch-all category includes typefaces that are strong, dramatic, and perhaps trendy. Use them to give a quick impression or to express a feeling that reinforces the content—not for paragraphs of text.

Some categories within the decorative classification include grunge and distressed, graffiti, tattoo, and retro. Figure 6.8 shows a variety of decorative typefaces.

HOW TO SELECT A TYPEFACE

With a new awareness of typeface anatomy and classification systems, you have the background knowledge to select the appropriate typeface for your project. Here are some things to consider:

- **Content.** Does the typeface reinforce the goals of your content?

- **Audience.** Is the typeface appropriate for the audience?

- **Display or body text.** Do you need a typeface for large titles and headlines, or are you selecting a typeface for the content, body text, captions, and labels? If you need both, ensure your selection works well in small and large point sizes.

- **Readability.** Will the body text be readable in all the point sizes you need, including the small screens of mobile devices?

Catfisch Script Pro

Brush Script

Edwardian Script

Lucida Calligraphy

Tekton Pro

FIGURE 6.7. *A varied collection of script typefaces.*

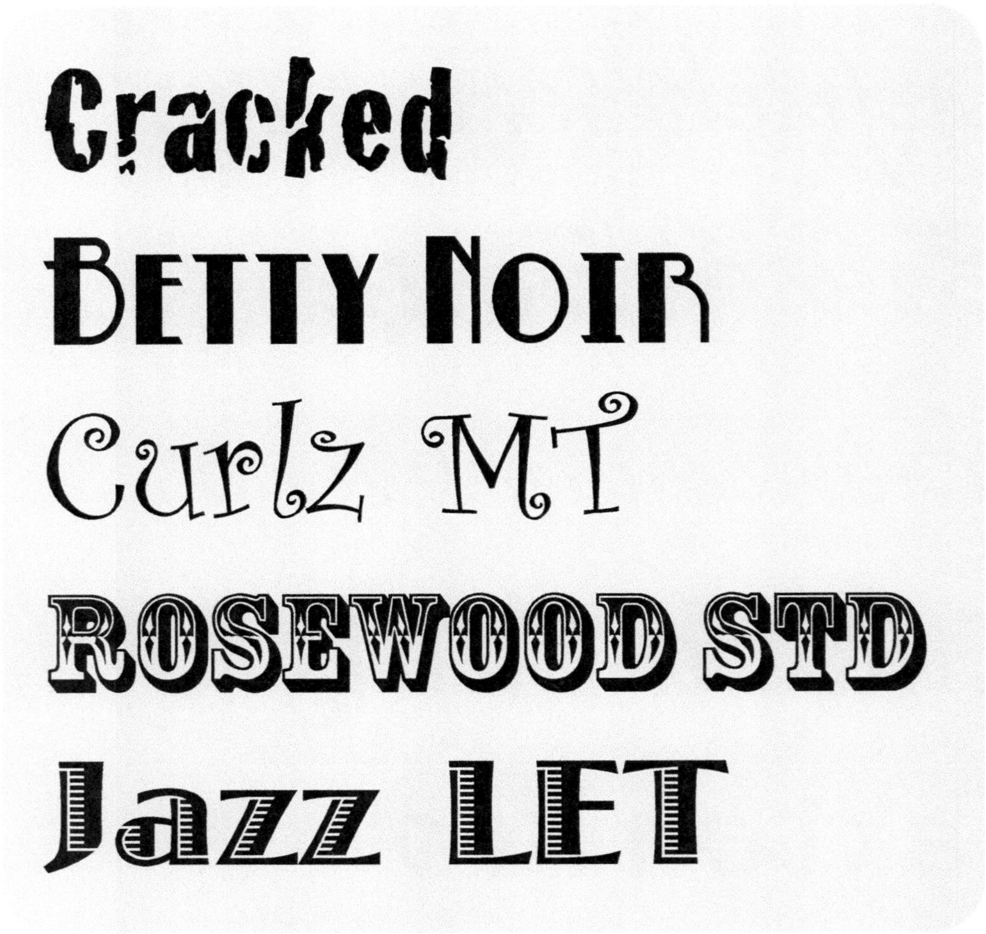

Cracked
Betty Noir
Curlz MT
ROSEWOOD STD
Jazz LET

FIGURE 6.8. *A collection of decorative typefaces, which include everything from grunge to retro.*

▩ **Type family.** Does the typeface come in the variety of styles and weights you want?

▩ **Screen or print.** Is the typeface for screen or print display? Many experts agree that sans serif typefaces are best for extensive reading on the screen and serif typefaces are best for body text in print, although this is not a hard-and-fast rule. Both Verdana (sans serif) and Georgia (serif) were designed for the screen. Consider web fonts for online display if you are creating web pages.

▩ **Platform and device compatibility.** Some typefaces are more readable on different browsers and mobile devices than others. Many projectors make text difficult to read. Test your chosen typeface on the device and browser where it will display. Ensure there is enough contrast between the text and the background and that the text is sized for readability (discussed later in this chapter).

▩ **Special characters.** Does the typeface have all the symbols you need?

▩ **Compression.** How does the typeface look after it is compressed by an authoring tool for online delivery?

▩ **Layout.** Will the typeface fit well in your layout?

▩ **Shapes and images.** Does the typeface resonate with the overall design, shapes, and images? For example, if your design is based on rounded shapes, you may want to use a typeface with rounded letter forms.

USING ONE TYPE FAMILY

Typographic expert Ina Saltz writes: "The more typographic choices we have as designers, the harder it is to practice restraint" (2011, p. 80). To put it another way, mixing and matching typefaces is fun, but it can get you into trouble. If you use too many, you lose the unity and consistency readers need to process information easily. That's why many designers recommend using one type family with many styles. When you require contrast, use variations in size, style, and weight to achieve this.

What Is a Family of Type?

A type family is a collection of typefaces designed to be used together. The related typefaces come in many weights and widths. A type family provides consistency because the letters in the family share common design traits, such as the same general proportions and the same x-height.

Extended Type Families

Any type family that has the basic variants you need, such as regular, italic, and bold, will suffice. But if you need many style variants, consider some of the larger type families: **Bodoni, Cheltenham, Futura, Gill Sans, Helvetica, Helvetica Neue, ITC**

Century, ITC Franklin Gothic, ITC Stone, Lucida, Minion, Mrs. Eaves/Mr. Eaves, Myriad Pro, FF Scala, Thesis, and Univers. See some of the styles in an extended type family in Figure 6.9.

GEEK SPEAK: TERMS DESCRIBING TYPE STYLES AND WEIGHTS

- **Bold.** A typeface with darker, thicker strokes so that it will stand out, good for headlines, titles, and subtitles.

- **Black.** Darker or heavier than a bold weight.

- **Condensed.** The Roman version in a narrow design for fitting letters into a small space.

- **Extended.** The Roman version in a wider design.

- **Italic.** The slanted version of a typeface that is script-like.

- **Oblique.** The slanted version of a typeface, similar to italic but lacking the script quality of a true italic.

- **Roman.** The upright or regular version of a typeface.

There are many benefits to using one extended type family because all of the styles you may need are available. Here are the options you can expect in an extensive family:

- **Variations.** A type family will often include regular, italic, bold, and semi-bold.

- **Type Weights.** A type family will include letterforms with varied darkness or heaviness. Common weights include thin, light, book (Roman or regular), bold, black, and extra black.

- **Widths.** Some type families include a condensed design (narrow characters) for fitting into small spaces and an extended width (expanded characters).

- **Small Caps.** A type family may include varied character sets, such as small caps, which are capital letters the size of the x-height. These can be useful when using capital letters within a sentence, such as for an acronym.

- **Ligatures.** A good family will include special characters known as ligatures. These combine two letters that would normally overlap or interfere with each other. For example, a ligature will prevent the dot above the *i* from running into the tip of the horizontal line of the *f*. The ligature is a more elegant single character that combines these two. Some common ligatures are *fi*, *fl*, and *ff*.

Type Families with Two Categories

Some type families may include both serif and sans serif fonts that were designed to be used together. These are known as superfamilies. See the example in Figure 6.10. Some superfamilies include:

- Base 12 Serif/Base 12 Sans

Myriad Pro Regular

Myriad Pro Italic

Myriad Pro Light

Myriad Pro Semibold

Myriad Pro Bold

Myriad Pro Black

Myriad Pro Condensed

FIGURE 6.9. *Some of the styles you will find in an extended type family.*

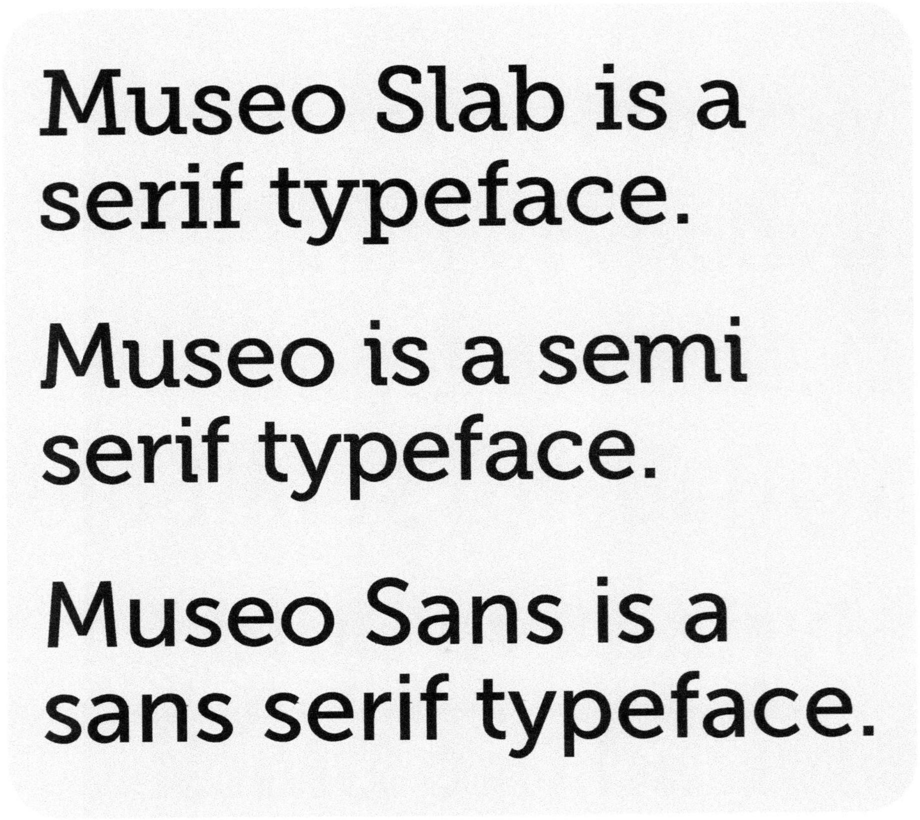

Museo Slab is a serif typeface.

Museo is a semi serif typeface.

Museo Sans is a sans serif typeface.

FIGURE 6.10. *A superfamily, such as Museo Slab, Museo, and Museo Sans, includes both serif and sans serif typefaces.*

- Fedra Serif/Fedra Sans
- FF Scala/FF Scala Sans
- Fontin/Fontin Sans

- ITC Legacy Serif/ITC Legacy Sans

- Museo Slab/Museo/Museo Sans

- PT Serif/PT Sans

- Scala Pro Scala/Sans Pro

- Thesis: TheSerif/TheSans

USING MORE THAN ONE FAMILY

If you choose to ignore the one family advice and want more than one typeface, there are helpful guidelines for selecting a second one. Be aware that combining typeface families takes more skill and experience than using one family. Examine your possible choices and think about them in two ways—look for both contrasts and similarities.

Think Differentiation

Similar to wearing three slightly different shades of black, things look amiss when visual features are just slightly different. That's why your second typeface should be quite distinct from the first.

To make things easy, select a typeface from another category and use it for a distinct purpose. If you choose a sans serif for the body text, then select a serif typeface for titles and subtitles. Or perhaps a sans serif for body text and a casual handwriting script for titles.

The second typeface should be noticeably different, yet its characteristics should not conflict with the first. For example, avoid two typefaces with dramatic and unique personalities, as this can cause visual dissonance.

Think Similarity

Although you want to pair typefaces that are distinct from each other, they should also look harmonious and complement each other. Find two varying typefaces that also have similarities. For example, use a second typeface with one or more similar features, such as:

- *Structure*: Similar proportions, x-height, body height, or stress

- *Weight*: Similar line weight

- *Strokes*: Similar transitions from thick to thin or uniform thickness
- *Impression*: Conveys a similar personality, such as the degree of formality or informality

Combination Examples

Mixing two typefaces involves both analysis and personal taste. Figure 6.11 shows a few examples of typeface combinations that contrast but don't conflict. See whether you find these combinations pleasing and whether they will successfully communicate your message.

LEGIBILITY AND READABILITY

When you apply your knowledge of typography to screens and pages, you will find that a typeface is useless if your audience can't read it. Two ways to measure how well a typeface is perceived and decoded are legibility and readability.

Legibility

Legibility is about perception. It's a measure of how clear the characters and symbols of a typeface are and whether a reader can distinguish between the letterforms. Think about the difference between the clear lettering on a highway sign and the psychedelic lettering on an old rock and roll poster. The highway sign, which must be seen from a distance, is more legible.

When your goal is to have the audience read with the least amount of difficulty, look for certain characteristics in a typeface. Features that make a typeface legible include:

- Letterforms that are distinct from each other,
- Sufficient contrast between the text and the background color,
- Large x-height,
- Large counter spaces (white space within the letters), and
- Simple, clean letterforms.

The detail of the letterforms should make it easier to distinguish one character from another. Legibility, then, is affected by the design of the typeface.

Garamond
Gill Sans

Caslon
Myriad

Museo Slab
Futura

Palatino
Tahoma

Droid Serif
Roboto

Baskerville
Franklin Gothic

FIGURE 6.11. *Some examples of typefaces that complement each other.*

Readability

Readability measures how easy it to read an extended amount of text. In addition, readability can refer to the appeal of the text. This is affected by how the text is arranged and the spacing between characters, words, and lines. Here are some guidelines for improving readability:

Consider the display medium. Readability is affected by the arrangement of the words. Ensure the organization and spacing of the words are ideal for the medium on which it will display. For example, a multi-column layout could be difficult to read on a smartphone.

Use the appropriate size. Use a point size that is readable for the medium where the text will display. Always check how much the text degrades after compression. Check the text on several monitors, particularly small ones, such as those on laptops, and inexpensive monitors, which are in abundance in the workplace. Check on mobile devices, if appropriate,

Use uppercase and lowercase. Avoid letters in all caps for longer sections of text. The shapes of words may be one of the visual cues people use to read quickly. Capital letters are all the same height so readers lose that cue.

Find the optimum line length. The length of a line of text can affect readability. If lines are too long, the reader's eye has to travel too far to get back to the start of the following line. This may cause eye fatigue or make it difficult to find one's place. If the lines of text are too short, the eyes are jumping around so that reading is choppy.

Emphasize or separate text. At times, you may want to clearly separate the text from everything else for emphasis or due to layout constraints. One approach is to use a lightly shaded color, like a dull highlight, behind the text to create contrast with the background. Another approach is to use a thin horizontal line to separate one section of text from surrounding elements. The lines can be placed above and/or below the paragraph.

ARRANGING TYPE FOR GOOD READABILITY

In *Thinking with Type*, author Ellen Lupton writes that "Design is as much an act of spacing as an act of marking." This is especially true when it comes to the arrangement of text for learning materials, where reading should be effortless.

You can improve the legibility and readability of a typeface by optimizing the space between letters, words, lines, and paragraphs. Although you may not have the time or the tools to set perfect spacing between every single letter, here are some all-purpose guidelines to use to your best ability.

White Space

The first thing to consider for improved readability is white space. Place ample white space around text, unless you want it to purposely interact with the graphic. Ensure margins are sufficiently wide, giving the screen or page an appealing lightness. Watch the white space between letters, words, and lines so that it is as even as possible for effortless reading.

Text Alignment

You have several choices when it comes to aligning text. You can align it to the left margin, to the right margin, or you can center it. You can also justify text. A general rule of thumb for alignment is to strive for consistency. Here are some accepted guidelines for text alignment:

Left aligned. For paragraphs of text, left alignment with a ragged right margin facilitates a smooth reading experience. Left alignment makes it easy for the reader to easily find the beginning of the next line.

Right aligned. Right aligned text adds a little design flair on a title screen or when it is aligned to a graphic that is placed to the right of the text. The ragged left edge makes it more difficult to read the text, so use it sparingly.

Center aligned. Placing text in the center may be effective on main title and section screens, for labels, and for short bits of text. But when used for screen and slide headings, it can look inconsistent if everything else on the screen is left-aligned.

Justified text. A block of text that is aligned on both the left and right margins is *justified*. In authoring and presentation tools, justified text can leave uneven and awkward gaps between words that interfere with reading. It is best to avoid using justified text.

Spacing Letters and Words

Many of the accepted guidelines for letter spacing assume the user is working with a professional publication tool for print. So what can you do with PowerPoint, authoring tools, and graphic programs?

When you design multi-screen courses or multi-slide presentations, you won't be able to spend hours adjusting inter-letter spacing throughout. But you may be able to adjust the spacing in your templates and to spend time on the most important slides, graphics, and blocks of text to make letter and word spacing consistent and even.

Kerning. In most typefaces, the spacing between two letters will be uneven at times. This becomes most obvious in large point sizes. Uneven gaps look random and stop the eye from moving smoothly across the text.

That's when you need kerning. It is the adjustment of the horizontal space between individual letters to improve their visual appearance in proportion to the font and the rest of the word. Notice the difference between text that is kerned and text that isn't in Figure 6.12. When possible, try to make the spacing pleasing on titles and subtitles and on the most important screens.

Letterspacing or tracking. Letterspacing refers to the overall spacing between the letters in an entire block of text. Try to make this even and in proportion with the size of the letters. Too much space hinders reading, too little space makes the letters difficult to discern. In blocks of text, you can tell when letters are spaced evenly, because the paragraph takes on an even color. When letter spacing is uneven, darker areas pop out.

Spacing for uppercase. If you use all uppercase letters in headlines and titles, you may need to adjust the letter spacing. Uppercase letters are not designed to be placed next to each other.

How kerning improves text.

Spacing Lines of Text

The vertical space inserted between lines of text is referred to as *leading* or *linespacing*. The term *leading* refers to the strips of lead once used to physically separate lines of metal type for printing. Although most applications automatically apply standard leading based on point size, intentional designers do not trust anything that is automated.

No parts of the letterforms from the line above (the descenders) should touch the letters below. When text has too little linespacing, the lines of text nearly touch or overlap, making the words difficult to read. On the other hand, lines of text that are too far apart vertically don't look like they are related. Like Goldilocks, you want to get the leading "just right."

Creating Optimum Leading

Leading is measured in point size. It is difficult to provide an exact measurement of what leading should be because typefaces and display mediums vary. Still, if you are interested in a general guideline for the optimum leading, try using a size that is 2 to 5 points more than the font's height. Thus, if you are using a 16-point font, consider making the leading anywhere between 18 to 21 points. But do not use this guideline without a visual check. You need to consider other factors, such as the medium where it will be read, size of the characters, weight of the type, and whether the letters are upper or lower case.

Small text or long paragraphs of text might need more leading. Upper case text (such as for a two-line title) may need less leading because there are no ascenders and descenders. As always, try to adjust leading in the templates rather than on individual screens or slides.

PLACING TEXT ON BACKGROUNDS

In eLearning and presentation design, you might want to place text on a gradient or textured background or overlay it on a photograph. Getting this right is crucial so that the background does not intrude on the text. A solid light background or barely visible texture with contrasting dark text is optimum for reading, but there are workarounds when you want to use an alternative approach.

Placing Text on Gradients

Gradients refer to the gradual blending together of two or more colors that fill a background or shape. Gradients usually have a range of dark to light or light to dark. The best technique for placing text on a gradient background is to make sure the gradient range is small, such as very dark gray to medium dark gray. That way, the overlaid text will consistently contrast with every color in the background, rather than blend in. When the range of values is large, it is difficult to find a text color that will be consistently visible against the background. See the comparison in Figure 6.13.

Placing Text on Textures

Avoid placing text on a highly textured or patterned background, because the busyness will interfere with seeing the letterforms. The solution is to overlay a solid or slightly transparent shape on the texture as background for the text. Adding a minimal amount of transparency to the shape brings unity to the slide because the textured background shows through ever so slightly.

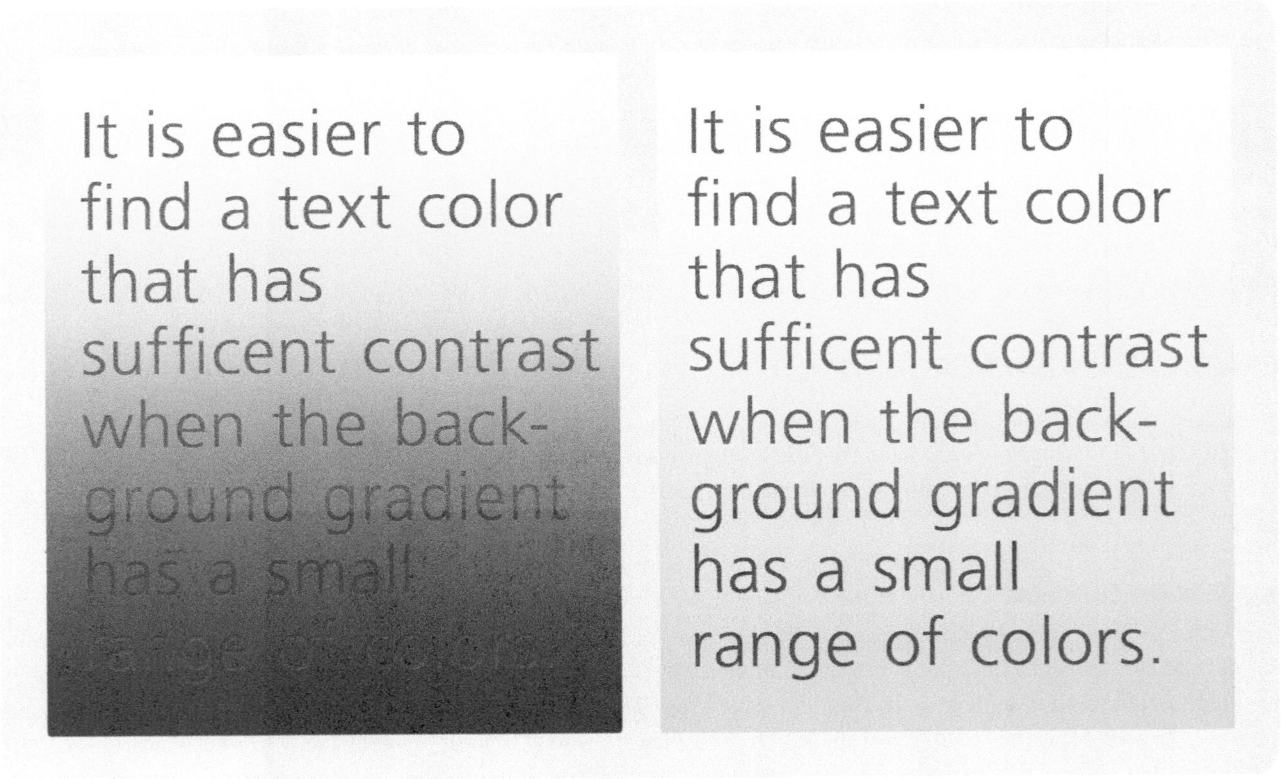

It is easier to
find a text color
that has
sufficent contrast
when the back-
ground gradient
has a small
range of colors.

It is easier to
find a text color
that has
sufficent contrast
when the back-
ground gradient
has a small
range of colors.

FIGURE 6.13. *Comparison of placing text on different gradients.*

Overlaying Text on Photos

If you want to overlay text on a photo, avoid placing it on a busy area of the image. Instead, look for a solid area of color, such as a section of blue sky or a smooth wall. If the image still seems to interfere with the text, use a solid or slightly transparent text box, as described above. One technique for short bits of text is to use a very large photo and then place a long thin rectangle across the width of the photo to serve as the text container. This provides an original look compared to the typical small text box that is often placed in the corner of the screen. See Figure 6.14 for an example.

MEETING STRATEGIES

Meeting Strategy 3: Hold different types of meetings for different types of information. Keep administrative meetings separate from tactical meetings.

FIGURE 6.14. *One approach for overlaying text on a photograph.*

THE **TAKEAWAYS**

- A typeface is a collection of characters that share a common design.

- Select a typeface that fits with the audience, content, medium, and overall design.

- The best option for novice designers is to use one typeface from an extended family. If you want to use more than one typeface category, consider choosing two from the same superfamily of type.

- Features that make a typeface legible include distinct letterforms, sufficient contrast, large x-height, ample counter spaces, and clean letterforms.

- To ensure readability, make the white space as even as possible between letters, words, and lines of text. Dark text on a light background is optimum for extended reading.

PART

3

POWER PRINCIPLES

The principles of design will eventually become tacit knowledge and run like a thread through your work. This section presents five compelling principles to apply to your designs. Let these principles guide your decisions from this point forward.

7

Use Color with Purpose

"In order to use color effectively it is necessary to realize that color deceives continually."
— Josef Albers

THE FRAMEWORK

THIS CHAPTER answers these questions:

- What are the psychological effects of color?
- How can I use color in learning materials?
- How do I design for people with color vision deficiency?
- How do I select a pleasing palette?

Color will demand a lot from you. It must work with the typography and images you select. It must also fit your content, your audience, and your purpose. But that's not all. Color is a chameleon. It changes appearance according to its surroundings. And to make things more difficult, people are known to perceive colors differently.

But you can't ignore color. It is a powerful channel of communication and an enigmatic aspect of visual design. It has both an aesthetic as well as a utilitarian purpose. Color creates a mood, attracts attention, and conveys meaning. It can add visual appeal, improve usability, and enable learning.

In this chapter, you will come to better understand color and see how to manage it. You will learn a bit about color theory and how to select a pleasing palette. You will also find out how to best express the message you want to convey through the intentional use of color.

COLOR AND EMOTION

Colors are known to evoke emotions and, as a result, are capable of affecting one's overall experience with colored materials. An individual's reaction to color may vary by his or her culture, past history, psychophysiology, and individual preferences (Taylor, Clifford, & Franklin, 2013). Even with all the variation among individuals, there are still some common associations and responses that people have to particular colors. The following comes from research mostly conducted in the United States and Europe.

- **Pleasure from Colors.** There is more consistency in the emotional effects of color brightness and saturation than there is to hue. People consistently experience pleasure from bright colors and, secondly, from saturated or vivid colors.

- **Color Preferences.** Color preferences are probably a result of the degree to which a color evokes positive or negative feelings (Kaya & Epps, 2004). Color preferences are not universal.

- **Stimulating Colors.** Yellow and red have a stimulating effect that results in psychological excitement or arousal. These two colors elicit more excitement than greens and blues. Yellow is often considered cheerful, and red is considered exciting.

- **Serene Colors.** Green and blue are often associated with a calm and relaxed feeling.

- **Dark Colors.** Generally, darker colors—defined as less bright—evoke feelings of dominance (strength), as do more saturated colors, which are more vivid or pure (Valdez & Mehrabian, 1994). In one study, black was associated with greater degrees of perceived aggression and wearing black uniforms led to higher levels of aggressive behavior in sports (Frank & Gilovich, 1988).

- **Bright Colors.** Vivid, bright colors are associated with "showiness," and duller colors are associated with "calmness" (Valdez & Mehrabian, 1994).

- **Neutral Colors.** Neutral colors, such as white and pale gray, are often seen as understated and elegant (Tucker, 1987).

- **Symbolic Meaning.** Many people associate colors with objects and events, so that previous experience influences their response to a color. For example, in the United States, while some people associate the color black with power or with being fashionable, others associate it with funerals (Kaya & Epps, 2004).

- **Colors to Avoid.** According to consumer research, colors not received well are bright orange, harsh pink, and lime green (Tucker, 1987).

USE COLOR TO ENHANCE LEARNING

From its psychological and emotional impact to properties that enhance perception, color has an influence on the learning process. Yet many designers use an arbitrary palette and fail to make the best use of color in learning design. Here are some techniques for leveraging color to promote learning.

Color and Motivation

Early in this book, I noted that design features of multimedia learning are known to evoke positive emotions. In two studies, these positive emotions boosted learners' intrinsic motivation and influenced them to perceive tasks as less difficult (Plass, Heidig, Hayward, Homer, & Um, 2014; Um, Plass, Hayward, & Homer, 2012). Color is one of the features that can create favorable feelings.

Although color alone does not guarantee that visuals will be effective, learners do tend to prefer color graphics over black and white. Also, colored visuals will sustain attention for a longer time than will black and white (Pett & Wilson, 1996).

Color and Meaning

One of the main goals of designing learning and informational materials is to reduce the cognitive effort required to understand them. Color can help with this because people derive meaning from colors, providing another dimension for sense-making. Some ways that color enhances meaning and improves learning are listed below:

- **Improves visual discrimination.** In situations when novices are learning to visually discriminate, such as materials that teach how to read radiographs, you can highlight hard-to-see markings with a very distinct color.

- **Improves retention with color coding.** Use color coding to coordinate text explanations with the corresponding parts of an illustration as a way to improve learning. An eye-tracking study demonstrated that this type of color coding improved the efficiency of locating information and signaled where learners should look. Color coding between text and an illustration has been shown to improve retention and transfer (Ozcelik, Karakus, Kursun, & Cagiltay, 2009).

- **Enhances storytelling.** Color is valuable for enhancing the meaning of stories. As an example, in an illustrated story, a red face conveys embarrassment or anger. Using color to convey an emotional response can improve comprehension of the story.

Color and Usability

Usability refers to the ease with which a product can be used, how easy it is to learn to use, and whether it provides a satisfying experience. It is the sweet spot where aesthetics and functionality converge. Usability should always be considered when designing learning materials, because a good experience creates a favorable impression. Here are some guidelines for improving usability with color:

- **Use color consistently.** Through the consistent use of color in a user interface, people associate specific colors with functionality. For example, if the feedback to interactive exercises is always presented in a box with an orange border, users will know what to expect when they see the box. This makes the user interface feel familiar and increases the user's level of comfort.

- **Use color as part of a visual hierarchy.** Color is one of the factors that allows you to rank elements on the screen to establish a visual hierarchy (discussed in the next chapter). Elements that are brightly colored will be noticed first and should be reserved for pointing out the most important information.

- **Use a limited color set.** People can perceive a limited number of different colors simultaneously. When color coding information graphics, such as graphs, with a legend, try to use no more than seven colors (Healey, 1996).

- **Create functional areas in a layout.** You can use color to differentiate and structure graphic space. Color is effective for separating areas of content, such as for navigation, sidebars, and blocks of text.

- **Use cues in addition to color.** However you use color, avoid using it as the only way of imparting critical information. This is one way to accommodate those with color vision deficiencies.

- **Use culturally appropriate colors.** Be aware of the symbolism associated with color when designing for an unfamiliar culture.

DESIGNING FOR COLOR VISION DEFICIENCY

When designing with color, it is important to consider color vision deficiency—also known as color blindness—as it affects around 8 percent of the male population and about 0.5 percent of females. There is a misconception that color blind individuals see in black and white. Rather, common color blindness is the inability to perceive differences between certain colors, most commonly reds and greens. Less common are those who cannot distinguish between blues and yellows.

RESOURCES: COLOR BLINDNESS SIMULATORS

Are your graphics accessible to everyone? You can check specific graphics and web pages using the tools below that simulate color blindness.

- color-blindness.com (select the simulator tool)

- checkmycolours.com

- vischeck.com/vischeck

During the design process, strive to create learning and informational materials that are inclusive and can be used by everyone. Also, accessibility is often required by governmental and other public organizations. You may find it helpful and informative to view some of your images or designs through a color blindness simulator. See the Resources box for suggested simulators.

Design Techniques

To meet the needs of people with color vision deficiency, users should never be required to distinguish between two colors as part of the learning process or as part of the user interface. A rule of thumb is to use redundant visual cues to make distinctions, avoiding color as the only signal. The guidelines below present specific ways to make visual designs accessible:

- **Hyperlinks**. Use an underline to indicate when text is also a hyperlink, rather than using color alone. I prefer to use a dotted line for the underline, as it is less intrusive but still noticeable.

- **Color coding.** Use more than color alone to convey conceptual categories or different sections of a course. For example, add a representative icon, shape, or text in addition to the color.

- **Keys and legends.** To distinguish areas in information graphics, such as graphs, charts, and maps, use line and dot patterns or variations in lightness and darkness in addition to color.

- **Adjacent colors.** When informational areas of color are adjacent, maximize their differences. If one color is light, then the adjacent color should be dark.

- **User selection of colors.** If for any reason users are required to select a color, name the color in text as well as showing the color.

THREE PROPERTIES OF COLOR

In order to make the best use of color in your designs, you will need to understand color theory so you can talk about colors and select a harmonious palette. The best place to start is with the three properties used to describe colors. See Figure 7.1 for a visual of each property.

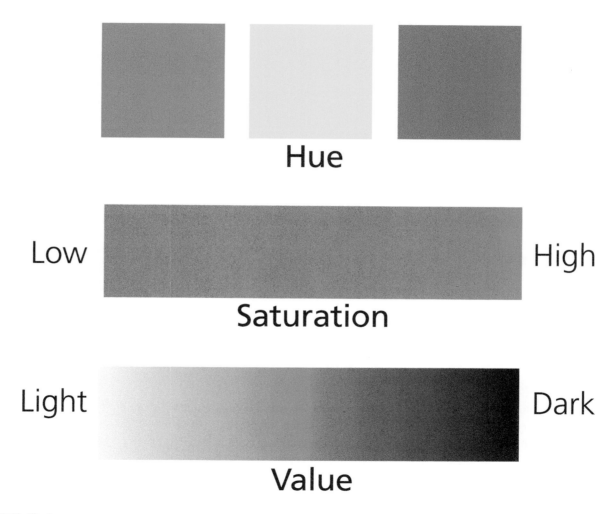

FIGURE 7.1. *The three properties used to describe color: hue, saturation, and value.*

- **Hue** is what we think of as "color," such as, red, yellow, and blue. It is the pure version of a color.

- **Saturation** is the relative vividness or intensity of a color. Sometimes it is referred to as chroma or tone. Technically, it is the amount of gray added to a color. In graphic applications, moving the saturation slider to 100 percent creates a vibrant version of the color. Moving it to 0 percent saturation turns it gray.

- **Value** is the relative brightness (lightness or darkness) of a color. The value of a color gets darker when black is added (shade) and lighter when white is added (tint). Each color has a wide range of values, from the pale blue of a summer sky to the dark blue of the ocean in the distance.

GEEK SPEAK: WHERE DOES COLOR EXIST?

The color of an object is not within it. Color appears as a reaction to the light that shines upon an object and is reflected or transmitted to our eyes.

Depending on the nature of the material and the wavelength of the light, light can reflect off an object, transmit through a transparent object, or be absorbed by the object. When there is no light, there is no color.

DO COLORS HAVE TEMPERATURE?

In addition to hue, saturation, and value, we can describe and understand colors by their temperature. Temperature is also a property of color and it is related to a color's wavelength. Here's how. What we see as color is electromagnetic radiation of a length and frequency that our eyes can detect. A wavelength refers to the distance between successive peaks or valleys of the wave. We perceive the longer wavelengths as yellow, orange, and red; the shorter ones as violet, blue, and green. This is significant because these two color groups are categorized into warm and cool colors, respectively. This reference to temperature refers to a perceptual or visual sensation, rather than heat.

Warm and Cool Colors

Recall that the red, orange, and yellow hues, considered to be the warm colors, are often thought of as stimulating or exciting. The green, blue, and purple hues, considered to be the cool colors, are typically associated with serene and calm feelings. When you look at a painting or a graphic, the warm colors seem to come forward and the cool colors appear to recede. Think of a bright sun nearly popping out of a painting and bluish-purple mountains in the distance.

To be more explicit, look at Figure 7.2. When you see a yellow circle on a blue background, the yellow shape seems to be closer, while the blue seems to recede. When the colors are swapped—yellow on the background and blue in the foreground—it's more difficult to tell which color is meant to be in front. If it works with your palette, use warm colors in the foreground and cool colors for a background.

FIGURE 7.2. *Warm colors (red, orange, yellow) appear to come to the foreground, and cool colors (violet, blue, green) appear to recede.*

Neutral Colors

Some colors are considered neutral; these are black, white, and gray. Tan, brown, and off-white are also neutral or near neutral. Neutral colors may tend toward warm or cool, depending on the colors that surround them. If you feel uncertain about choosing a color palette, any color paired with a neutral is a reasonably safe—although not guaranteed—choice.

THE COLOR WHEEL

Many different color models help designers and artists understand and work with colors. Color wheels illustrate a color model and show the relationships between colors for selecting a pleasing palette. One commonly used color wheel is based on the red-yellow-blue or RYB model. This model identifies three primary colors, three secondary colors, and six tertiary colors. Think of the color wheel as an organizational tool and a way to think about colors.

GEEK SPEAK: COLOR SPACES

You can work with several different color spaces in graphic software. A color space provides a way to reproduce colors. These are common color spaces you will come across.

1. **CMYK** stands for cyan, magenta, yellow, and black. It is the color system used for printing images.

2. **RGB** stands for red, green, and blue. Use RGB for graphics that will be displayed on screens.

   - RGBA allows for the display of colors with varying transparency. The "A" value specifies opacity information.

   - **Hexadecimal codes** describe RGB colors in HTML. The code consists of six digits, including 0 to 9 and A to F. A to F represents the numbers 10 to 15. The format is #RRGGBB. Example: #0000FF is displayed as blue because red and green are set to zero and blue is set to its highest value—FF.

3. HSV stands for hue, saturation, and value and is another way to specify colors in the digital world. It reflects the three properties used to describe colors.

The RYB (Red-Yellow-Blue) Model

There are twelve colors in the RYB color wheel, and you'll see how the arrangement of the colors offers the option for many harmonious palettes. Each color group or slice of the wheel in Figure 7.3 displays the hue or true color in the widest ring. The lighter colors in the inner rings are the tints (white is added to the hue), and the darker colors in the outer rings are the shades (black is added to the hue). You may hear the terms tint and shade used interchangeably in everyday language.

This color wheel includes the following colors, shown in Figure 7.4:

Primary colors. In the RYB model, the primary or pure colors are red, yellow, and blue. They are considered primary because they can't be created by any of the other colors and are the *source* of other colors.

Secondary colors. The secondary colors are orange, green, and violet, which are created by mixing two primary colors.

Tertiary colors. There are six tertiary colors made from mixing the adjacent primary color with a secondary color, giving each hue a two-part name. The tertiary colors are red-orange, yellow-orange, yellow-green, blue-green, blue-violet, and red-violet.

Complementary colors. Any two colors that are opposite on the color wheel are complementary: blue and orange, red and green, and yellow and purple.

CHOOSING A COLOR PALETTE

A color palette or color scheme is the limited set of colors you use in a design. Choose your palette deliberately and stick with it. If you are writing a style guide, you will want to include the color palette in the guide. When designing learning and informational materials, there are at least four things you can hope for from a color scheme. Your color palette should:

- Promote a positive experience,
- Avoid causing eye fatigue,

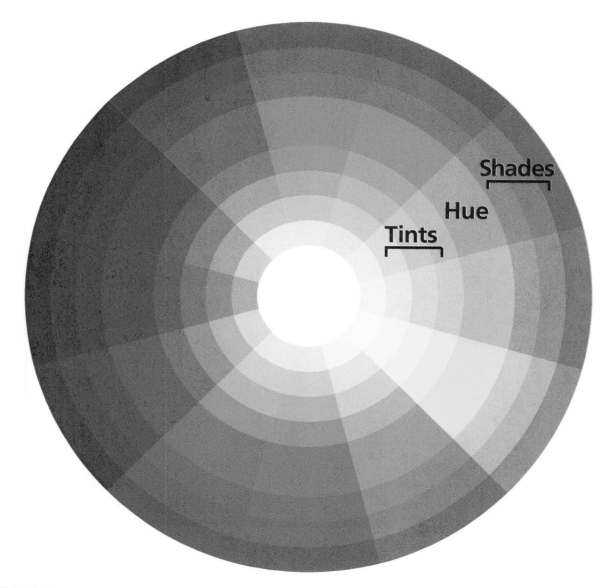

FIGURE 7.3. *The color wheel showing the hues, tints, and shades.*

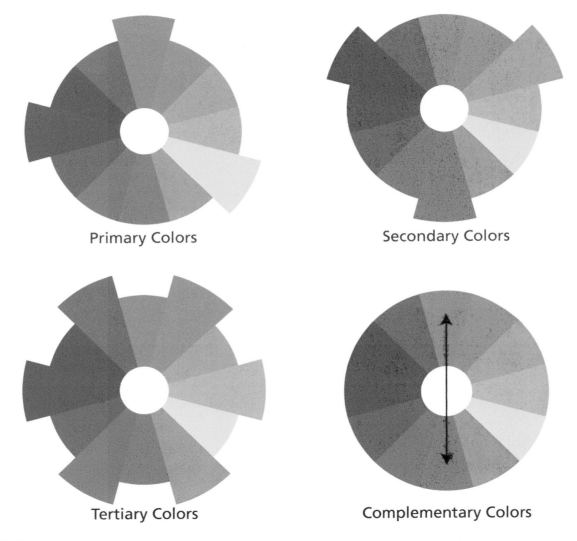

Primary Colors

Secondary Colors

Tertiary Colors

Complementary Colors

FIGURE 7.4. *The primary, secondary, tertiary, and complementary colors of the color wheel.*

- Project the appropriate mood or personality, and
- Be appropriate for the audience and content.

How Many Colors?

The number of colors you need may vary with the project, but it's better to be stingy with your colors than overly generous. Too many colors can be overwhelming and confusing, making it hard to extract information. It's also more difficult to find harmonious combinations when you use too many colors.

A fairly safe formula is to start with three colors—a base color and two accent colors. Then choose a neutral or light background color.

Use Shades and Tints

You greatly expand your palette options when you look beyond pure colors to include ones with varied values. Recall that a color's value is the relative lightness or darkness of the color. When selecting colors for a palette, be sure to include the full range of values in your options.

Background Colors

Because most people find it easier to read dark text on a light background, choose a lighter color that is restful on the eyes for the background and a contrasting dark color for the text. Light neutral colors, such as white, light gray, and tan, are usually a safe bet for a background.

Although a light background is best for extensive reading, there is no harm in reversing this guideline for short bits of text, such as topic titles and user interface elements. In these cases, placing light text on a dark background can be effective for contrast purposes.

When to Use a Dark Background

In a few situations, you may want to have a dark background. One is when slides are projected to a large room. On many projectors, a white background displays an annoying shimmer. A dark background is best in this case. You may find other situations when a dark background is best. If you design with intention, you will make the right decisions for your content, audience, and environment.

Eight Ways to Choose a Palette

If you have trouble choosing a palette, you're not alone. This is a challenge for many of us, which is why there are so many possible approaches. Here are eight of them:

1. **Branding.** The branding colors of a company or organization are part of its symbolic identity. The chosen colors convey the message that the organization wants to promote. You may have little choice in the color scheme if you are required to use the branding colors. If you find them distasteful or inappropriate for learning materials, present your case to your department's leadership or to the marketing department as to why they won't work. Another approach is to try to use subdued shades or tints of the branding colors, and perhaps you can slowly slip away from the distasteful ones.

2. **Based on audience.** Use your knowledge of the audience to choose a color palette. Is this course for baristas of a high-energy coffee chain or for employees of a conservative financial institution? Check out the colors on the websites created for a similar demographic, if possible. Make your color scheme something that relates to the audience.

3. **Based on photos.** Perhaps you have a set of photos that will make up the bulk of your content. In that case, you can choose a palette based on the key colors in your photos. For example, in a story-based course, you can emphasize the color of the main character's clothing, hair color, or setting by using those colors in your palette. To select the exact color, use a graphic program or utility color picker to choose the colors from a photo. You can also automate the process by uploading photos to an online palette generator. It will then create a palette based on your photo. See Figure 7.5 for an example of this auto-generated palette.

4. **Symbolism.** Colors are associated with meanings that vary by culture. If symbolic color has emotional relevance to your audience, consider selecting colors with this in mind. It will add a rich dimension to the communication. The flip side is to ensure that the colors you choose will not be offensive or misinterpreted, especially when you are designing outside of your own culture.

5. **Psychological impact.** Consider choosing a palette for the psychological effect you would like to have on the audience. For example, if the subject is about a serious illness, you might choose a palette of unobtrusive pastels. But to build enthusiasm in volunteers who run charity events, you may want colors that are bright and exciting.

6. **Industry conventions.** Some industries use a conventional color palette that you may want to adopt because it will feel familiar and comfortable to the audience. For example, the healthcare and finance industries often use a blue palette, political organizations often use the colors of their country flag, and environmental companies often use green. You get the idea.

FIGURE 7.5. *Online tools can generate a palette from a photograph. This one was generated using Adobe Kuler.*

7. **Borrow from nature.** People usually find the colors in a flowery meadow or the hues of the sky, ocean, and sand aesthetically appealing. We tend to find nature's color palette pleasing and harmonious. If you're not sure which colors to pick for a palette, look to the colors in the natural environment for inspiration.

8. **Use color harmonies.** The color wheel introduced earlier provides a framework for understanding color theory and for selecting a color scheme. The diagrammatic representation of colors in a wheel makes it easy to select a palette based on formal rules of color harmony. Next, you will learn how to choose a color scheme based on the RYB color wheel.

COLOR HARMONIES

Just as audio harmony sounds pleasant to our ears, color harmony is pleasing to the eyes. You can create tasteful color combinations through several specific relationships described next, known as color harmonies. Designing with color harmonies improves a person's aesthetic experience and can make learning and informational materials enjoyable to use. Here are some different approaches to achieving a harmonious color palette. Remember that you will want to select from the tints and shades and, most likely, will not be creating a palette of only true colors.

Analogous Palette

One easy way to find a color scheme is to select three colors that are adjacent to each other in the color wheel. These colors appear harmonious because they partially share the colors adjacent to them. You may find it best to choose three warm or three cool colors.

Select one of your colors as the dominant one and then select a color on either side, as shown in Figure 7.6. If blue-green is your dominant color, in an analogous scheme, your other two will be blue and green. An analogous color scheme can be subtle and sophisticated, although it often lacks contrast. For a more nuanced palette, experiment with varying the saturation (intensity) and value (lightness and darkness) of the colors. This is an easy method for creating color harmony.

Complementary Palette

Another choice is to create a palette using two complementary colors. These are directly opposite each other on the color wheel, such as blue and orange. Two complementary colors provide the greatest contrast and the widest variation in a color scheme, as shown in Figure 7.7. But they can be overly intense when used in equal amounts of brightness. The complementary palette is best when the saturation of one color is modified or when one color is dominant and the second one is used as an accent. Consider the split complementary for a palette that's easier on the eyes.

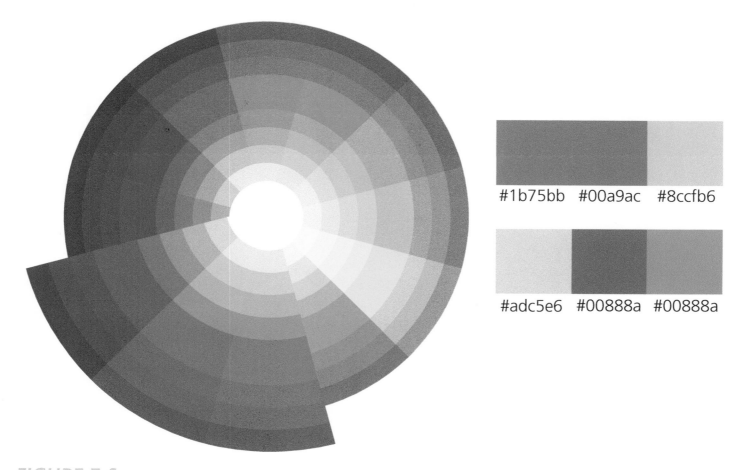

FIGURE 7.6. *An analogous palette uses three adjacent colors.*

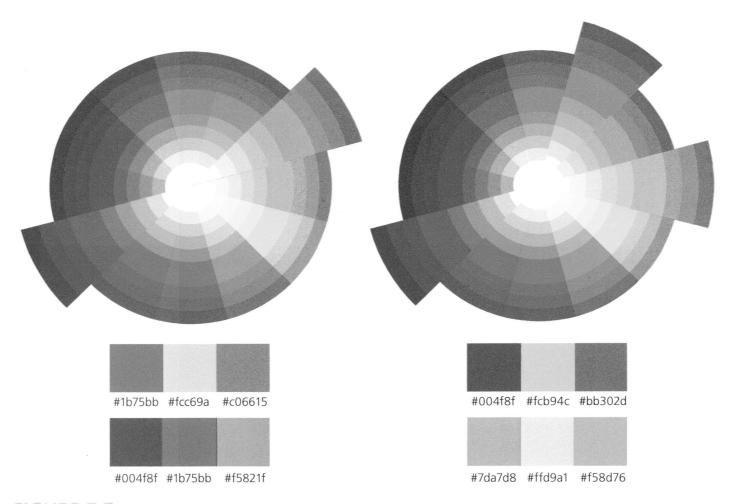

#1b75bb #fcc69a #c06615

#004f8f #1b75bb #f5821f

#004f8f #fcb94c #bb302d

#7da7d8 #ffd9a1 #f58d76

FIGURE 7.7. *A complementary palette and a split complementary.*

Split Complementary

Figure 7.7 also demonstrates the split complementary palette. Rather than using the complementary color as your second color, select the two colors adjacent to the complementary color.

Triadic Palette

To create a conventional triadic palette like the one shown in Figure 7.8, select three colors that are equidistant from each other on the color wheel, such as three secondary colors—orange, purple, and green. Again, the pure version of the colors may be too bright for your needs, so adjust the colors in saturation and value. The triadic palette provides a good deal of contrast. As with all intense palettes, select one color to be dominant and the other two for emphasis and accent.

Modified triadic palette. For a modified version of the triadic scheme, select a dominant color and two colors that are one space away on either side.

Monochromatic Palette

Yes, you can create an entire color palette using just one color. Start with a color that is easy on the eyes and then add lighter or darker versions of the color. Figure 7.9 demonstrates a monochromatic palette of blues. This is an easy way to find a sophisticated color harmony with an elegant appeal. Your ability to show emphasis with this palette is limited due to the lack of color contrast.

> ## RESOURCES: ONLINE PALETTE TOOLS
>
> - kuhler.com
> - colourlovers.com/palettes
> - colorexplorer.com
> - pictaculous.com (online palette generator)

Achromatic Palette

There may be times when you require a subtle color scheme. Consider an achromatic palette that uses colors without a strong hue, such as the neutrals and near neutrals. The achromatic colors include black, white, gray, brown, and tan. Explore this option and play with the neutral colors. It might be ideal if you need an understated design.

Using Online Tools

When selecting a color scheme, you can use the color wheel in this book for reference or use one of the many online applications for choosing a palette based on the color relationships just described. See the *Online Palette Tools* resource for some of these

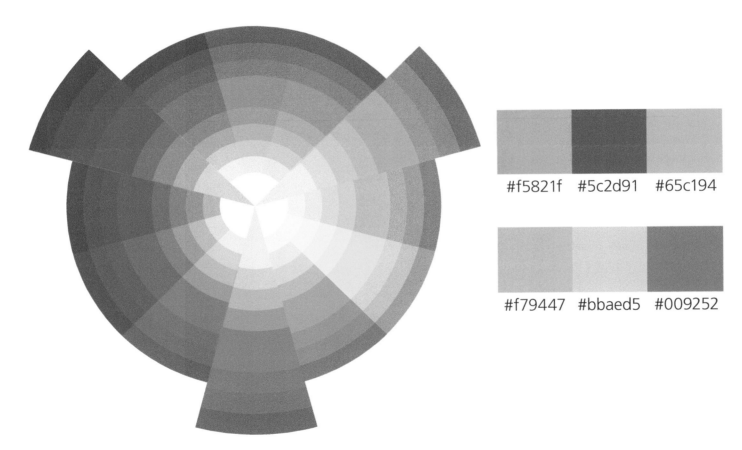

#f5821f #5c2d91 #65c194

#f79447 #bbaed5 #009252

FIGURE 7.8. *The colors in the triadic palette are equidistant from each other.*

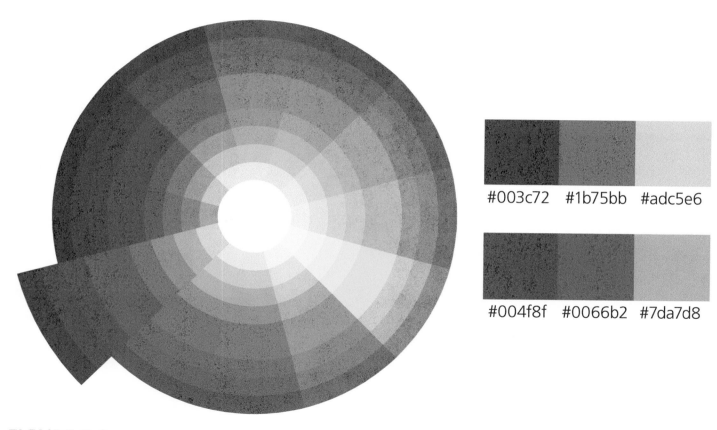

#003c72   #1b75bb   #adc5e6

#004f8f   #0066b2   #7da7d8

FIGURE 7.9. *A monochromatic palette uses tints and shades of one color.*

sites. There are also mobile apps that allow you to sample colors from the environment and export them as color palettes for use on the computer. You can find these in the app stores.

COLOR INTERACTIONS

Working with colors can be complicated because we rarely see a color in isolation. Rather, we see many colors simultaneously in relation to adjacent colors. This means we see colors in relative rather than absolute terms because each is affected by the hue, saturation, and value of its surrounding color. For instance, notice how the bright green circle in Figure 7.10 appears less vivid on a gray background than on a highly contrasting yellow background.

To have some control over your design, begin to notice how colors interact. What follows are some common interactions in the way people perceive juxtaposed colors.

- **Light and dark effects.** The same color will look lighter on a dark background and darker on a light background, as demonstrated in Figure 7.11.

FIGURE 7.10. *Notice how the same color appears to vary when placed on a different background.*

FIGURE 7.11. *The same color looks lighter on a dark background and darker on a light background.*

■ **Emphasis from complementary colors.** Recall that complementary colors are opposite each other on the color wheel. They have the greatest contrast. To create emphasis, place complementary colors next to each other. Both colors will seem to have a greater intensity or saturation. For extreme contrast and increased saturation, place the complementary colors on a gray background.

■ **Contrast through value.** Another way to create contrast is to choose colors of differing value (lightness or darkness). If you are using a pale orange, then a bright, vivid orange will create a subdued contrast.

■ **Shifting adjacent colors.** When non-complementary colors are placed next to each other, particularly when they are adjacent colors in the color wheel, both colors appear to shift toward their complementary color.

■ **Gray effects.** Gray is adaptable, appearing warm on a blue background and cool on a red background, because it tends to take on the complementary color of its surroundings.

THE **TAKEAWAYS**

- Color is known to have potent psychological and emotional effects. Choose a palette with care.

- Use color to increase motivation, enhance understanding, and improve usability.

- To make materials accessible to all, do not require learners to discriminate or recognize important information based on color alone.

- Some ways to choose a color palette include colors from a photograph, branding colors, industry colors, and color harmonies.

- Use the color wheel to select an anesthetically pleasing palette based on specific harmonious relationships.

- Colors are not seen in isolation, as they are affected by the colors that surround them.

Establish a Visual Hierarchy

"Much of visual communication has been left to intuition and happenstance."
— Donis A. Dondis

THE FRAMEWORK

THIS CHAPTER answers these questions:

- How can I control where viewers look?
- How do people scan a screen or page?
- How do I create a visual hierarchy with visuals and text?

Did you ever hike through a forest that had poorly marked trails and you were unsure of what path to take? With no visual cues to mark the route, you weren't sure how to proceed. When it comes to visual design, users have a similar experience. When looking at a screen or slide, they need help finding their way. Otherwise they become confused or they waste effort, unsure of what to look at first.

As a designer, your job is to provide an obvious path for the viewer's eyes to follow. You can achieve this by creating a hierarchical structure of dominant and subdominant forms. In this chapter, you will learn techniques for establishing a visual hierarchy. You will begin to see that, without a visual hierarchy, a design falls flat.

WHAT IS A VISUAL HIERARCHY?

Look at both graphics in Figure 8.1 and notice what happens to your attention as you view each one. Were you unsure of where to focus when viewing the graphic on the left? Did you scan the graphic for meaning and eventually start reading from the top in a downward direction? This graphic was not designed with a visual hierarchy, so your eyes probably fell into a default reading pattern.

What about the graphic on the right? Were you quickly drawn to the largest and brightest shape connected to the dotted line? The graphic on the right establishes a visual hierarchy that directs your eyes to a focal point—the largest shape. The graphic on the left has no hierarchy. Nothing stands out.

Purpose of a Visual Hierarchy

When you create a clear visual hierarchy, you are telling the viewer two things: what to look at first, second, and third and how the eye will travel from one point to the next. With a hierarchy, you control the sequence in which viewers see information. This can affect how well the audience understands what you are presenting.

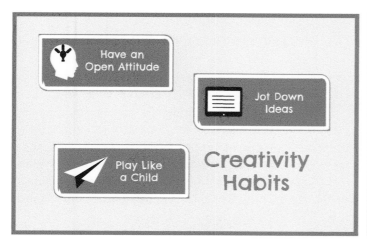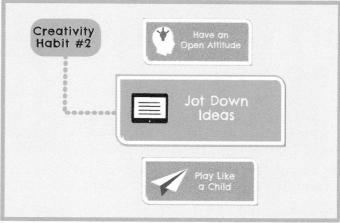

FIGURE 8.1. *Comparison of a graphic with no visual hierarchy (on the left) and one with an established visual hierarchy (on the right).*

Without an intentional hierarchy, a viewer's eyes may wander randomly around the screen seeking information and looking for meaning. When all the elements are of equal weight, they demand equal attention. Your message may be lost when nothing has prominence.

Aesthetically, visuals with a clear hierarchy are more appealing because there is a focal point that draws in the viewer. Without a focal point, a design can appear dull because nothing pulls the eye or grabs attention. There are many ways to establish a visual hierarchy. To make the process easier, let's first see how people typically navigate through visual information.

GEEK SPEAK: HOW OUR EYES MOVE

Our eyes have two main types of movement that help us see: fixations and saccades. During fixations, the eyes are relatively stable, as the viewer focuses on the visual scene and processes visual information.

During the saccades, the viewer's eyes move rapidly from one point to another. We don't see the blurry image that would result from the saccades. Instead, we see what appears to be a continuous stream of visual information as the brain integrates the input from eye fixations.

Follow the Eyes

There are some typical patterns that a person's eyes follow when scanning a screen or page. You can leverage these patterns by placing important information in their path.

Many of the investigations into eye movement patterns employ eye-tracking technology. This technology measures where a subject is looking or it captures the motion of the eyes as the person views a screen or a page.

Two Eye-Scanning Patterns

The most common eye-scanning movements of people who read in left-to-right languages occurs in an F-pattern. The next most common is the Z-pattern, which is how people tend to read print newspapers and magazines. In both patterns, readers start from the top left position and read horizontally across the upper content, which you cansee in Figure 8.2. From there, the reading patterns differ. You can infer from these patterns that readers are trained to think that information at the top of the screen is of the greatest importance.

Note that actual eye-tracking data is not as clean as a simple *F* or *Z* letterform. You will see squiggles and zigzags if you look at the data. But the F- and Z- shapes are sufficiently visible that researchers speak of the patterns in those terms. For example, a reader may stop short of a complete horizontal scan or may form the Z-pattern many times on one page.

As a designer, you can use this knowledge of eye-movement patterns to place critical information in a location that is commonly scanned. It is good to note, however, that a strong visual hierarchy can disrupt the typical eye-movement patterns. If you want to send viewers on a different path, there are many design techniques for directing eye movements. First, you'll need to plan the visual hierarchy by thinking through the purpose of each particular screen.

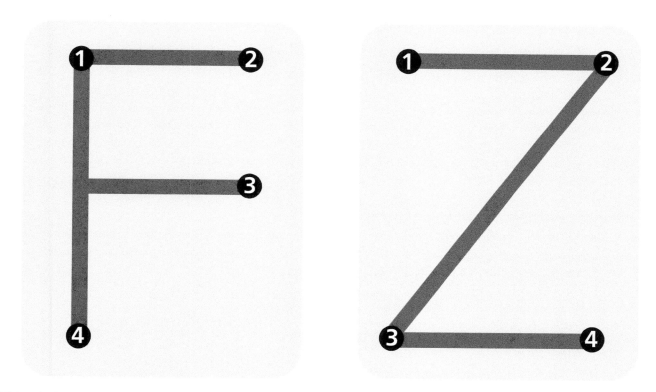

FIGURE 8.2. *Two common eye-scanning patterns are the F- and Z-patterns.*

PLANNING THE HIERARCHY

Before you place elements in a layout, determine the purpose of the screen or slide and identify the corresponding elements that will fulfill this purpose. Assign each element a rank using two or three levels. At the most, identify elements that are of a primary ranking, then a second, and then a third. This type of ordering will help you form the structure for directing the viewer's eyes through a planned sequence.

Considerations for the Hierarchy

How can you assign a ranking to visuals or text? Ask yourself these questions and see the example that follows:

1. What is the instructional or informational point of the screen or slide?

2. Then, what does the audience need to see, understand, or do first?

3. What element (visuals or text) provides the greatest support for what the audience needs to see or do first?

4. In what sequence do learners need to interact with the remainder of the content?

This approach will help you make the best design choices for establishing a visual hierarchy and for assisting an audience through the content. When you know the ranking of importance, use the techniques presented next to implement the hierarchy.

If you are designing an extensive course, you do not need to ruminate over every screen. Eventually, these types of considerations will become second-nature to you and you will be able to quickly create a hierarchy. Also, you can make use of flexible templates that embody a hierarchy to speed up the process.

Visual Hierarchy Example: Explaining a Concept

For a simple example of how to plan a hierarchy, suppose you are designing materials to explain how to create a personal learning network (PLN). You will use a diagram that shows five resources that learners can use and a text-based explanation. Here is how I would answer each of the questions to plan the hierarchy shown in Figure 8.3.

1. What is the instructional or informational point of the screen or slide?

    The key point is to introduce five resources for developing a personal learning network in a way that helps the learner create a mental model.

2. Then, what do learners need to see, understand, or do first?

    Learners first need to see the diagram title, which provides the context of the graphic.

3. What element (text or visual) provides the greatest support for conveying the first message?

    The circle in the center with the title text.

4. In what sequence do learners need to interact with the content?

    Title first, then the five entities of the diagram, then the explanatory text is at the third level.

This example uses variations in typography to build the hierarchy—from a boldface font for the title, to a regular weight for the entities and a light weight for the definition. The use of color and scale also helps to establish the hierarchy. There are many techniques for creating dominant and subordinate elements. These are discussed next.

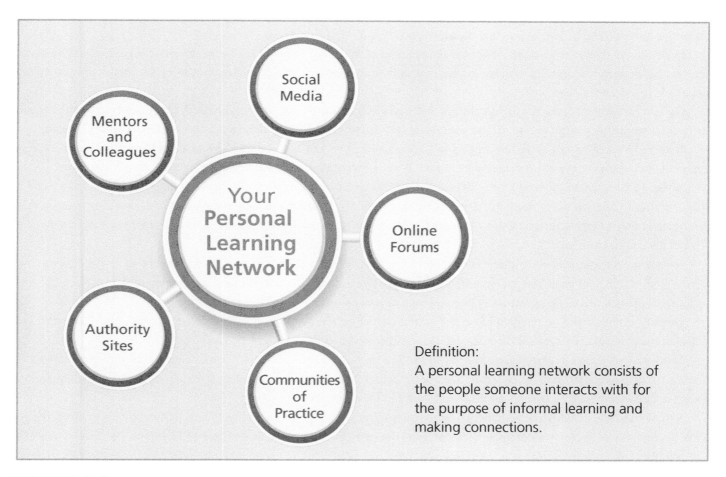

Social
Media

Mentors
and
Colleagues

Your
**Personal
Learning
Network**

Online
Forums

Authority
Sites

Communities
of
Practice

Definition:
A personal learning network consists of
the people someone interacts with for
the purpose of informal learning and
making connections.

FIGURE 8.3. *A visual hierarchy at three levels—large title in the center, five smaller entities, and then explanatory text.*

Techniques for Creating Emphasis

Here are several ways to make elements have greater prominence over the other elements on the screen. Combining several techniques at once can help to assure that the hierarchy is clear.

Position. All things being equal, graphics and text placed at the top or upper left of the screen will be noticed first because the eyes of Western readers tend to move left to right and top to bottom. This is why logos on websites are usually placed in the upper left or top of the page.

Color. Our eyes are more sensitive to bright and warm colors like yellow, orange, and red. If you apply any of these colors to your hierarchy, they seem to pop off the screen and will usually attract your audience. See Figure 8.4 for an example.

Images. What draws your eye first when you see a website or pick up a newspaper? Most likely the pictures leap out at you. Images tend to pull the eye more than blocks of text. Also, viewers are highly attuned to pictures of people and faces.

Scale. Scale refers to the relative size of elements. Scale creates a visual hierarchy because larger elements seem as though they are closer to the viewer; thus, they have more visual weight. Viewers notice larger elements first, making contrasts in size an excellent way to create several levels of hierarchy. Make sure the size differences are clear and obvious. You saw this at the start of the chapter in Figure 8.1.

Isolation. You can use white space around an object to isolate it, which increases its dominance in a visual hierarchy, as shown in Figure 8.5. Objects that are surrounded by white space draw attention because the element contrasts with the empty space. Also, if you place one object away from a group of related objects, it indicates importance.

Density. Another way to create a hierarchy is to group objects very close together so that there is very little white space between the elements. This makes them appear dense or heavier, and this too attracts the eyes.

Motion. Our eyes are extremely attracted to motion because we are sensitive to any changes in the environment. The simulation of movement, such as dynamic lines or an action photo, is a way to create dominance. Avoid using animation to attract attention, however, if there is no meaningful reason for doing so.

Visual cues. Most audiences will likely follow visual signals, like arrows and dashed lines, that are known to direct the eyes. This is another way to create a dominant element. Find out more about visual cues in Chapter 12, Show Them Where to Look.

Numbering. If everything else is equivalent, you can use numbering to create a hierarchy. Readers are most likely to start at the number 1, which makes the first element the most dominant and provides an order of visual flow.

Short and powerful phrases. Short lines of text will attract the eyes more than longer blocks of text. That is why websites use phrases such as "Buy Now" or "Click Here" on buttons designed to persuade people to take action. In a learning context, we can use similar phrases, such as "Show Me How," to attract attention.

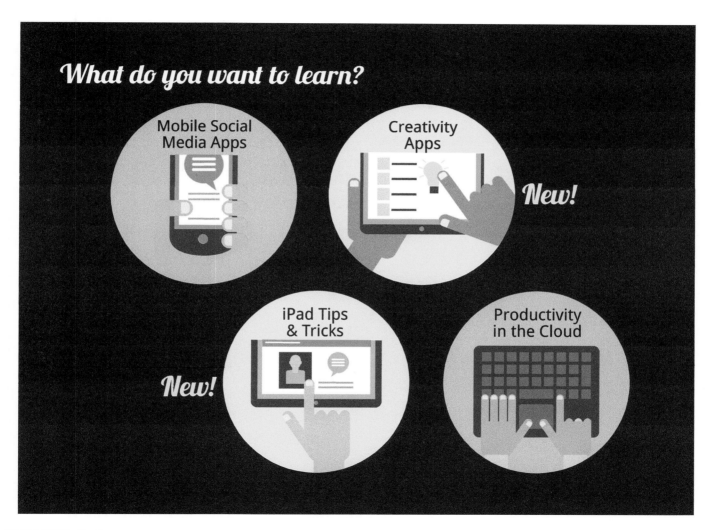

FIGURE 8.4. *Use bright or warm colors to create dominance over other elements.*

Fire Safety

Use demagnetized extinguishers in rooms containing MRI units.

FIGURE 8.5. *Isolating an object or person* is a way *to give an element dominance.*

The Squint Test

How can you know whether a visual has the hierarchy you intended? How can you ensure that the elements don't compete with each other? You can ask others to look at the design and ask what they noticed first. The alternative is to employ the tried-and-true squint test. Examine each screen while squinting to see the overall impression it projects. Are the appropriate elements prominent? If not, you will need to exaggerate some attributes and minimize others.

DESIGNING THE VISUAL HIERARCHY

During design, the element of primary importance will become the focal point or center of interest in your layout. It is the first thing that draws a viewer's attention, regardless of whether it is a captivating image, a colorful shape, or a large title. Because our brains seek meaning, people will notice when an element is emphasized and assume that the emphasis is significant. For example, if instructions for completing an exercise are of primary importance, you might place them at the top of the screen overlaid on a brighter background.

But you don't want your audience to stop at the focal point. You have important information they need to see. Next, you will want to create an intentional visual flow from the most dominant element to the next subordinate element. For subordinate elements in the hierarchy, you can use the same or varied techniques, but in a more nuanced and subdued way. If you are using color and scale to create a hierarchy, then your second-level elements will be less vivid and smaller than the primary elements.

Because your time and budget are limited, try to plan for a visual hierarchy design in reusable templates.

A HIERARCHY OF TYPE

Most likely, you have much experience creating a visual hierarchy with type. In documents, slides, and eLearning, you differentiate the importance of information by using headings, subheadings, and body text.

As you know, with a typographic hierarchy, the most important information stands out to influence the sequence in which viewers read text. A hierarchy also creates an entry point to start reading and a way for viewers to quickly scan information. Although you can use many of the previously mentioned techniques to create a hierarchy with text, such as position, size, and color, you have some additional options with text. Here are more techniques you can use to create dominant and subordinate elements using typography.

Techniques

Contrasting typeface. Use a contrasting display typeface to bring attention to a headline or title. See Chapter 6, Working with Type, for approaches to selecting a typeface.

Type weight. The darkest text on the lightest background will establish prominence because it has the greatest contrast. For titles and subtitles, you can invert the text by placing light text on a dark background for a striking effect.

Rules. Figure 8.6 shows how you can use horizontal lines, also known as *rules*, to separate an area of space and draw attention to the text in that space. You often see this approach in newsletters and magazines. There are many options for line types—single

FIGURE 8.6. *Adding horizontal lines or rules adds emphasis to the text in that space.*

or double, thick or thin, or a combination. Rules are more effective than underlines because they provide a noticeable structure to the graphic space. Also, underlining text may confuse your audience because it can signify a hyperlink.

White space. Use space to establish a hierarchy by grouping blocks of related text together. Also, add empty space around text to attract attention to it.

Indentation. Indenting text is a simple way to create differentiation and adds to a hierarchy, showing where new paragraphs or sections of text begin.

Short text. Shorter text is read more often than longer blocks of text. Short text can be scanned more quickly.

Pull quote. This is a quote taken from the main text that is set in a larger point size or contrasting typeface and placed outside of the text block in such a way that it captures attention. Pull quotes may be set in a different color than the body text and in a bold or italic style. Ensure there is a strong visual contrast with the rest of the text.

Drop capital. The "drop cap" is a way to create prominence by setting the initial letter of the first word in a paragraph in a larger point size than the rest of the paragraph. See Figure 8.7. Because the capital letter is aligned with the top of the text, it "drops" below the line.

Drop caps are a way to create prominence by setting the initial letter of the first word in a larger point size than the rest of the paragraph. Because the capital letter is aligned with the top of the text, it drops below the line.

FIGURE 8.7. *A drop capital gives prominence to a block of text.*

THE **TAKEAWAYS**

- A visual hierarchy provides a way to navigate content and define the order of importance in which visual elements should be viewed.

- Two common eye-movement patterns that people use to scan a screen or page are the F-pattern and the Z-pattern.

- To plan a visual hierarchy, identify the purpose of the screen and then determine what the viewer will need to look at first, second, and third to convey the message.

- You can create a dominant to subordinate visual hierarchy through position, color, use of images, scale, isolation, density, motion, visual cues, numbering, and use of short phrases.

- Some techniques for creating prominence that are specific to text include use of a contrasting typeface, separating the text with rules (horizontal lines), using pull quotes, and drop caps.

CHAPTER

Unify the Design

"Speak with one visual voice."

— Timothy Samara

THE FRAMEWORK

THIS CHAPTER answers these questions:

- What is a unified design?
- How does a unified design affect learning?
- What strategies can I use to create visual unity?

A unified design may seem like an ethereal concept, but it is similar to how you would think about unity in any other context. When a group is unified, the people have some type of bond or there is a consensus among members. Likewise, when a design is unified, there is a relationship among the elements and these elements are in agreement, visually or conceptually. A visually unified design is one where the layout, images, shapes, and typography work together as a whole and are well-integrated. A unified design conveys one harmonious message.

Unity is an overarching ideal of successful visual design that most of the other principles support. For example, achieving a balanced design through the distribution of visual weight contributes to unity. Consistent styles of imagery and a consistent color palette also create a unified design.

As you work with the techniques that support visual unity, there is a risk that your design may become monotonous. That is when you need to add some distinctive elements for interest. This chapter will look at ways to achieve a cohesive, unified design and also how to add a touch of variety.

UNITY AND WHOLENESS

People generally see the whole before they see the parts of a visual. The principle of unity can also be understood in this light—a unified design works as an integrated whole rather than being seen as distinct parts. It is the result of making intentional rather than haphazard design choices. Even designs with tension, asymmetry, and intentional chaos can be unified when the elements are visually related.

Unity and Gestalt

Wholeness is more than integration. A unified design generates a gestalt—where the sum is more than its parts. In design, this means that the message created by the wholeness of a composition may be quite different from the parts alone in impact and meaning. Figure 9.1 provides a graphical example of this concept. Most people will see the arrow before seeing the

FIGURE 9.1. *In a graphic, people perceive the whole before seeing the parts. This is also true for an entire design.*

individual shapes. Likewise, when your design is seen as a unified whole, it might be quite different—and more powerful than—the individual elements.

Two Levels of a Unified Design

There are two levels of unity that need your attention. There is the unity within each screen or slide and the unity of an entire course, slide deck, or website. Strive to unify all the different screens so they look as though they come from the same source and that they project the same message. This is one benefit of designing with templates and grids. Both templates and grids introduce a level of consistency that is difficult to achieve otherwise.

A UNIFIED DESIGN SUPPORTS LEARNING

Unity is the extent to which the organization and graphical elements are coordinated with one another. With unity, all the elements in the design are working toward one common goal. Not only is this aesthetically pleasing, but the consistency of a unified visual experience supports learning in several ways:

- **Reduces cognitive effort.** When there is similarity among the elements and conformity in the layout, learners know what to expect. They won't waste cognitive effort trying to figure out each screen or slide as though it is a new experience.

- **Creates a focused message.** In a unified design, the message is clear and uncluttered. To intentionally make a design harmonious, you often need to remove extraneous elements so that the relationships are easy to discern. A fragmented or unintentional design is confusing; a unified design is focused and has a strong message. This is demonstrated in Figure 9.2.

- **Improves the aesthetic experience.** An important theme in learning and information design is that an appealing look and feel provides a favorable experience. Visuals that work as a unified whole contribute to a pleasing and tasteful design.

Through the strategies of repetition, similarity, and alignment, presented next in this chapter, you will find ways to ensure your design communicates meaning.

REPETITION

One of the most effective ways to achieve unity is through the repetition of a design element. Repetition creates a rhythm—a sense of visual motion—that establishes a unified look. You can reuse the same element, such as a shape, grid, pattern,

FIGURE 9.2. *A confusing message from a fragmented design for a job aid (left) versus a strong message from a unified design (right).*

typeface, or image style, for this purpose. You can also repeat visual features, such as color, line type, or texture. For example, you might:

- Consistently use a thin line above and below all titles to make them stand out.
- Use consistent, but unusual, typography for titles and subtitles.

- Organize the layout of slides using the same underlying grid so that margins and title placement are consistent on screens that present the same type of information.

- Use the same shape as the dominant element in a design. Use the same overall design for interactive screens.

- Place navigation in eLearning and on web pages in a consistent location that never varies.

- Use the same color and thickness of the border around photos.

The repetition of elements and visual features is an effective way to show that each screen, slide, or page is related and that the elements within it are connected. Figure 9.3 demonstrates the cohesiveness of repetition in the user interface design for an eLearning course about nutrition. The shape formed from utensils is repeated as the menu button. Repetition in the color palette and the location of navigation elements brings an attractive unity to the design.

Although repetition is a sure-fire way to achieve unity, you may also find that the use of similarity works well for your projects. This is discussed next.

CREATE VISUAL CONNECTIONS

You may need other strategies for composing visuals that appear unified. In addition to repetition, there are ways to create a connection between elements through the use of similarity and alignment. These techniques help ensure that the shapes, images, and typography in a design correspond to each other in a way that shows they are in agreement.

Similarity

Related to the concept of repetition is the nuance of *similarity*. Whereas repetition refers to repeating one object or shape, similarity refers to creating variations of the same shape, line type, colors, textures, and use of space. Similarity could mean using overlapping photographs throughout a project in different ways or drawing with dotted lines rather than solid ones whenever lines are used, although their thickness might vary. Another approach to similarity might be using different colors of the same patterned background for different topics, as shown in Figure 9.4. Similarity is more like creating a visual theme.

This type of variation makes for a visual environment where the elements are connected. Within this backdrop, it is easy to create a contrasting focal point when you need an element to appear prominent.

Use Implied Lines

Alignment, which is discussed in Chapter 4, Organizing Graphic Space, is another way to show that elements are connected to each other. Figure 9.5 shows how any element that is placed in a layout creates implied horizontal and vertical axes at its edges. You can make a strong visual connection by aligning graphical elements with each other along these axes.

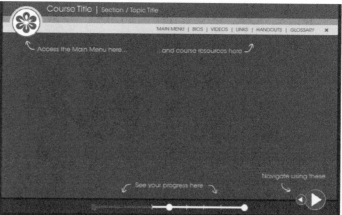
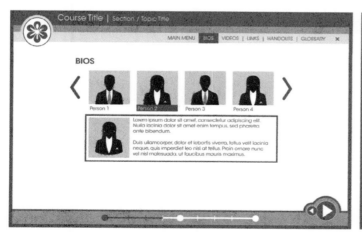
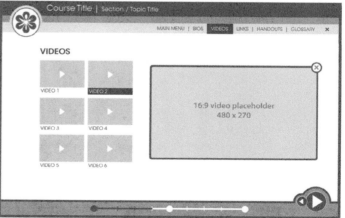

FIGURE 9.3. *Repetition of shape, user interface elements, and colors are some ways to create a unified design. eLearning screen designs by Kevin Thorn, NuggetHead Studioz, and Trina Rimmer, Rimmer Creative Group.*

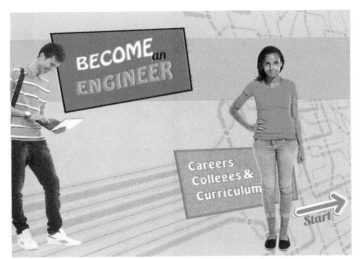

FIGURE 9.4. *Similarity refers to repeating visual elements with variation, as in this course design about engineering careers.*

Unless you have a reason to do otherwise, align all elements on the screen or slide with one of these implied lines. It demonstrates a visual relationship that creates cohesion. If you place an element out of alignment, do so purposely to convey something meaningful. Resist the inclination to place text and objects randomly.

It is not always easy to create a sense of connectedness and harmony out of disparate visual elements. You can rely on most of the general design principles to create unity, as well as the particular strategies of repetition, similarity, and alignment. As you make design choices, keep the unity principle in mind as a guidepost for the direction you want to follow.

UNITY NEEDS SOME VARIETY

Although unity provides cohesion, viewers are also drawn to contrast—to the visual elements that appear different from the rest. Thus, striving for unity alone is not enough, because without variety a design can become dull. Variety is a necessary balance to unity.

FIGURE 9.5. *To create unity, align elements to the implied lines that are created through the layout process.*

What Is Variety?

"Variety is the range of line, shape, color, and texture that is used in a composition," explains design educator John DiMarco (2010, p. 86). It is the diversity in elements and features that breaks the spell of uniformity. The creative challenge is knowing when to add variety and how much to add. Although this will vary with the project, use variety in a way that is meaningful. Use variety for impact or to highlight informational differences. Here are two things to consider when using variety.

What needs to stand out? Every screen or slide has an element that is most important and becomes the focal point. You can use variety to make the center of interest prominent. For example, in a multimedia presentation on product training, make the specific product being discussed much larger than the others. Or show all the products in black and white and show the item under discussion in color. This adds variety.

Where does the design seem monotonous? When you find a dull place in the design, such as a screen where you think a viewer will lose interest, use variety to add freshness or surprise, but try do it with meaning. Use a bright arrow to point out important text, tilt an important photo so it is skewed or add a humorous sticky note.

By introducing some variety to a design, you can find a balance between the need for a unified whole and the need to keep viewers interested and attentive.

THE TAKEAWAYS

- A unified design is one in which the individual parts work together as a harmonious whole.

- Uniformity in a design can impact learning by providing a familiar structure that lets viewers know what to expect, which reduces cognitive effort.

- Some ways to achieve unity include the repetition of elements and creating connections between elements through similarity and alignment.

- Introducing variety into a design by slightly modifying repeated elements makes meaningful differences stand out and adds appeal.

10

Create Contrast

"The brain loves a difference."

— Alberto Cairo

THE FRAMEWORK

THIS CHAPTER answers these questions:

- Why is visual contrast important?
- How can I create contrast?
- How can I use contrast to communicate?

It may be difficult to understand the joys of spring without knowing the hardships of winter. You may not appreciate the taste of finely prepared food without eating meals that taste bland. It is through contrasting experiences that we develop a meaningful understanding of the world.

This is also true in design. Contrast is a visual difference that attracts the eye and informs how a person understands a graphic. You can create noticeable contrasts in your designs through the use of dissimilar characteristics, such as large and small elements, dark and light colors, or shiny and dull textures.

Unity and contrast are in a symbiotic relationship. They need each other. Through unity you create a harmonious design. Through contrast you break the unity to create a focal point or center of interest. Without the cohesiveness of unity, contrast might not be visible.

In this chapter, you'll find out why contrast is important and how you can use contrast to improve visual communication.

CONTRAST AND THE BRAIN

Contrast is a power principle because it is based on how the brain works. During vision, we look for similarities and differences to recognize and identify objects. The brain seeks these differences to make sense of the environment.

We initially detect that an object is different from its surroundings through processing areas of light and dark as well as edges (Marmor & Ravin, 2009). The degree of contrast determines how easily and quickly we perceive it. The higher the contrast and the sharper the edges, the easier it is to detect a form. The lower the contrast and the more the edges blend into the surroundings, the more difficult it is to distinguish forms. You can see examples of degrees of contrast in Figure 10.1.

FIGURE 10.1. *The greater the contrast, the easier it is to detect a form.*

Contrast Is Relative

In visual design, contrast requires strong differences between elements that are juxtaposed. The more striking the contrast, the more impact it will have. People see contrasts by making comparisons, seeing the relative differences between features rather than remembering the absolute degree of the feature (Marmor & Ravin, 2009). For example, a color will seem brighter when it is placed next to a dull color. Text will seem heavier when placed next to a typeface that is light in weight.

Leveraging Pre-Attentive Attention

During pre-attentive perception, the brain gathers sensory information before a person is paying attention to it. At this time, certain features stand out among others in the visual environment. Some of the strongest visual features of a graphic that pop out during pre-attentive attention are color, orientation (direction), size, depth, and motion or the appearance of motion (Ware, 2012). You can take advantage of this by creating contrast with any of these features.

THE EFFECTS OF CONTRAST

Contrast is a fundamental principle of design because it provides a potent way to visually communicate. Use it to make shapes prominent, to add visual appeal, and to organize information.

Contrast Creates Emphasis

When you place visual elements with opposing features in proximity, the contrast between the features attracts the eye. In this way, contrast creates emphasis. It makes an image, shape, or text dominant compared to other elements in the design.

Contrast affects the order in which a viewer looks at the parts of a graphic. Using varying degrees of contrast is a way to establish a visual hierarchy. Figure 10.2 uses contrast in an employee portal design to lead the user's eyes to an orientation video. It demonstrates how contrast conveys an immediate message that the dominant form is the most important.

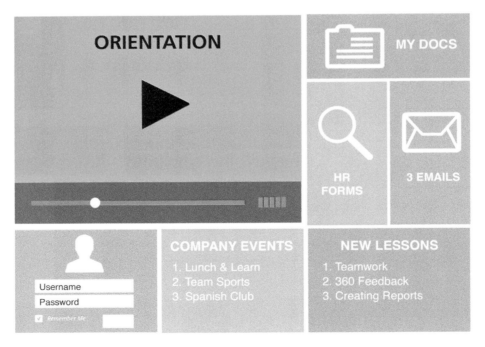

FIGURE 10.2. *In this employee web portal design, contrast creates emphasis and attracts the eye, conveying an immediate message that the orientation video is most important.*

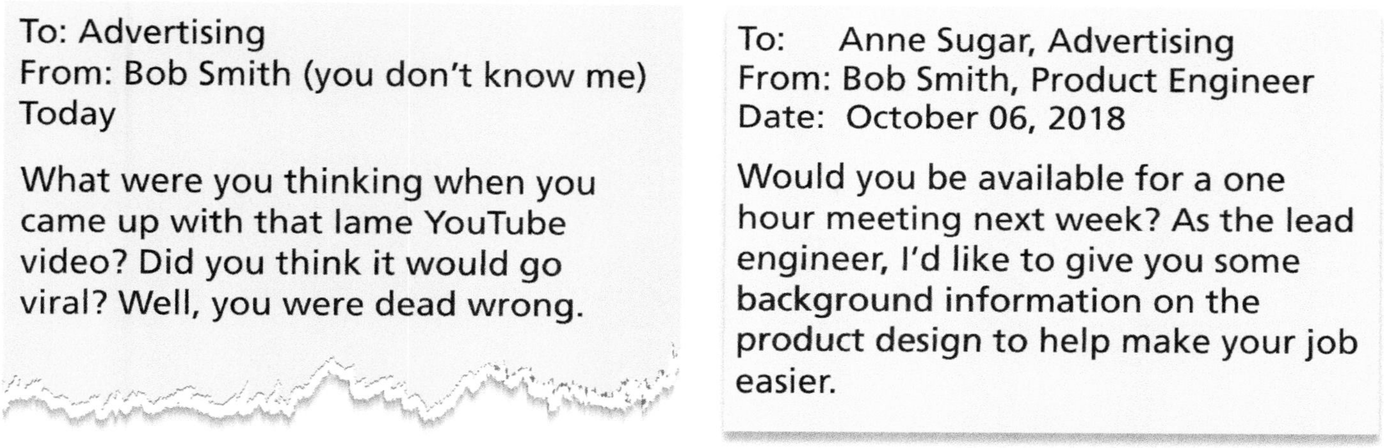

To: Advertising
From: Bob Smith (you don't know me)
Today

What were you thinking when you came up with that lame YouTube video? Did you think it would go viral? Well, you were dead wrong.

To: Anne Sugar, Advertising
From: Bob Smith, Product Engineer
Date: October 06, 2018

Would you be available for a one hour meeting next week? As the lead engineer, I'd like to give you some background information on the product design to help make your job easier.

FIGURE 10.3. *Contrast is effective for demonstrating comparisons.*

Contrast Creates Visual Interest

Because the brain seeks differences, contrast adds visual appeal. Viewers tend to become bored with monotony. Without contrast, a design is neutral. There is nothing specific to attract attention, which can make it difficult to understand the point. Use contrast to grab and sustain attention.

Contrast Creates Meaning

Contrast is an aspect of visual language that creates meaning in the same way that powerful words communicate a strong message. In instructional and informational materials, use contrast in these ways to convey and amplify your message.

Comparisons. Contrast can signal that something is different when making comparisons. Look at the example in Figure 10.3. It compares the correct and incorrect way to write a workplace memo using exaggerated elements in the background to convey the message. By placing the incorrect example on a torn paper shape and the correct example on a clean, straight-edged shape, the comparison is stronger.

Importance and scale. Scale or size is an effective way to show contrast when the goal is to convey importance. In Figure 10.4, the most important person in the story is larger than the others, which brings him into the foreground. Color contrasts also help. Most audiences will recognize that the largest object or person is the most significant.

FIGURE 10.4. *Use contrasts in scale to show importance.*

FIGURE 10.5. *Two different patterns express two different emotions.*

Emotions. If you want to express emotions, use strong contrasts between very dissimilar elements, such as two different patterns. In Figure 10.5, a pattern with dissonant jagged lines conveys tension, while the opposite is true for a pattern of serene circles.

HOW TO ACHIEVE CONTRAST

There are countless ways to create contrast, as long as the two elements are very different. When the two elements are only slightly different, you may create conflict rather than contrast (Williams, 2009). To help designers find novel ways to create contrast, design educator and author Alex White produced a helpful list of opposing compositional elements (White, 2011).

In Table 10.1, I've modified this list for learning designers. On any row, Features 1 and 2 are opposing and can be manipulated to create contrast. This should be more than enough to get you started intentionally designing with contrast.

TABLE 10.1. **Opposing features that can create contrast.**

Contrast Type	Feature 1	Feature 2
Spatial contrast	Filled space High density	Empty space Low density
Layout contrast	Top High Right Isolated Symmetrical	Bottom Low Left Grouped Asymmetrical
Form contrast	Simple Representational Geometric Angled	Complex Abstract Organic Curved
Direction contrast	Vertical Static	Horizontal Moving
Style contrast	Technical and precise Playful	Hand-drawn and irregular Serious
Size	Large Long Wide	Small Short Narrow
Color contrast	Dark Black and white Warm colors Vivid	Light Colorful Cool colors Muted
Texture contrast	Fine Smooth	Coarse Rough
Typographic contrast	Serif Roman style (regular)	Sans serif Bold style

COLOR CONTRAST

Color contrast deserves special attention because there are so many ways to use this property to enhance a design. In his book, *The Art of Color*, Johannes Itten (1997) explains several ways to use color contrast.

- **Contrasting hues.** The most obvious type of contrast is to use different colors. The more separated they are on the color wheel, the more they will contrast.

- **Complementary colors.** A common technique for creating contrast is to use two colors that are opposite each other on the color wheel, such as violet and yellow. One of these can be the main color and the other can be the accent or highlight color.

- **Contrasting values (light and dark).** You can contrast values by juxtaposing black and white or dark and light colors. You can also contrast values using just one color in a monochromatic design.

- **Contrasting temperatures (cool and warm).** With this approach, contrast the cool colors (blue and green) with the warm ones (yellow and orange).

- **Contrasting saturation.** Use a vivid color next to a color that is less saturated, meaning it is mixed with gray.

HOW TO SHOW EMPHASIS WITH TEXT

You knew the value of typographic emphasis the first time you scribbled an important word in large print or used a brightly colored crayon to make your point. Increased size and colored text are still effective for creating contrast in typography. For your communication to be most effective, consider whether certain words are more significant than others and emphasize them through contrast. Here are some techniques for creating contrast with text.

Headlines and Titles

It's no surprise that headlines and titles draw attention because the size and weight of the text contrasts with the body text. Also, placement at the top of the screen conveys importance, although you can place titles in other areas, too.

Reverse Colors

Use light text on a dark background to create contrast for headings, titles, and buttons.

Sideways Direction

You can create contrast by placing short titles in a vertical position next to body text. Although this shows emphasis, make sure it can be read by your audience.

Typeface Contrast

When it makes sense in your design, select a contrasting typeface to convey the meaning of the words. For example, use an expressive typeface that contrasts with the body text for an emotional title. In Figure 10.6, the display type adds tension to the word.

Scale

Sometimes you only need to emphasize one idea. Make this text much larger and bolder than everything else on the screen. For example, perhaps there is one principle or guideline that needs emphasis, as shown in Figure 10.7. Show that text in as bold a way as you can, with large and heavy type. It will attract attention.

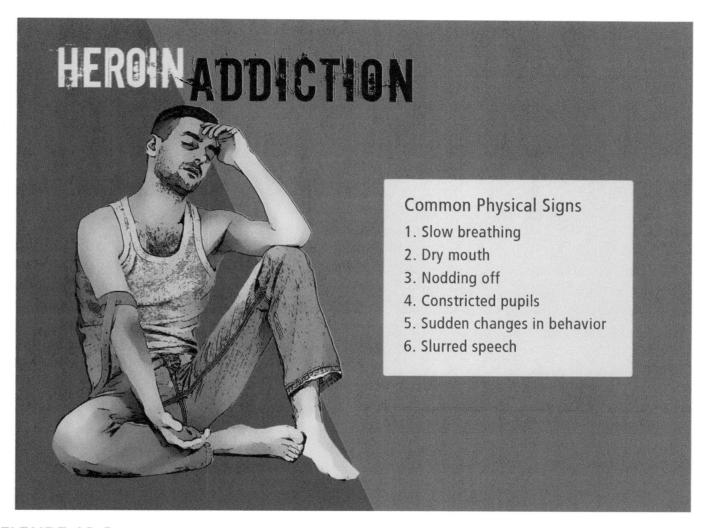

FIGURE 10.6. *When it will help convey meaning, use an expressive typeface for screen titles that contrasts with the body text.*

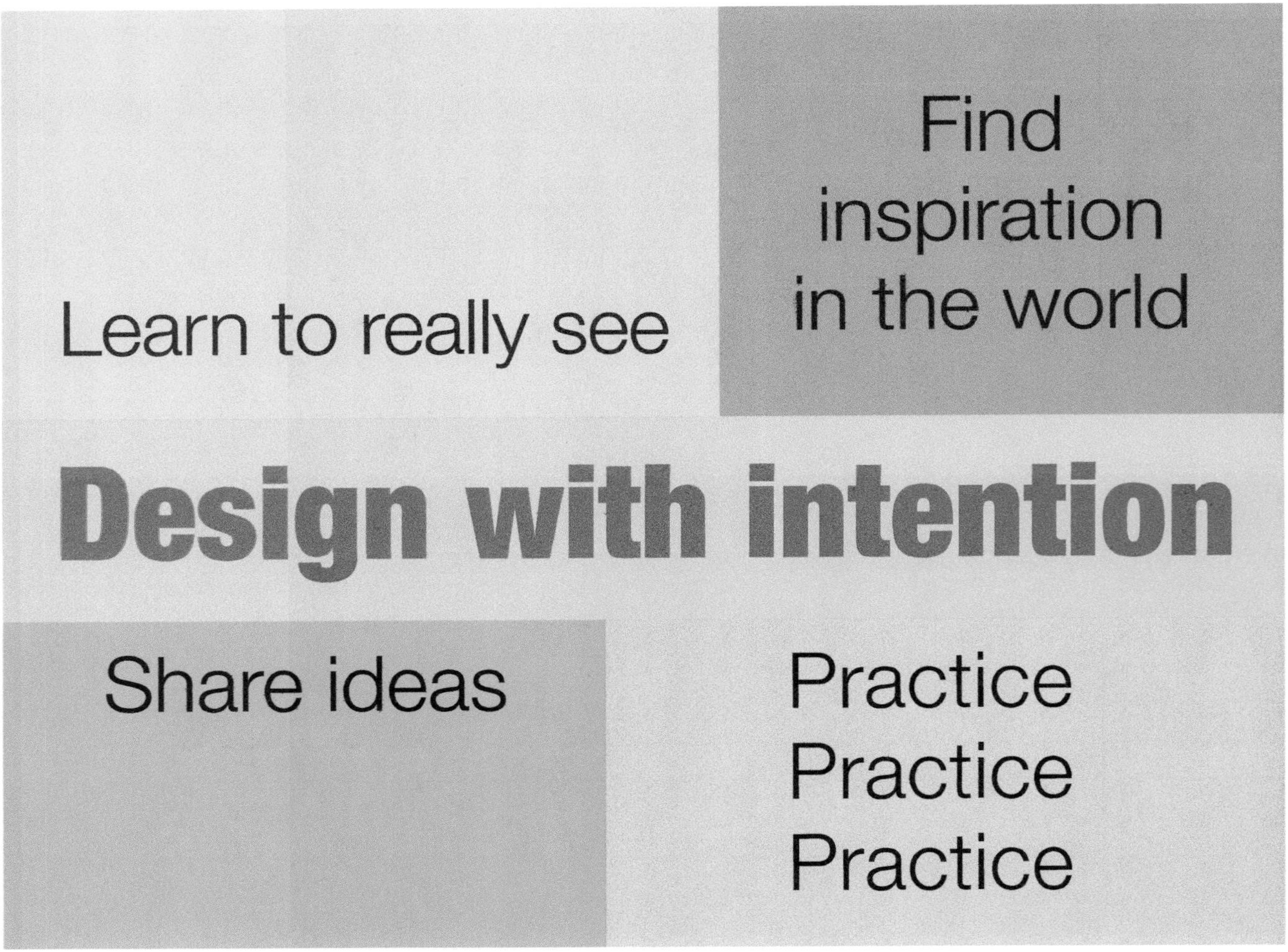

Find
inspiration
in the world

Learn to really see

Design with intention

Share ideas

Practice
Practice
Practice

FIGURE 10.7. *Using scale, weight, and color to create typographic contrast.*

THE **TAKEAWAYS**

- Our brains naturally look for differences to make sense of the environment.

- Contrast is a visual difference you create by placing elements with opposing features next to each other.

- Contrast creates emphasis, generates visual interest, and enhances meaning.

- Some easy ways to create contrast are through the use of complementary colors (opposites on the color wheel), opposing values (light and dark), different shapes (geometric and irregular), and varying the scale of elements (large and small).

CHAPTER

Group for Meaning

"Good information design depends on strategies for reducing the perceptual and cognitive effort required to understand an image."

— DeCarlo and Santella

THE FRAMEWORK

THIS CHAPTER answers these questions:

- Why is grouping important to learning?
- What visual conditions create grouping?
- How can grouping help me communicate?

Did you ever arrive in a foreign culture and feel confused? Things look unlike anything you've seen before. It takes a while to become oriented in an unfamiliar place—to structure the scene so you understand what's going on. If you were aware of the sensory information picked up by your eyes when you first look at a graphic, it would be an analogous experience. Sensory information is a jumble of disorganized input until we structure it and give it meaning.

The brain organizes sensory information into patterns, based on certain mechanisms of perception. If you structure your graphics into these easily recognized patterns, they are likely to be understood quickly and clearly.

In this chapter, you will learn ways to make graphics more meaningful by organizing visual information into groups.

IMPORTANCE OF GROUPING IN LEARNING

One of the key ways that people understand a graphic is by initially seeing the groups in it before they see the individual parts. In Chapter 9, Unify the Design, you saw an example of how seeing the shape of an arrow supersedes seeing the individual elements that make up the shape. This organizing principle is so strong that it is difficult to visually break apart the group, as demonstrated in Figure 11.1.

FIGURE 11.1. *People see groups before seeing individual elements—under certain conditions.*

Visual grouping is one of the most powerful techniques a designer can use to communicate. It lets learners know what elements in a visual are related to each other. Showing relationships conveys meaning so that your graphics are interpreted correctly and remembered accurately. By showing the parts of a graphic that are associated, you are using visual language to improve your message. Grouping enhances learning in several ways:

- **Affects speed of perception.** Grouping helps learners perceive relationships quickly and efficiently.

- **Supports comprehension.** Research consistently shows that organizing information using grouping principles helps learners accurately perceive meaningful relationships among elements and facilitates the process of learning (Vekiri, 2002; Winn, 1991).

- **Reduces cognitive load.** Grouping techniques support visual chunking, which happens automatically, prior to conscious awareness. When a process is automatic, it reduces cognitive load because it shifts the processing burden off of working memory.

- **Facilitates recall.** A key goal of learning design is to help learners retain and accurately recall information. Grouping reduces the number of items to remember, facilitating recall. As one educational researcher explained, "Rather than having to recall each individual item, one can recall the chunk and 'unpack' it to see what is inside. Helping people chunk materials by arranging them in clusters on the screen or slide has proven effective for a variety of memorization tasks" (Winn, 1991, p. 221).

- **Improves visual hierarchy.** When elements are grouped, there are fewer individual forms scattered around a design. This makes it easier to understand the visual hierarchy, which guides the learners' eyes so they see the most important information first and subordinate information second.

Conditions for Grouping

How can you ensure that your designs are accurately interpreted through grouping? By knowing and understanding the visual patterns that cause it. Several conditions compel viewers to perceive individual elements as groups rather than as isolated objects. These are considered principles of perception and include:

- The principle of proximity,
- The principle of similarity,

▓ The principle of uniform connectedness, and

▓ The principle of enclosure.

The rest of this chapter demonstrates how to apply these principles in your designs to create the conditions for grouping.

GROUPING AND PROXIMITY

Spatial proximity has a strong impact on how viewers organize visual information. During perception, objects that are close together, overlapping, or touching are seen as one entity, and objects that are far apart are not. Because people seek meaning from visual cues, placing objects in close proximity implies there is a relationship between them. Notice that in the scatter plot graph shown in Figure 11.2 it is clear that the data points in close proximity are part of a group and that the isolated point in the upper left is an outlier.

Applying Proximity in Design

Use proximity when you want to show that elements in a graphic have a common function or meaning. The closer the elements are to each other, the more likely they are to be seen as having an association. Use sufficient white space in between groups to make it clear which items belong together and which do not. This works for people as well as objects.

eLearning scenarios. In eLearning scenarios, leverage the proximity effect to tell a story. For example, in Figure 11.3, proximity clearly indicates which people are members of the same social circle and which person is an outsider.

Diagrams and maps. When adding labels to a diagram or map, overlay the labels on the elements or place them very close to the element they represent to show they belong together.

User interface design. When designing a user interface, position buttons with similar functionality close to each other. For example, place all of the navigations buttons in close proximity to demonstrate they have a common function.

Beware of unintended grouping. A corollary of this principle is that viewers can find unintended associations and relationships when objects are placed too close together. Watch for accidental groupings when you are laying out a design. Figure 11.4 is an example of unintended grouping. The proximity of each set of labels to the two food groups makes it difficult to determine which label is associated with which group.

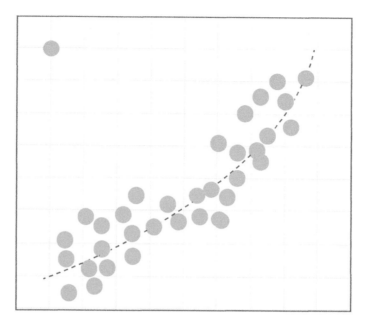

FIGURE 11.2. *Proximity shows what is related and what is not.*

GROUPING AND SIMILARITY

The way people interpret graphics is often based on real-world experience, and this is true for the principle of similarity. When you see a group of people with very similar features, you may think they are part of the same family group. Likewise, in visuals, we tend to see similar elements as one group, such as when they are similar in size, color, and shape.

Notice the examples in Figure 11.5. On the left, all of the rectangles are equidistant from each other. A viewer might see these shapes as four rows or four columns. On the right, changing the similarity of one attribute—color—creates the perception that the shapes are horizontal groups or rows.

FIGURE 11.3. *You can use the grouping principle to convey a message in eLearning scenarios.*

Similarity in Design

The principle of similarity is most useful in charts, diagrams, maps, and other information graphics. When you want the audience to associate specific elements in an information graphic, give the elements similar features. You can see how this works in Figure 11.6, which compares the salaries of women by level of education with the salaries of men in the United States (sorry for the bad news, women). Bars with a common color will be perceived as belonging to the same group.

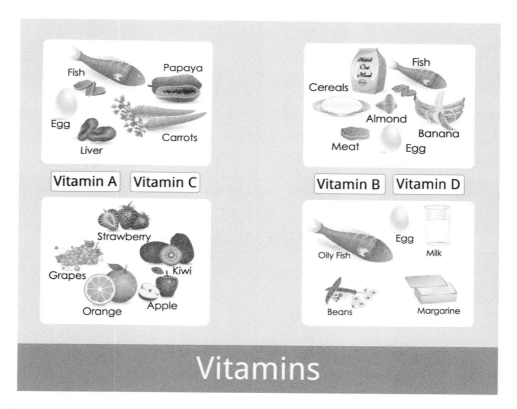

FIGURE 11.4. *Unintended proximity can cause incorrect groupings. Here, it is difficult to tell which label is associated with which group.*

You can also use similarity to group elements in an interactive design as a way to show they have related functionality. For example, in a drag-and-drop exercise, use one design style for all of the drag objects and another for the target objects, as shown in Figure 11.7. When viewers see graphical elements that are similar, they assume they are associated.

FIGURE 11.5. *Because we perceive similar items as a group, we tend to see vertical or horizontal groups on the left and only horizontal groups on the right, where the shapes are similar in color.*

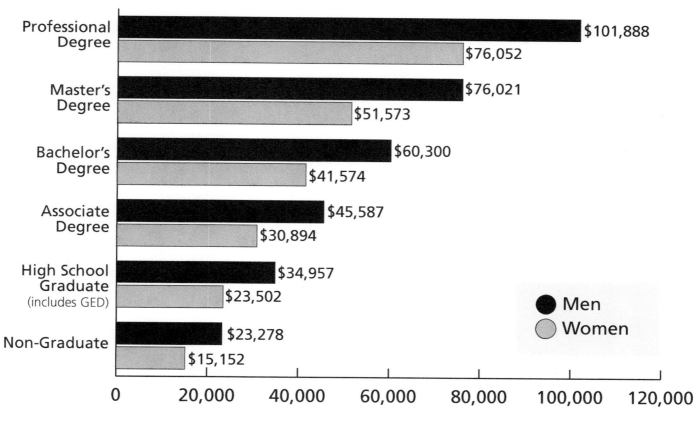

MEDIAN EARNINGS BY EDUCATION AND GENDER IN U.S.
(People 25 years and over)

Professional Degree — Men: $101,888 — Women: $76,052

Master's Degree — Men: $76,021 — Women: $51,573

Bachelor's Degree — Men: $60,300 — Women: $41,574

Associate Degree — Men: $45,587 — Women: $30,894

High School Graduate (includes GED) — Men: $34,957 — Women: $23,502

Non-Graduate — Men: $23,278 — Women: $15,152

● Men
● Women

0   20,000   40,000   60,000   80,000   100,000   120,000

Source: U.S. Census Bureau, 2012

FIGURE 11.6. *Objects of the same color or shape are perceived as a group.*

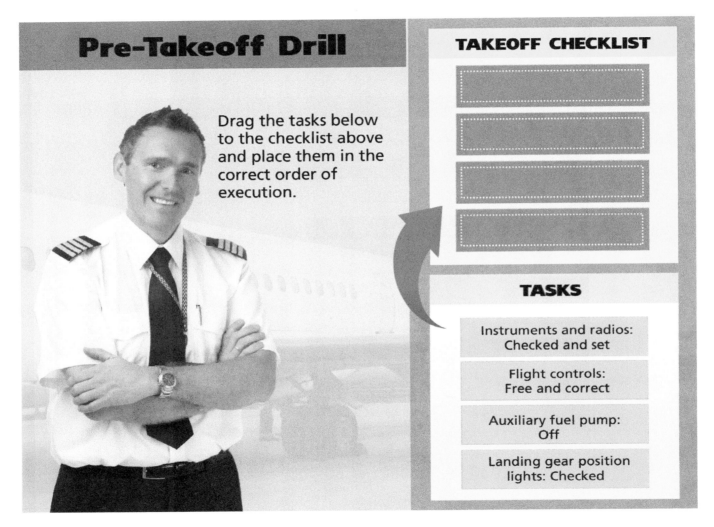

FIGURE 11.7. *Using similar styles in user interface design shows which elements are related. Here, the drag objects (bottom) are all similar, as are the targets (top).*

GROUPING AND UNIFORM CONNECTEDNESS

Uniform connectedness explains why you see an organization chart as one unit. When elements are connected by a line or common edge, we perceive them as part of a group. This may seem obvious, but notice how powerful the connectedness is in Figure 11.8. This is an example of how a connecting line can override the principles of both proximity and similarity. In this case, the line connects dissimilar shapes and the shapes that are the farthest apart, yet we still see the connected elements as a group.

Applying Connectedness in Design

Use lines, arrows, and other types of connectors between elements to convey that they are associated with each other. You can also align shapes so they share a common edge, as in the borders of counties on a map. In particular, connectedness can convey that concepts are related and that steps of a process go together. Figure 11.9 uses a ribbon shape to connect concepts.

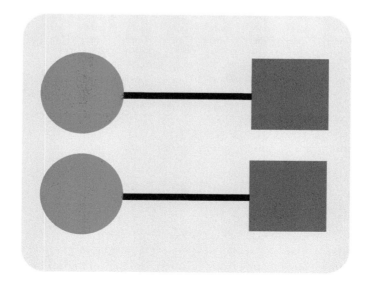

FIGURE 11.8. *Placing a line between objects creates a condition for perceiving the connected shapes as a group.*

FIGURE 11.9. *Using a ribbon for a connecting line.*

GROUPING AND ENCLOSURE

Imagine an aerial view of a neighborhood where the fences indicate property lines. Everything within the fence is perceived as one unit. The principle of enclosure works the same way. We see elements as grouped into a unified whole when they are enclosed by a boundary, even though they would otherwise be seen as distinct entities. Figure 11.10 demonstrates this principle using a map. The three houses enclosed by a dashed boundary line appear to be part of one group.

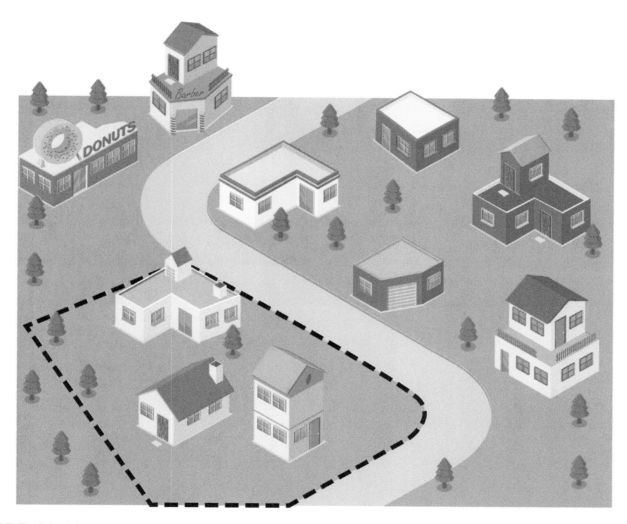

FIGURE 11.10. *The dashed boundary line around the houses suggests they are a group.*

Applying Boundaries in Design

A simple technique to convey that elements are related is to create a common region around them—a geometrical enclosure, an irregular shape, or a flat area of color. Use an enclosure around a set of buttons in the user interface or place a filled area of color in the background of a map or diagram. Enclosure is a compelling way to provide meaning.

The four perceptual conditions that create grouping—proximity, similarity, connectedness, and enclosure—provide much impact for little effort. They are not difficult to implement, yet they speak volumes in visual language.

THE TAKEAWAYS

- The brain detects patterns in order to provide structure and meaning to sensory information.

- Grouping helps learners quickly perceive relationships and reduces the effort required to understand the associations in a visual.

- People structure individual elements into groups when the elements are near each other, similar to each other, connected to each other, or enclosed by a boundary.

PRACTICING DESIGN

An effective design communicates a message, clarifies information, and engages the audience. This section provides practical solutions and ideas to ensure your designs are a success.

CHAPTER

Show Them Where to Look

"There can be no guarantee that anyone will view and read an image you have created the way you would like them to."

— Marc Galer

THE FRAMEWORK

THIS CHAPTER answers these questions:

- What are visual cues?
- How can visual guidance improve learning?
- What types of visual cues should I use?

Imagine you are walking down a city street. While pausing to look up at the tall buildings, you become aware of a pleasant breeze. Your mind travels to the movie you saw last night, but you are interrupted by a passerby who asks for directions. Sound typical? At any given moment, a person might be attending to sensory information or an internal conversation or responding to a situation. How does anyone ever focus?

Fortunately, we all have the ability to use *selective attention*, which allows us to attend to what is important in an ocean of sensory information and internal dialogue. Through selective attention, a person decides what information is processed and what is not. The rest is filtered out.

This also applies to seeing visuals in a course or presentation. What people notice while intentionally using selective attention is different from what they notice while aimlessly looking at a graphic with no goal in mind.

In this chapter, you will learn how to guide the viewers' eyes to ensure they pay attention to what is most important in your design.

VISUAL CUES ARE PERCEPTUAL SIGNALS

If you allow a viewer's eyes to freely wander around a design, he or she may overlook the visual element or text you consider most important to the message. This is where visual cues are useful. A visual cue can be a graphical device or a technique. You can create a visual signal with an arrow or by using a contrasting color in the form of a highlight. The eye gaze of a photograph can serve as a directional cue. Also, there are common typographic cues that make text prominent.

These perceptual signals become part of the visual hierarchy, controlling where viewers look. They help viewers know which part of an image or text is being emphasized so they can effectively focus their attention. Figure 12.1 shows four examples of visual cues. We'll look at each of these types and a few others in subsequent pages. Pick the type that will work best in your design to satisfy your purpose.

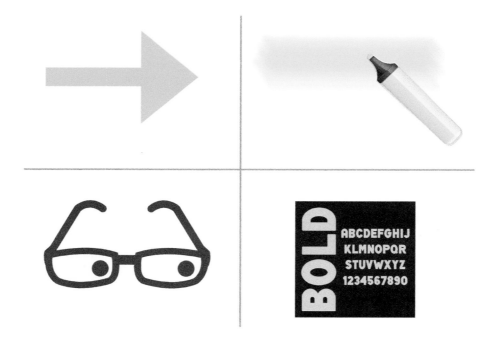

FIGURE 12.1. *Four types of visual cues that guide the eye.*

VISUAL CUES AND LEARNING

Are visual cues really necessary? Eye-tracking data consistently show that perceptual cues do guide attention to relevant information (Ozcelik, Arslan-Ari, & Cagiltay, 2010). Learners selectively attend to the signaled area for a longer period of time as a result of a visual cue compared to non-cued areas. Also, visual signals help viewers select the *appropriate* visual information when it corresponds to explanations in narrations or text (Clark & Lyons, 2010). For example, visual cues help learners know where to look while simultaneously listening to audio and scanning a complex diagram.

When a person's eyes scan a photograph, illustration, or paragraphs of text, brain resources are used that could be more effectively devoted to learning. Visual cues make this process more efficient by improving the speed of finding relevant information. Research also shows that visual cueing can improve the retention of information (Jamet, Gavota, & Quaireau, 2008).

PUTTING VISUAL CUES TO USE

How do you know when to use visual cues? If there is a possibility that a learner will not know where to look or will miss an important part of an image or text, a visual cue will be helpful. This might occur when the screen displays a complex graphic or when it is hard to distinguish one element from another. You might need a visual cue any time important information—image or text—doesn't jump out at the viewer.

Some specific examples of learning situations when a visual cue would be helpful are

- Using arrows to indicate the most significant data points in a graph,

- Highlighting parts of the user interface in a tutorial teaching a new software application, and

- Adding color to highlight a component of a black-and-white drawing as it is explained by a narrator.

Unintentional Cues

When you understand how visual cues work, you can ensure your designs don't contain unintentional cues. This happens when images or text of lesser importance inadvertently draw the eye because they were designed with attention-getting features, such as a colorful border, as in Figure 12.2. This could be misinterpreted as a highlight. To be safe, always review a design from the user's perspective to confirm you are not using perceptual cues that have the opposite effect of your intent.

Information Technology
Learning Portal

Information Technology

Information technology (IT) is the application of computers and telecom equipment to store, retrieve, transmit and manipulate data, often in the context of a business or other enterprise.

Summer Class Schedule	
HTML5 for Beginners	June 1
JavaScript Clinic	June 1
Usability Testing	July 1
Advanced PHP	July 1
Wordpress Workshop	Aug 1
CSS Styles	Aug 1

Select a class to register.

FIGURE 12.2. *An unintentional visual cue, like this colorful border, could be interpreted as a highlight.*

Limit Visual Cue Styles

You may find it tempting to use any type of visual cue that comes to mind. But haven't we been taught to avoid temptation? This is true in design as well. Viewers will find it confusing if you use an abundance of styles. They won't know what to expect when one graphic has red arrows, another uses yellow highlights, and a third uses a pink circle to signify importance.

Whenever possible, use only one type of visual cue. If you need a second style due to the nature of your graphics, use the same type of cue for the same purpose. For instance, always use a yellow highlight to indicate important text. When you repeatedly use a consistent perceptual signal, you train the viewer to be on the lookout for these alerts. Whatever type of cues you choose to use, document it in your visual style guide. Now let's look at the different types in more detail.

DIRECTIONAL CUES

A natural way to focus attention is to use a picture of a finger or an analogous symbol pointing to an object. The pointing gesture is a fundamental act of communication, making it easy to understand its purpose. Here are some directional cues you can use to show viewers where to look.

RESOURCES: VISUAL CLUES

You might find new ways to think about visual cues by borrowing from other fields, such as Information Design and Wayfinding. See the books below:

- *Design for Information* by Isabel Meirelles
- *The Information Design Handbook* by Jenn Visocky O'Grady and Ken Visocky O'Grady
- *The Wayfinding Handbook* by David Gibson

Pointing Hands and Fingers

You can easily find photographs and illustrations of a hand or a character pointing in the right direction to signify the location of where the viewer should look. An alternative is the old-fashioned illustration of a finger pointing, known as a *printer's finger* or *manicule*. Even before the printing press was invented, these graphic devices were used as visual guidance, drawn in the margins of books to point out lines or paragraphs of interest. Use this stylized pointer as a humorous or whimsical option to focus attention if it makes sense with your message. You can see an example of the printer's finger in Figure 12.3.

Arrows

Arrows take the place of a pointing finger and convey a similar message. Because the arrowhead converges to a point, these symbols can focus attention on a very specific area, such as directing viewers to a particular data point on a graph. Arrows have their own visual language. As you modify the arrow's parts—head, shaft, or tail—you can change the communication. See some of the varieties of arrows in Figure 12.4 and think about the different messages they communicate.

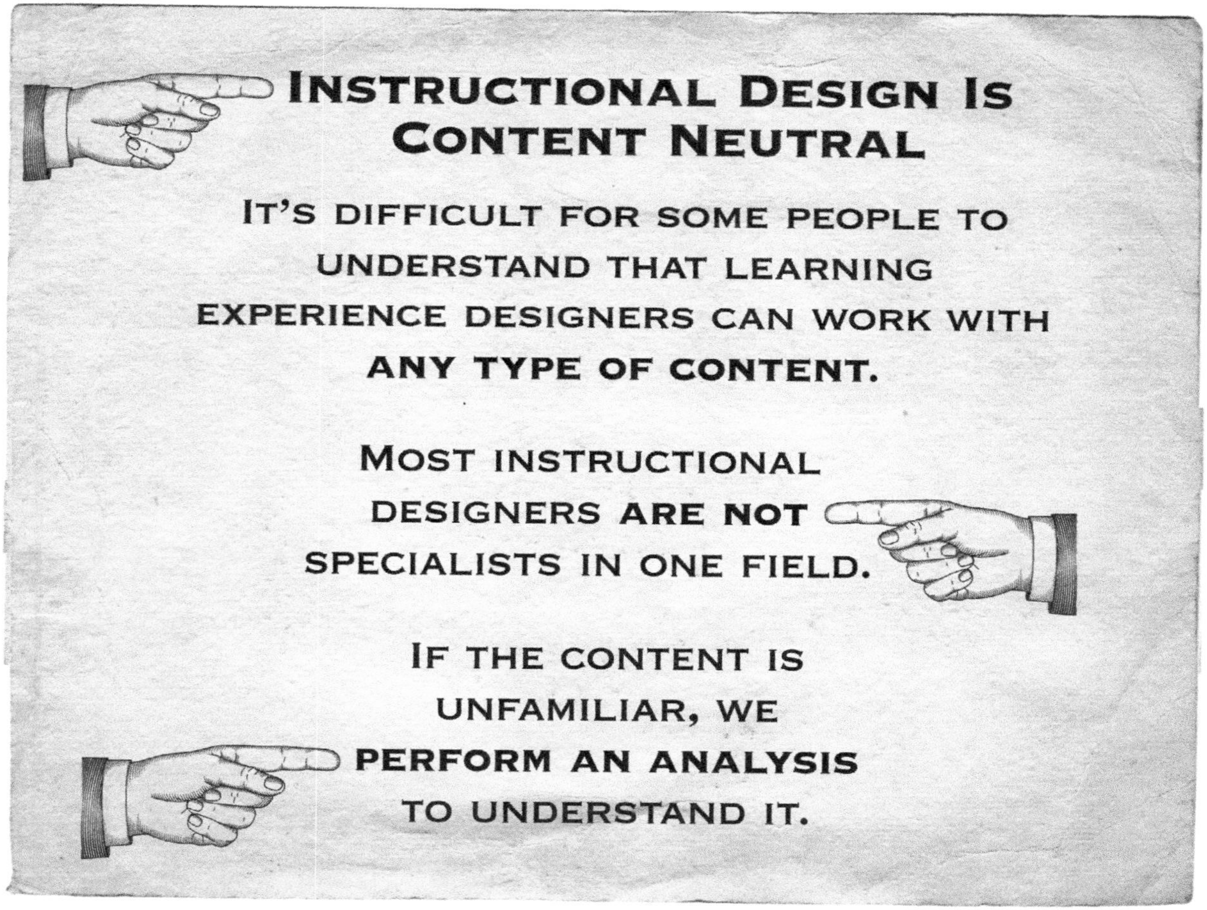

INSTRUCTIONAL DESIGN IS CONTENT NEUTRAL

IT'S DIFFICULT FOR SOME PEOPLE TO UNDERSTAND THAT LEARNING EXPERIENCE DESIGNERS CAN WORK WITH **ANY TYPE OF CONTENT.**

MOST INSTRUCTIONAL DESIGNERS **ARE NOT** SPECIALISTS IN ONE FIELD.

IF THE CONTENT IS UNFAMILIAR, WE **PERFORM AN ANALYSIS** TO UNDERSTAND IT.

FIGURE 12.3. *The printer's finger has worked as a visual cue for centuries.*

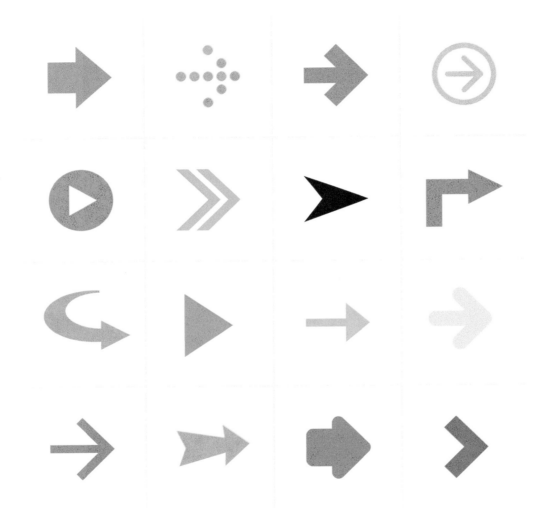

FIGURE 12.4. *When using directional cues, take advantage of the wide variety of arrow types to make the most effective communication.*

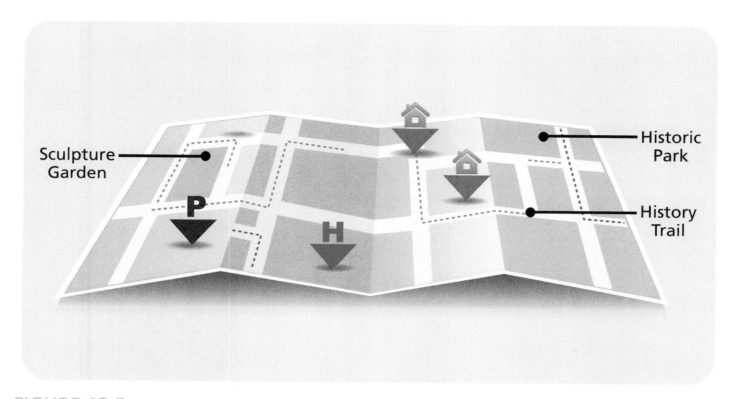

FIGURE 12.5. *Simple geometric shapes, such as triangles and point callouts, are also effective for pointing.*

Pointing Shapes

Several basic geometric shapes are naturally good for pointing, like those in Figure 12.5. These include an elongated triangle, a simple line, or one with a circle at the tip. Thin lines and point callouts are effective for accurately identifying small parts in tight spaces. They can also overlay an image without obscuring it as an arrow might.

COLOR CUES

From bright red stop signs to yellow highlighting pens, people are familiar with the use of color as an intentional visual cue. When a bright color is used as a signal of importance, it helps viewers filter out extraneous information and shows them where to place their attention. Color cues shorten the search for important information and free up brain resources for other cognitive tasks (Jamet, Gavota, & Quaireau, 2008).

Not just any bright color will do, however. The color must contrast sufficiently with the surrounding elements and background to automatically capture attention. Consider a complementary color or a bright yellow, orange, or red. The color should coordinate with the palette, but also be clearly visible. Keep in mind that the most common type of color blindness is the inability to distinguish between red and green, so do not require viewers to make this distinction. Here are some ways to signal importance through the use of color.

Color Transformations

Use a change in color to draw the eyes to an important area of focus. For example, in an interactive anatomical illustration, change the color of the body part that the user clicks to indicate what was selected. In animations, a change in color is effective for highlighting important information that might be missed if it goes by too quickly. Figure 12.6 demonstrates the use of a color transformation.

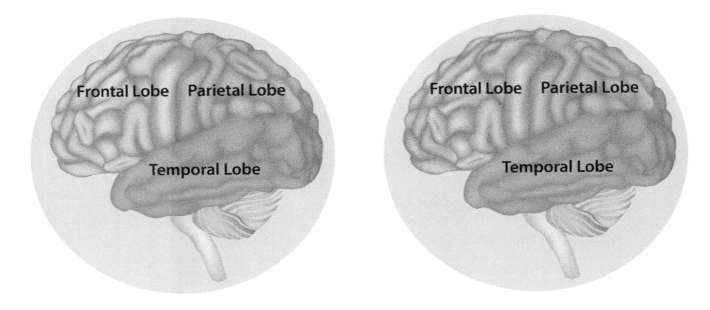

FIGURE 12.6. *Use a change in color to focus attention on an element that is selected.*

Highlights

By definition, a visual highlight is a perceptual signal. Here are four ways to make use of colored highlights:

1. Create a colored shape and use this as a highlight to focus attention. The highlight can be partially transparent and overlaid on text or a graphic.

2. Place an opaque highlight behind elements that have a transparent background.

3. Add numbers to a circle highlight if the order of viewing is important, as in Figure 12.7.

4. Highlight an object by placing a bright border around it as another way to focus attention.

Spotlight Effect

A visual spotlight works just as it does in the theater. As you can see in Figure 12.8, darken the less important parts of an image and place a partially transparent white or light yellow spotlight shape on the area of significance. You can also use this effect in storytelling to feature the main character. Although this style of visual cue may not be practical in many cases, it is dramatic.

EYE GAZE

If you find it surprising to think of eye gaze as a visual cue, think of the last time you saw a crowd of people looking up. Most likely, you immediately looked up, too. Whether our brains are wired to do this or it is a learned act of curiosity or survival, it is well known that people quickly follow eye gaze. Make the most of it.

You can take advantage of this quirk of human behavior by using eye gaze as a visual signal to guide attention. Place an image of a face or person so the eyes are looking in the direction of the object you want to single out. If you want viewers to look at an area of the screen, use a photograph of a person looking in that direction. Notice how, in Figure 12.9, the direction of eye gaze works like an arrow to the text.

As a general rule, always place the image of a person so he or she is looking into the slide rather than out of it. This keeps the viewer's eyes on the content.

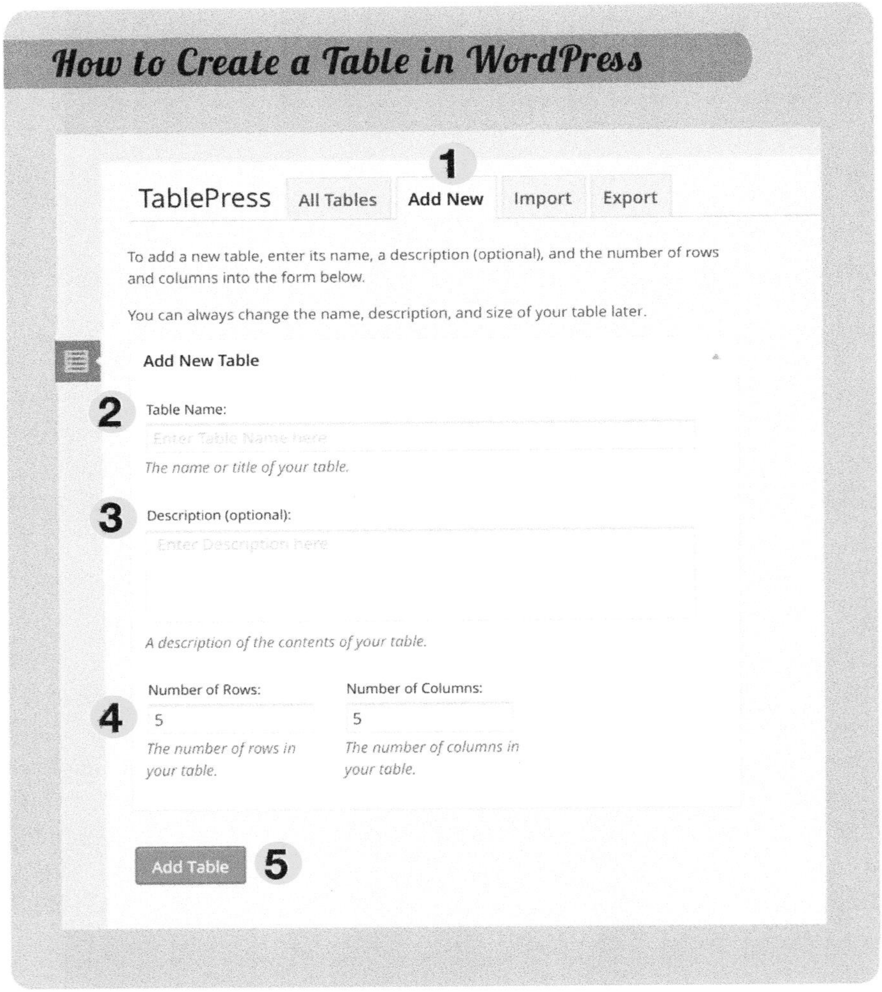

FIGURE 12.7. *The colored highlight is another way to focus attention. Add numbers when the viewing order is important.*

FIGURE 12.8. *A spotlight effect focuses attention.*

FIGURE 12.9. *Eye gaze works as a directional signal to guide the viewer to relevant information.*

OTHER APPROACHES

Both visual and written languages are rich with options. If your design requires unusual ways to signal importance, consider these approaches.

Typographic Cues

Typographic cues are useful for finding information more quickly and for pointing out important words, like glossary terms. In addition to increasing the size of text and using a bold style, other ways to signal importance are with italics, colored text, brackets, and indentation. Within blocks of text, use typographic cues sparingly. Too many instances of bold, italics, and colored text will interfere with reading.

Radiating Lines

You can make text or a graphic prominent by surrounding it with radiating lines, as shown in Figure 12.10. Some viewers might interpret this as a playful approach, so tread carefully when you are working with more serious content.

Stamp It

In prehistoric times (before the digital age), people used a physical stamp and ink pad with the word "IMPORTANT" to indicate that certain information was a priority. This convention is still with us today, though it is digitized. Figure 12.11 demonstrates this, using a stamp typeface, to bring attention to important points.

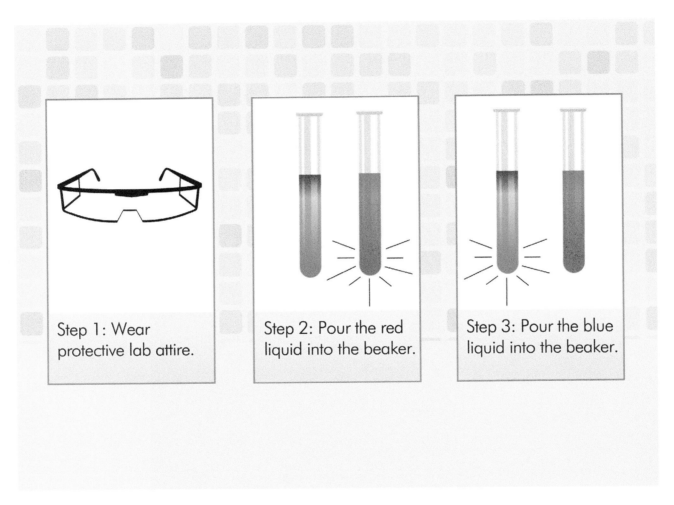

FIGURE 12.10. *Radiating lines signal importance.*

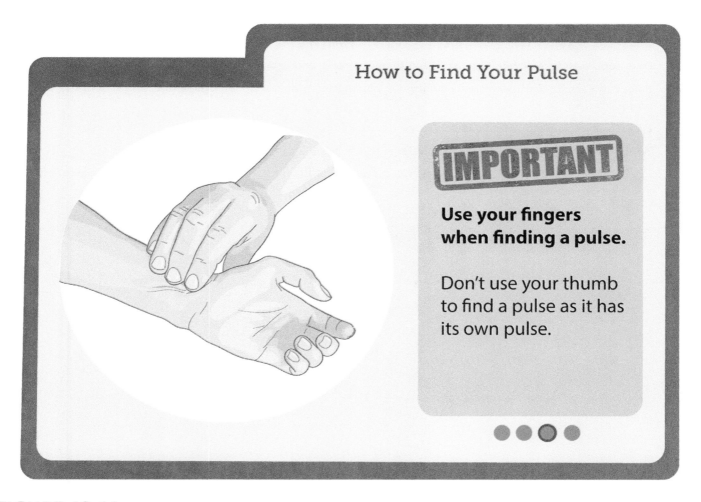

How to Find Your Pulse

IMPORTANT

Use your fingers when finding a pulse.

Don't use your thumb to find a pulse as it has its own pulse.

FIGURE 12.11. *A stamp effect is another type of visual cue that attracts attention.*

THE TAKEAWAYS

- Visual cues guide attention to what is important so viewers will not overlook significant information.

- Directional cues include pointing hands and fingers, arrows, and geometric shapes.

- Color cues include changing color or brightness, highlights (partly transparent shapes and bright outlines), and the spotlight effect.

- Eye gaze is a visual signal that compels viewers to look in the direction of the gaze.

- Typographic cues, such as bold, colored, or large text, provide a hierarchy of relative importance.

13

Add Some Excitement

"Design is improvisation."

— Jessica Helfand

THE FRAMEWORK

THIS CHAPTER answers these questions:

- How can I create an exciting design?
- How can I avoid using lots of bullet points?
- How can I surprise and delight the audience?
- How can I add visual interest on a low budget?

The design process is like walking a tightrope. On the one hand, you want your design to be clean and clear, so the audience can easily understand the content or find the information they are seeking. On the other hand, you want it to be dynamic and energetic, to keep the audience interested and motivated. When you add visual interest, your design will have more appeal.

In this chapter, you will find ways to add visual excitement that won't interfere with the audience getting the message. These ideas are just the start. Once you start, you will find lots of ways to add visual interest yourself.

BULLET POINTS TO GRAPHICS

Fortunately, screens filled with bullets are out of fashion. But not everyone has caught on. With a little care and attention, it's not that difficult to convert bullet points to graphics and improve the visual interest of the screens.

You don't need to exterminate every last bullet list, as they do make important points easy to read. Yet, too many bullet lists becomes repetitive and boring, and what may be even worse, they have a bad reputation. Give the audience a break and try some of these more graphical approaches.

Where to Start

How do you go about it? When you see you have three, four, and five bullet points in a list, stop and imagine whether this same content can be expressed visually using icons, shapes, or images. Here are some alternatives to bullet lists.

Place Text in Shapes

Probably the easiest way to replace bulleted text is to place each point within a shape that you are repeating in the design. Figure 13.1 shows this approach. You can take this one step further by adding a relevant icon to each shape to make it memorable and aesthetically pleasing.

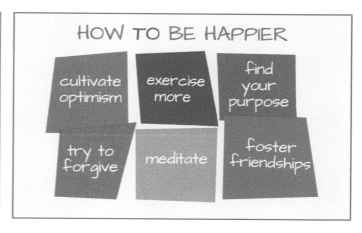

FIGURE 13.1. *Using varied shapes with an expressive typeface is one way to replace bullet points and convey a mood.*

Use the bullet with the most text to judge the size shape you will need, or consider using varied shapes and sizes. You can make that work, too. Then arrange the shapes in a way that will make it easy for learners to read, expresses your message, and looks cohesive. This is often, but not always, a symmetrical or grid pattern.

Place Text Next to Photos

Whenever possible, find photos that express the content of the bullet points. Try to find photos that have a solid area of color or you can create a slightly transparent rectangular shape to hold the text. Look beyond conventional associations to find images that are unique. Then place the text on the photo and remove those bullet points. See Figure 13.2.

Replace Bullets with Word Balloons

When you use people cutouts to "speak" your points, no one will suspect that these were once bullet points. Use photographed cutouts of people or illustrated versions. Place a word balloon near each person and add the text that was in your bullet point. Now you have a set of characters that are, hopefully, tied to the rest of your course presenting your text. The simple act of having a person "speak" the point can make it more meaningful.

FIGURE 13.2. *Place text on a flat area of color in a photo (left) or on a slightly transparent shape that overlays the graphic (right).*

FIGURE 13.3. *Use word balloons instead of bullet points. People cutouts courtesy of eLearning Art.*

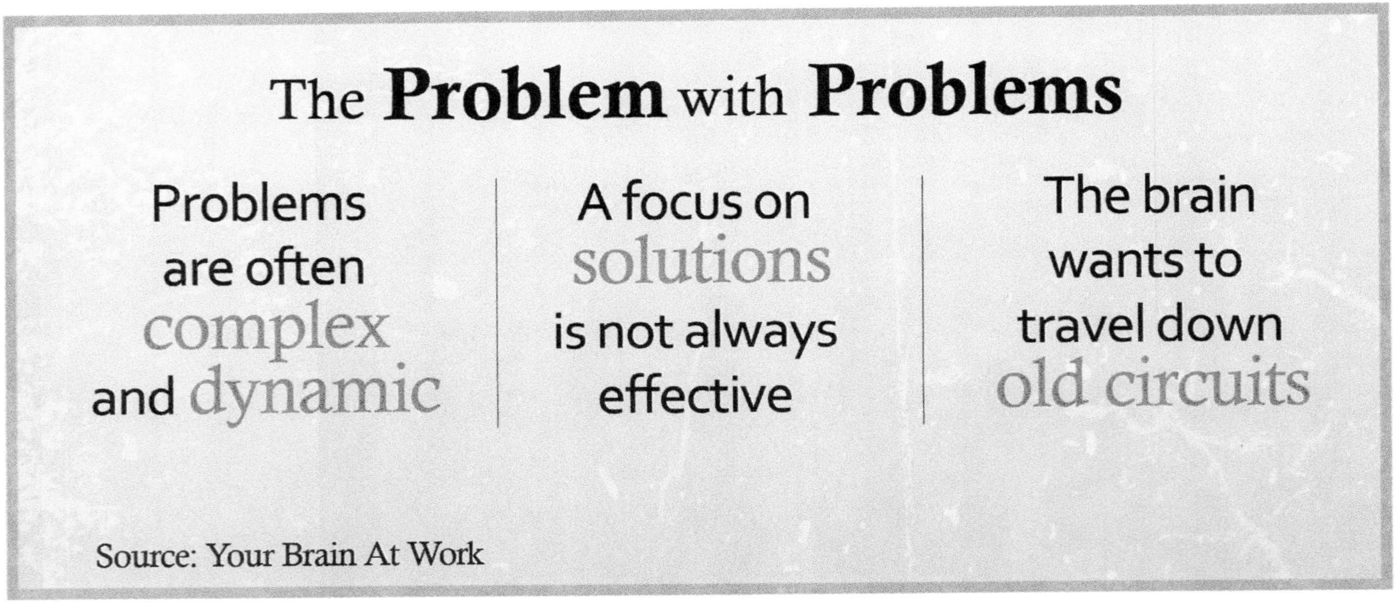

The **Problem** with **Problems**

| Problems are often complex and dynamic | A focus on solutions is not always effective | The brain wants to travel down old circuits |

Source: Your Brain At Work

FIGURE 13.4. *Place text on a panel and replace bullet points with vertical lines.*

Place Text on a Panel

Make your visual presentation more engaging by placing the bullet list horizontally on a panel, using typographic emphasis to enhance it. Enlarge important words for emphasis. Then separate each point with a thin line or rule. As shown in Figure 13.4, this approach is effective when you only have a few bullets. Otherwise, it will be crowded.

Think of Text as an Image

A typeface is a visual form that can be used in a graphical approach. To replace bullet points, try treating the text more like an image. Figure 13.5 shows how a "do not" list can be changed from bullet points to a more graphical treatment. The text is crooked and lightly crossed out (so it can still be read), which conveys the message, "avoid these mistakes."

Do you make these
COMPUTER SECURITY MISTAKES?

I open all email attachments

I click on browser pop-ups

I use an older browser

I download files from unknown sources

I don't back up my work

FIGURE 13.5. *Ditch the bullets by giving text a more graphical treatment. Here, things to avoid are lightly crossed out and displayed in a distressed typeface.*

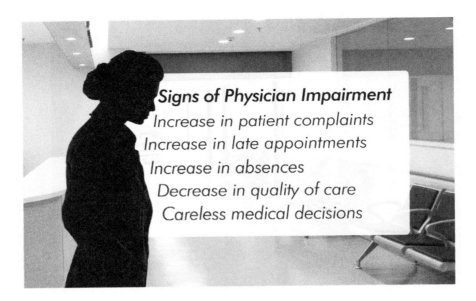

FIGURE 13.6. *Wrapping text around a silhouette is an alternative to the bullet list.*

Wrap the Text Around a Silhouette

Figure 13.6 shows how you can use the outline of a silhouette as the path for lining up text that was previously listed as bullets. Start with a compelling silhouette, such as a person performing a relevant action or an object associated with the text. Then work with each line of text as a separate text box and place it around the silhouette or shape, gently following the outline. This is one way to make image and text interact.

Draw a Diagram

Simple diagrams can replace bullet lists. Think through whether the information in the list is non-hierarchical (all on the same conceptual level) or hierarchical and select the most appropriate diagram type. For flat information, use a diagram that has no hierarchy. You can find them on stock photo sites, like the one in Figure 13.7, or create them yourself.

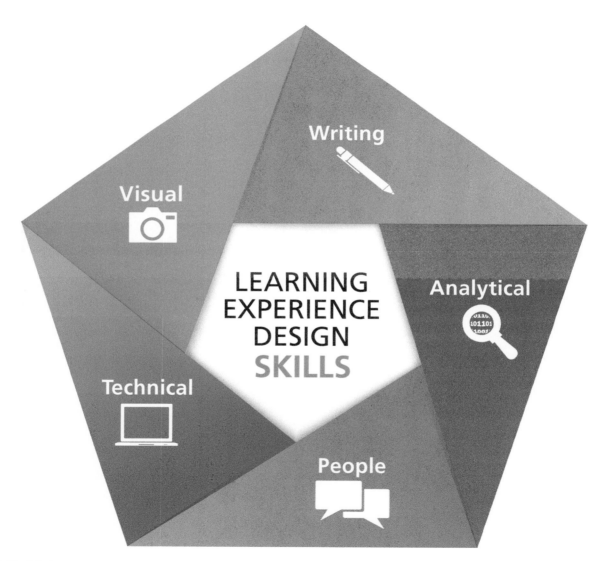

FIGURE 13.7. *Example of a non-hierarchical diagram replacing text bullets.*

A radial diagram is easy to create and effective for flat information. Place the topic or category in a circle in the center. Then place spokes around the circle in the form of arrows or pointers. Place one key point at the end of each spoke.

For hierarchical information, a diagram that conveys levels, such as an organization chart, works well. Find out more about designing diagrams in Chapter 14, Enhance Meaning.

Create a Table

Upon analysis, you might discover that one or more bullet lists can be grouped into a single common category. In this case, consider using a table format, which can handle words or numbers. Figure 13.8 shows how a bullet list of difficult personality types can become a table organized by personality type.

Difficult Personalities At Work

Downers
- Negative
- Critical
- Judging

Complainers
- Whiny
- Blaming
- Accusing

Clams
- Indecisive
- Overly passive
- Disengaged

Explosives
- Irritable
- Angry
- Bossy

Note: most people have some of these traits on a bad day.

Difficult Personalities At Work

Downers	negative	critical	judging
Complainers	whiny	blaming	accusing
Clams	indecisive	overly passive	disengaged
Explosives	irritable	angry	bossy

Note: most people have some of these traits on a bad day.

FIGURE 13.8. *When information can be categorized, use a table format instead of a list of bullets.*

BEYOND THE BOX

If "think outside the box" were not such a tired cliché, it would be a great description of the following techniques for creating visual interest. Instead, let's think of it as breaking boundaries. Even though many images come to us as rectangles, there are lots of ways to go beyond the boxy look. Visual boundaries are not physical limits.

Extend Image Beyond Boundaries

A common use of boxes in eLearning is as backgrounds for cutout people or objects to make a clickable element. A simple technique for breaking out of the box is to change where you place the person or object in relation to the box. As shown in Figure 13.9, enlarge the foreground element so that it extends beyond the box's borders. This makes the image more dynamic, and the background shape draws the eye due to contrast.

Cut Out a Portion of an Object

If you look at most eLearning courses or slides, you might think there are there only two ways to display photographs: with a solid background or with a transparent background. A third and less-used alternative is to cut out only a portion of the photograph, as a way to make the image more distinct. Using the approach shown in Figure 13.10, you will leave the portion of the photo that provides meaning, such as a desk or a bookshelf, to depict a person in an office. This gives a photograph an irregular shape that breaks the boxy look.

Circular Photos

What about displaying photographs in other shapes as a way to bust out of the rectangular habit? Consider cropping photos in a circle or placing them in a circle for a different approach. This is an effective way to present one or more people, such as when introducing characters in a story.

To work in a circular format, find the focal point of the photograph. The focal point should be based on the concept or idea you want to communicate. If you want to show more than one person, the people must be in close proximity to fit in a circle. In Figure 13.11, the photographs of experts are cut out and placed in circular shapes. This gives the design a distinctive flair. Don't stop with circles. Your photographs might work in other shapes, too.

FIGURE 13.9. *Add visual interest by breaking through the boundary lines of a box. Cutout people courtesy of eLearning Art.*

FIGURE 13.10. *Break the boxy look by cutting out only a portion of the photograph. Leaving the large gavel conveys the heavy hand of the law.*

FIGURE 13.11. *Cropping photographs into circles or placing them in non-rectangular shapes avoids the typical boxy look. Website design by d'Vinci Interactive.*

RIBBONS, STICKERS, AND TAGS

If you are looking for a way to charge up a design, consider using simulated ribbons, stickers, and tags. You see these types of graphical ornaments on websites as the background for titles, navigation bars, and announcements. Why not use them in eLearning and presentation designs?

Lots of Variety

There is no shortage of these inexpensive elements for purchase at stock photo sites. They come in diverse colors, textures, styles, and orientations. Use what you know about contrast to make them stand out as much as your need requires. For example, a large bright red ribbon will be prominent on a white background, as compared to a narrow light gray ribbon, which will be more subdued on the same background.

Use for Design Impact

Ribbons, stickers, and tags draw the viewer's attention because of their contrast and novelty. If a design seems a bit monotonous, a ribbon for titles or navigation might add the punch you are seeking. Figure 13.12 shows how the use of a ribbon for the title of

FIGURE 13.12. *Using a ribbon on a title graphic or web page can liven up a design.*

a learning game enhances the design. Although ribbons may add a whimsical feel, they can also be elegant and sophisticated, depending on their color, texture, and use.

Use for Emphasis

Tags and stickers are effective at focusing a person's attention. Figure 13.13 demonstrates some ways to use these ornaments. Hang a tag off of an object to show its category. Or place important information in a sticker to ensure it is noticed. You can also turn them into clickable hyperlinks.

How Many?

You can probably imagine a slide that uses too many ornaments or a course that uses them too frequently. Any element that adds flourish has the potential for adding clutter. Use ribbons, stickers, and tags for a true design purpose, and select or create a style that aligns with the content and the audience.

THE JOY OF DINGBATS

You may recall from Chapter 5, Selecting and Creating Images, that dingbats can be a source of illustrations. They are typographic symbols and pictograms that consist of little pictures, bullets, and shapes that display in place of characters. In the world of printing, a dingbat was known as a printer's ornament and was used for things like ending a chapter or a section in a book.

Types of Dingbat Typefaces

There is an overwhelming variety of dingbat typefaces, each with its own unique illustrations. The first digital dingbat typeface was Zapf Dingbats, followed by many others, including Wingdings and Webdings. Most likely, one or both of these come with your computer operating system. In addition, you can find scores of free dingbat typefaces online in different categories, such as cartoons, sports, animals, and borders. If you're not familiar with dingbats, refer to Figure 5.7 in Chapter 5 for some examples.

How to Access Dingbats

Think of dingbats as a free source of digital clip art. If you're using PowerPoint, insert a dingbat character from the Insert Symbol panel with one of the dingbat fonts selected, such as Wingdings. In a graphics program, select one of the dingbat typefaces and explore the illustrations by typing letters and numbers.

Once you select a dingbat object, you can increase its size, change the color, rotate it, and flip it. You can also combine several dingbats together, partially overlapping them to create a unique illustration. You can also save dingbats as pictures and bring them into other programs.

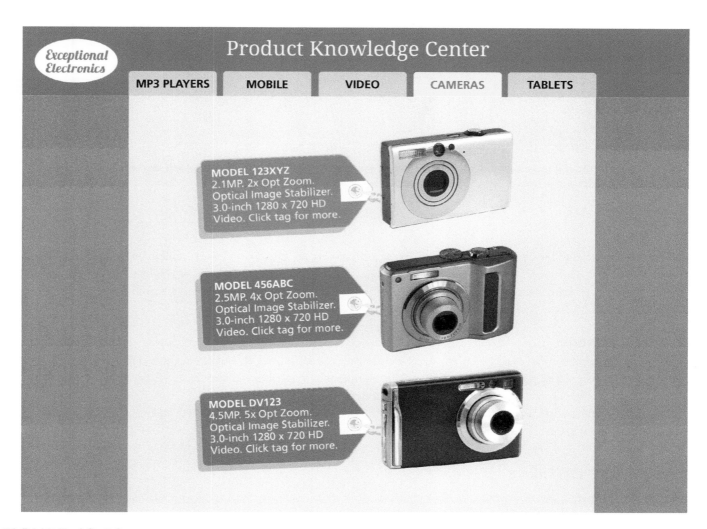

FIGURE 13.13. *Use ornaments, like these tags, to focus attention on important information.*

FIGURE 13.14. *Dingbats make excellent icons. Create a unified look by placing each one on the same background shape.*

Use for Icons

Dingbats make excellent icons because they are crisp illustrations that are clearly visible at small sizes. To create an icon from a dingbat, place each dingbat picture on a similar background shape. Figure 13.14 shows how you can make use of dingbats to represent categories of information. Display these types of icons to organize concepts, as a mnemonic device, or as interactive buttons that are part of a user interface.

Use as an Illustration

By increasing a dingbat symbol to a large point size, you can use it as an illustration in your designs. Then arrange it just as you would any image, combining it with text. You can see an example of a dingbat as the prominent feature of a title slide design in Figure 13.15. It provides a crisp illustration that scales well to any size.

A single large illustration like this, created from a free dingbat typeface (Birds of a Feather) makes an impressive focal point in a design, and few will suspect that it is a very large dingbat character.

TEXTURES AND PATTERNS

In the digital domain, texture is the optical surface that appears as an overall tone. A visual texture can have properties that make it seem smooth or rough, or it can simulate an actual surface, such as stone, canvas, or wood.

A pattern is often similar to a texture, but it refers to the rhythmic repetition of a motif in which the individual shapes are more distinctive than a texture. Figure 13.16 shows the difference between a texture and a pattern.

FIGURE 13.15. *Example of using a very large dingbat character (the bird) as an illustration.*

FIGURE 13.16. *Comparison of textures (on the left) with patterns (on the right).*

There are many ways to use textures and patterns to add visual excitement and to amplify your message. Here are a few ideas for doing this.

Use in Backgrounds

Add a textured background to your design as a way to enhance your communication. As a general rule, don't let busy backgrounds detract from learning or from finding information. But you can weave a relevant texture into content to add meaning. For example, Figure 13.17 demonstrates how a brick texture is effective for introducing a scenario or content that is associated with an urban scene. The texture adds vibrancy to the design and creates the appropriate mood and setting.

FIGURE 13.17. *A textured background is an excellent way to convey a mood. Cutout person courtesy of eLearning Art.*

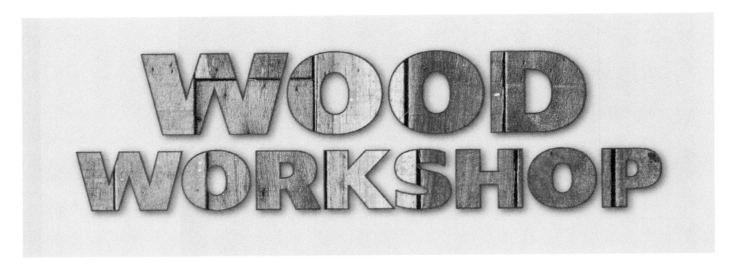

FIGURE 13.18. *Fill large type with a texture to add appeal.*

You can also use patterns to enliven a design, adding a pleasing aesthetic to the experience. A bright and playful pattern on title and section graphics can create an upbeat mood. Vivid textures and patterns can become tiring, however, so avoid overuse.

Consider breaking up a design with a partial texture or pattern, such as using the pattern on the bottom half of the screen. As always, avoid placing text on busy backgrounds.

Textured Type

Figure 13.18 demonstrates how adding a meaningful texture to type can make a point and add an attractive touch. This is most effective when using a typeface set in a large point size, such as for a title or similar screen. You can fill text with a texture in PowerPoint and in graphic programs.

VIGNETTE EFFECT

A final way to add excitement is the vignette effect. This is a technique for focusing attention on the central point of an image by softly filtering out the edges with either a dark or a light area of color. The distinguishing feature of the vignette is that the inner

FIGURE 13.19. *The vignette effect creates a softly filtered edge.*

edge of this area of color is not cut out as a precise line. Rather, it gradually fades out until it becomes transparent, a technique known as feathering. This effect makes the unwanted outer portions of an image recede into the background.

Dark and Light Vignettes

Although you may associate the vignette effect with old photos and movies, it can look classy and contemporary, too. Notice how this technique works as a blended dark shadow effect on the edges of Figure 13.19. To create a strong focal point, use the vignette effect in an extreme way, by blocking out most of an image. To simply add an elegant touch, use it as a subtle border.

Although less common, you can also use the vignette technique with a light color. In this case, select a color from the image so that the vignette appears unified with the graphic. To create an old-fashioned look, convert photographs to a sepia tone and overlay a sepia vignette.

How to Create a Vignette

To use the vignette effect, start with a feathered shape that has a transparent center. The best way to create this is with a graphics program. Once the shape is created, overlay it on any photograph or illustration.

THE **TAKEAWAYS**

- Visual excitement attracts attention, adds impact to a design, and makes visuals more distinctive.

- Some ways to convert bullet points to graphics include placing text in shapes; integrating the text with a photo; replacing bullets with word balloons; and wrapping the text around a silhouette.

- Create an energetic design by breaking out of the boxy look; designing with ribbons, stickers, or tags; using dingbat characters; carefully integrating textures and patterns; and creating a vignette effect.

14

Enhance Meaning

"Meaning is what the brain performs in a dance with the external environment."
— Colin Ware

THE FRAMEWORK

THIS CHAPTER answers these questions:

- How can I use visuals to improve comprehension?
- How do I ensure my graphics are interpreted correctly?
- How can I avoid overwhelming the audience?

If you typically create meaning through words, you will enjoy increasing your use of visual language to provide another channel for creating meaning. A key goal of visual design is effective communication. Helping the audience make sense of information through the visual dimension adds clarity to explanations.

As you generate ideas for visualizing content, you'll discover there are many ways you can extend the meaning of an idea or concept by using the suggestions discussed next.

In this chapter, you'll learn practical ways to make content more meaningful through the use of cultural conventions, visual metaphors, chunking, visualizing, and other techniques. These approaches are effective because they are attuned to how we understand and learn.

■ ■ ■

START WITH CULTURAL CONVENTIONS

If you want to achieve clear communication, a good place to start is by using your culture's visual language. In every culture, there are commonly accepted meanings and uses of imagery and icons that most people recognize and understand. When people become fluent in their culture's visual vocabulary, they are considered visually literate.

Visual Literacy

Visual literacy refers to the ability to understand and use visual language. This affects a person's understanding and interpretation of a graphic. People from other cultures and other literacy backgrounds may interpret visuals differently. For example, when you see a picture in which a person or an object is partially obscured, you assume it means the object is behind something in the foreground, as shown in Figure 14.1. You know that the image depicts three-dimensional space, which you have learned to

FIGURE 14.1. *When an object or person is obscured, you know it is hidden because of how you interpret depictions of three-dimensional space.*

interpret from years of looking at pictures. Yet, in a pre-literate culture that is not familiar with photographs or a culture that conveys perspective in a different way, the viewer might see the object as cut off or missing a part rather than obscured.

The same goes for how you interpret the form of a silhouette. You know that the shape represents an object or person, but this might not be clear to someone who has never seen a drawing of a silhouette. Perhaps he or she would wonder what happened to the person's face and clothes. Interpreting pictures as you do demonstrates your level of visual literacy.

Visual Language Promotes a Shared Understanding

It is important to become aware of your culture's visual language and that of the cultures for which you are designing. Visual language includes techniques like 3-D perspective, and it also includes symbolic representations, such as:

- *Alphanumeric symbols*—example: an asterisk can indicate a footnote,

- *Shapes*—example: an octagon sign implies "stop," and

- *Spatial cues*—example: entities close together indicate a relationship.

Using a culture's learned visual vocabulary helps to ensure that all members of an audience interpret a message in a similar way. Acknowledging this shared visual language is important because it is no less than "the cognitive map—the record of experiences, previous perceptions, and learned concepts stored and arranged in the brain—that allows us to see," wrote educator James Mangan (1978, p. 245). As a designer, you have the power to use visual language so it is most effective.

Common Conventions

To reduce cognitive effort and to promote meaning, adhere to cultural conventions that your audience will understand. Commonly used visual conventions are recognized quickly and are more likely to be interpreted accurately than are unfamiliar symbols and techniques. Using red to convey "danger" and yellow to convey "caution" are standard practices in many cultures. You would not want to use the color green to represent "danger" when a green traffic light indicates "proceed." It is good practice to think through the symbols you choose, to ensure they enhance rather than conceal the meaning.

Common Symbols

When looking for appropriate symbols, choose icons that look like tangible objects or select symbols that are widely known, like those shown in Figure 14.2. Iconic graphics that have characteristics in common with what they stand for are the easiest to understand. These are common in application interfaces, such as when a pencil icon stands for "edit" and binoculars or a magnifying glass stands for "search" functionality. Because these functions represent something in the physical world, they are

FIGURE 14.2. *Use familiar and distinct symbols that won't interfere with learning.*

fairly intuitive. Familiar symbols that are learned are also easy to interpret, such as displaying a checkmark for a correct response and an "X" for an incorrect one.

To maintain clear communication with your audience, there is no need to reinvent your own symbols. Use the ones that are standard in the culture for which you are designing and that have a common interpretation. In addition, select symbols that are distinctive to avoid ambiguity in meaning.

VISUAL METAPHORS

Another way to enhance meaning is through the use of a metaphor, which is a type of analogy. Suppose you wanted to communicate the idea that 21st century citizens are overwhelmed with data and information. Would you use words to explain that we are awash in data, or would you show someone isolated in a boat surrounded by a sea of data? The latter approach—a visual metaphor—is likely to have more impact because the image is striking, as shown in Figure 14.3. If you want to persuade or make a memorable point, a visual metaphor will enhance its meaning.

FIGURE 14.3. *A visual metaphor makes an idea memorable.*

Metaphors Improve Understanding

Analogies and metaphors underlie human thought. When we see a new type of object or hear a new concept, we relate what is unknown to something familiar in order to shed light on it. We seek an analogy or metaphor to understand it. Although we usually think of a metaphor as a figure of speech, it is just as helpful—if not more so—when it is in visual form. In a verbal metaphor, the elements of a new concept are mapped to something we already know. Visual metaphors work in a similar way, with the advantage of being able to map the visual elements as well.

Typically, effective metaphors compare two things that are superficially different. They provide context and meaning by connecting to previous knowledge. Comparing human information processing to a funnel, for example, is an effective way to show that only a small amount of sensory input ever reaches long-term memory (see Figure 14.4).

Metaphors Evoke Emotion

Metaphors are also effective because they can add an emotional layer to content, depending on the image selected. If you want to convey that a person is tense from overwork, portraying the person with smoke blowing out of his head is evocative. The smoke metaphor is more expressive than simply showing a tense office worker at his desk, as shown in Figure 14.5.

What about using a more abstract metaphor? To convey psychological overload, you might use a gauge with the pointer on full to indicate the extent of the overload in a novel way. Using a metaphor like a gauge is a unique way to express the degree of an emotion that an audience may find appealing.

Metaphors Persuade

Visual metaphors can be used for persuasive purposes, too. Rather than triggering previous knowledge, a persuasive metaphor asserts that there is an association between two objects or events by showing that one is figuratively like the other. Once this comparison is understood, the metaphor begins to seem reasonable (Phillips, 1997). This is how advertisers persuade people to associate drinking a particular soda with a carefree life of beach parties. *If only this were true.*

You can use metaphors when you are attempting to modify the values, habits, or biases of an audience. For example, in a presentation about smoking cessation, the designer made a cigarette look like it was a corpse (see Figure 14.6).

Other Benefits of Visual Metaphors

Visual metaphors can also capture attention, not only because people are attracted to pictures, but also because metaphors are often surprising or clever. Some metaphors serve as a memory aid because a learner can mentally fit the key elements of a

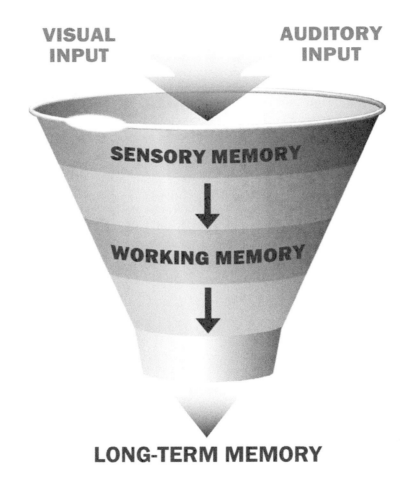

FIGURE 14.4. *Information processing compared to a funnel clarifies the concept that more information enters our senses than is permanently stored in long-term memory. Graphic courtesy of Get My Graphic.*

FIGURE 14.5. *Metaphors can express the degree or extent of an emotion.*

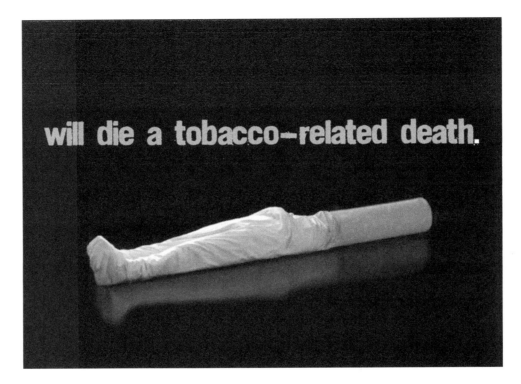

FIGURE 14.6. *Using a cigarette as a corpse is a persuasive metaphor. Slide design by Empowered Presentations.*

concept into the pictorial metaphor and remember it in its graphic form. In the example shown in Figure 14.7, a target is the metaphor for a business process.

In user interface design, visual metaphors provide an intuitive way to understand and learn the functionality of software and devices. Users transfer their experience in the physical world to the applications. For example, deleting a document is similar to throwing paper into a trashcan and tracking changes is similar to editing with a red pen.

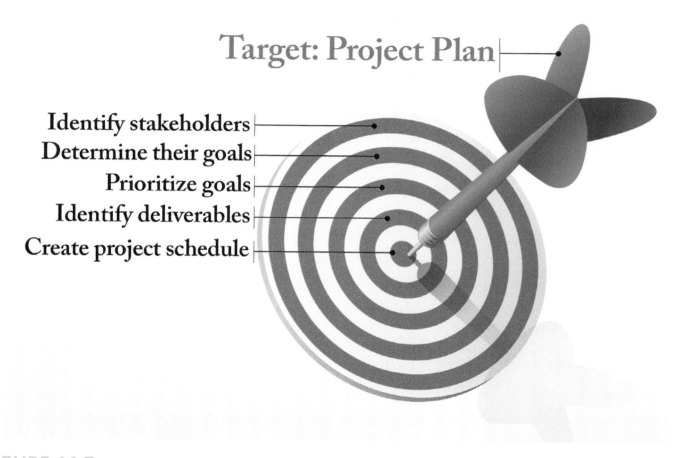

FIGURE 14.7. *Visual metaphors can act as a memory aid. Graphic courtesy of Get My Graphic.*

Using Visual Metaphors

To use visual metaphors, think of a physical corollary to the concept you want to communicate. Find something that has a clear association related to the unfamiliar concept and that is well known to the audience. If you are having difficulty thinking of visual metaphors, start with this list of conventional ones for initial brainstorming purposes. Here are ten well-known visual metaphors to get your wheels turning (metaphor intended):

1. Compare a problem to the tip of an iceberg.

2. Compare a sequential design process to a waterfall.

3. Compare a digital organizational system to a paper filing cabinet.

4. Compare embarking on a difficult project to a winding path through difficult terrain.

5. Compare working through a process to climbing up a ladder or climbing stairs.

6. Compare a repetitive procedure to a wheel turning.

7. Compare an overarching principle to a building with pillars (the concepts) that support the building.

8. Compare a concept that connects ideas to a bridge.

9. Compare a gap in understanding to a chasm.

10. Compare a quantitative increase to something going through the roof (see Figure 14.8).

Guidelines for Using Visual Metaphors

Any type of verbal or visual metaphor can potentially confuse a learner, so follow the guidelines listed here:

■ Ensure the metaphor is clear and does not distract from understanding a concept.

■ Use the right metaphor for the audience—ensure they will be familiar with it.

■ Ensure the tone of the metaphor is appropriate for the content.

■ Overused metaphors can become tired quickly.

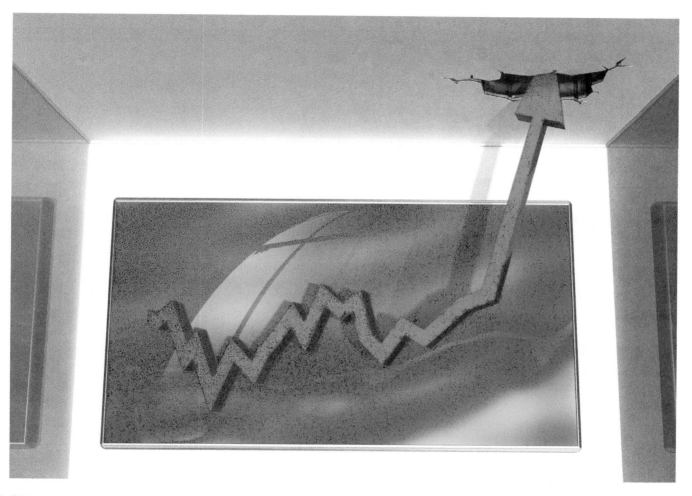

FIGURE 14.8. *"Going through the roof" metaphor works for concepts like sales, prices, and inflation.*

BREAK IT DOWN

Recall that a key feature of how the brain works is that people only process a small amount of information at one time. Although we are surrounded by sensory input, we can only attend to and make sense of a small amount of it. Modern research tells us that working memory has a limited processing capacity and also that we can attend to around four chunks of information at one time (Cowan, 2001).

This number is quite small relative to the amount of information presented in a typical eLearning screen or presentation slide. That is why you need to break up complex information into smaller, meaningful units. It helps people attend to and process information more effectively—a few units at a time—slowly constructing knowledge.

Breaking down content applies to the design of visuals, too. When you think a graphic will overload the audience, you can restructure and chunk the information in a variety of ways. Not only will this enhance meaning, but when a graphic is quickly apprehended, it uses fewer attentional resources than an overwhelming visual. Some visual ways to break content into meaningful units is to place the content into a text table, to sequence the information, and to build it in layers. Let's look at each technique.

Text Tables

Placing content into a table visually organizes information into simple units that can be displayed simultaneously or one row or column at a time. When the content has no hierarchical or sequential order, use the table as a device for an improved layout that serves to break down information.

Figure 14.9 demonstrates the placement of content into a table. According to the grouping principles discussed in Chapter 11, Group for Meaning, viewers will see each cell as a separate entity because the elements are separated by a boundary line or region. This encourages the processing of one chunk of information at a time. In addition, imposing a visual structure or pattern on information may make it more memorable.

Sequencing

Whereas a text table makes use of spatial layout, sequencing has more to do with temporal organization. Sequencing works well for content that has a beginning, middle, and end, such as narratives, timelines, and step-by-step instructions (shown later in this chapter).

When using timelines to create a sequence, consider the meaning that underlies the orientation of the line. For example, Figure 14.10 makes use of an upward pointing diagonal line rather than the conventional horizontal timeline. The ascending line represents positive progress and achievement of the on-boarding technique depicted in the timeline.

Basic User Interface Concepts

Affordance	Drag and Drop	Hover-Reveal	Modal Window
How the physical properties of an object influence its action possibilities or function.	An action in which an object is dropped into another position, as when arranging photos.	The display of information or tools when the mouse pauses over an object.	A child window that requires an action before the user can return to the main window.
Object Selection	**Pop-Up**	**Spotlight**	**Toggle Selection**
When a UI element is selected directly on the object.	Windows that cover part of the screen and appear automatically without the user's permission.	A momentary highlight that indicates when a change has been made.	When a UI element is selected in an on or off state, such as with a checkbox.

FIGURE 14.9. *The text table is a way to chunk content. It breaks down information into simple units.*

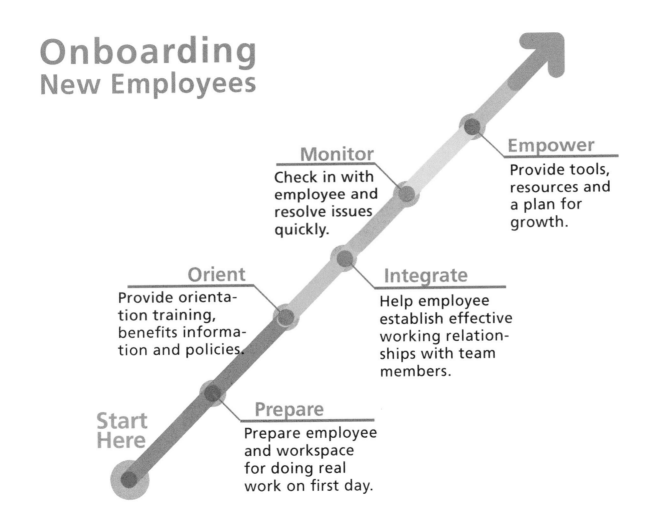

Onboarding
New Employees

Monitor
Check in with employee and resolve issues quickly.

Empower
Provide tools, resources and a plan for growth.

Orient
Provide orientation training, benefits information and policies.

Integrate
Help employee establish effective working relationships with team members.

Start Here

Prepare
Prepare employee and workspace for doing real work on first day.

FIGURE 14.10. *A sequencing technique, such as a timeline, is effective for chunking and ordering information.*

Sequences allow you to adjust the pace of a presentation to reveal the contents progressively. For eLearning, sequences provide a way to make content interactive, giving the learner control of the pace. If the viewer will need to integrate the individual segments into one entity for learning purposes, display them all together at the end. This is important for processing and integrating the information as a single unit in working memory (Kulhavy, Stock, & Kealy, 1993).

Layering

You can also use layering as another way to enhance meaning. Layers refer to chunking information into overlapping surfaces. Unlike the previous approaches, a layered visual builds on top of itself.

To create a layered graphic, begin with a base visual, which serves as a container for holding the rest of the content and the starting point on which the image will build. For example, in a diagram of the human body, the base layer would be the outline of the body or a silhouette, as shown in Figure 14.11. Then group the information into meaningful layers and overlay them one at a time.

VISUALIZE WITH DIAGRAMS

The diagram is an excellent visual choice for enhancing explanations. Regardless of whether it is drawn by an illustrator or made out of boxes and arrows, a well-planned diagram is an effective cognitive aid. Diagrams are flexible. They can depict the parts of an object or the steps of a procedure as well as represent intangible ideas. Because people benefit from concrete representations, you can almost be assured that an effectively designed diagram will improve understanding.

Benefits of Diagrams

Diagrams have so many uses and are written about so often that they have many definitions. In the context of this chapter, I refer to a diagram as a schematized visual that represents objects and concepts using distilled images and symbols. One reason explanatory visuals seem to be more effective than words alone is because "relatively large sections of static pictures and diagrams can be understood in parallel," writes Professor Colin Ware. "We can comprehend the gist of a complex visual structure in a fraction of a second, based on a single glance" (2012, p. 328).

Showing Parts and Structure

An excellent use of the diagram format is to help learners understand the parts and structure of an object. These are pictorial diagrams often illustrated in line art. To create a diagram that demonstrates the parts of an object, draw, trace, or find a clean depiction or cross-section of the object and remove all of the unessential details. Keep the diagram in a simplistic form and label its parts, as shown in Figure 14.12. A schematized version of an object is easy to understand and is effective for simple

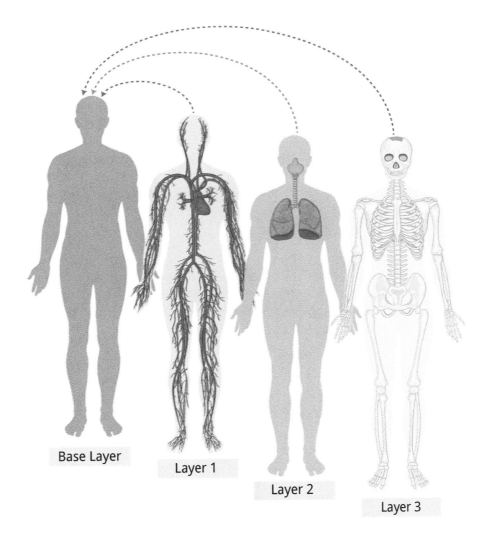

Base Layer

Layer 1

Layer 2

Layer 3

FIGURE 14.11. *Use layers to chunk information in the depth dimension to create overlays.*

Violin Parts

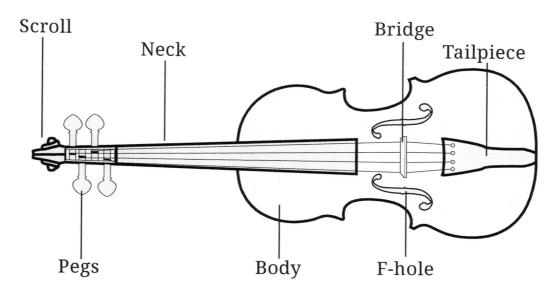

FIGURE 14.12. *A simplified parts and structure diagram enhances meaning.*

structures. For more complex structures where parts are obscured, you may need to have an illustrator create a cutaway drawing, in which some of the surface elements are removed to make both internal and external features visible.

Explaining Systems

If the audience needs to see the big-picture view of a system, organization, or entity, use a diagram to depict an overview of it. Adult learners prefer to have a framework for constructing future knowledge. In the diagram, include the components of the system and use connecting lines to indicate relationships between entities. A common diagram for showing the big picture is the hierarchical diagram used for organization charts, but there are many others, depending on the structure of the system. Notice in Figure 14.13 that using icons and simple images to represent components not only extends the meaning, but it adds visual interest to a diagram.

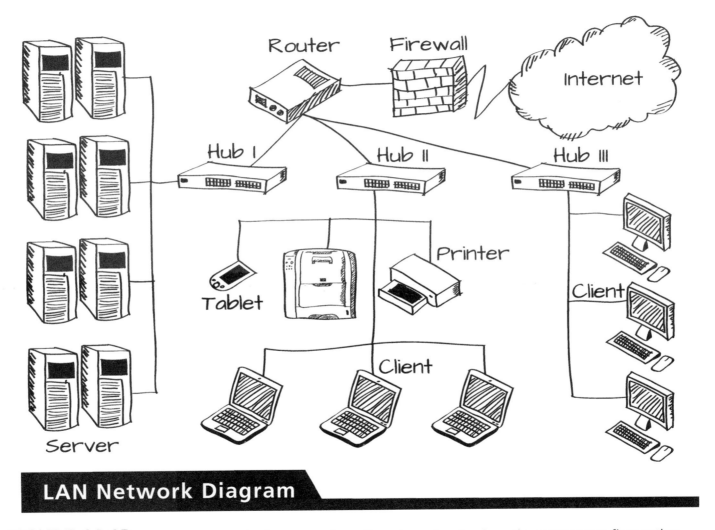

Router Firewall Internet

Hub I Hub II Hub III

Printer

Tablet

Client

Client

Server

LAN Network Diagram

FIGURE 14.13. *Use diagrams to depict an overview of a system, showing how the components fit together.*

Explaining Flow and Movement

Whereas the system diagram focuses on components and their relationships, a diagram that shows flow demonstrates the *movement* of information or energy in a system. This is important when the audience needs to know how something works, whether physical or conceptual. Diagrams that show movement can explain many things, from how a machine works to the flow of information in an organization.

Rather than using connecting lines, as in a system diagram, use straight or curved arrows to show the direction of the flow, as demonstrated in Figure 14.14. Clear and concise static diagrams like this can be as effective as animations for learning (Tversky, Morrison, & Betrancourt, 2002).

Notice in this illustration that the strokes of an engine are depicted in a phase diagram. A phase diagram is a series of static frames that convey the key stages of a dynamic event. The phase diagram is often a more effective approach than a single diagram for helping learners gain an understanding of how something works.

You can also depict movement in a diagram using dashed or dotted lines, as shown in Figure 14.15. In this example, the lines represent the swing of an ax. Research shows that conveying movement in a diagram format can help viewers construct appropriate mental models when explanatory text or audio is presented simultaneously (Mayer, 1993).

Demonstrating How to Do Something

There are times when the audience needs step-by-step instructions to perform a procedure or other type of action. Procedures refer to an ordered sequence of steps or operations performed to achieve a goal, such as how to perform a medical procedure or how to do an exercise routine. Because "how-to" instructions are typically done in the same way each time, it is helpful to document them visually. In the cooking instructions in Figure 14.16, notice how the addition of numbers to a series of steps makes the demonstration easier to follow.

Explaining Concepts

Another use for diagrams is to make abstract concepts concrete. When done well, the visual improves the clarity of the concept and may improve retention. To diagram concepts, use geometrical shapes to represent each component and show relationships through proximity and connecting lines, as demonstrated in Figure 14.17. If the concept is complex or will be difficult for the audience to understand, you may find that a visual metaphor is more helpful than a generic diagram.

Four-Stroke Engine

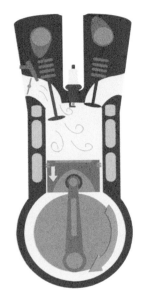
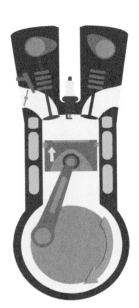
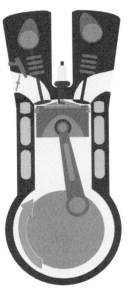

Intake Stroke　**Compression Stroke**　**Power Stroke**　**Exhaust Stroke**

Small arrow: piston motion
Large arrow: crankshaft motion

FIGURE 14.14. *Arrows depict the flow of information or energy.*

FIGURE 14.15. *Dashed or dotted lines are another way to convey movement. Illustration by Eleanor Underhill.*

FIGURE 14.16. *Use step-by-step visual explanations to demonstrate how to do something. Adding the number of each step makes the progression clear.*

The Elements of User Experience

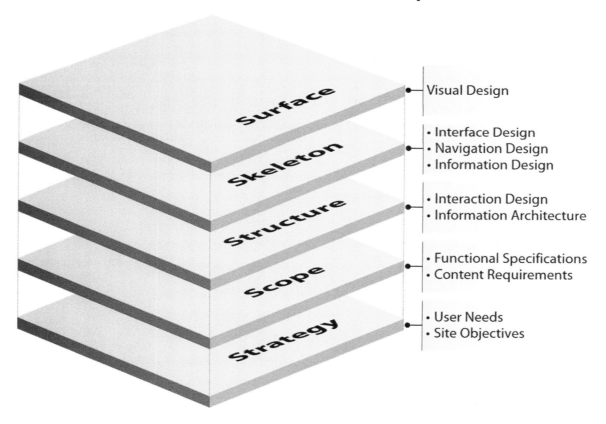

Visual Design

- Interface Design
- Navigation Design
- Information Design

- Interaction Design
- Information Architecture

- Functional Specifications
- Content Requirements

- User Needs
- Site Objectives

Source: Jesse James Garrett

FIGURE 14.17. *Use diagrams to represent abstract concepts. Diagram courtesy of Get My Graphic.*

SEMANTIC COHERENCE

Did you ever see a graphic that seemed clear at first glance until you realized that it was illogical? The failure often occurs because some part of the graphic does not correspond to its message. To overcome this problem, ensure that all aspects of your visual representation are aligned with their intended meaning. I call this semantic coherence, and it is one more way to enhance meaning.

Understanding on Many Levels

Let me explain. Pictures are understood on many levels. The most *literal* level is what the picture depicts. When you see a line drawing of an airplane, you recognize the shape and features of the object and identify it as an airplane.

On another level, the *context* of the picture provides meaning. The same picture of an airplane on a freeway sign means that an upcoming exit will take you to the airport. This is a different context than a photograph of an airplane you may see in an airline advertisement, which suggests a persuasive rather than an informational purpose. Understanding the meaning of the picture depends on the context of where the picture exists.

Another level of meaning is based on the style of the graphic. This is expressed in many ways, such as through symbols, spatial layout, and accepted conventions. For example, certain attributes of an illustration indicate when a drawing is an architectural blueprint and when it is a scientific illustration.

There are also *metaphoric* meanings in some graphics, as discussed earlier in this chapter. Metaphors convey meaning beyond a simple depiction and provide another layer of meaning.

Consistency on All Levels

When a graphic has semantic coherence, it is consistent with what you are communicating at every level of meaning. This way, it is more likely to be understood as you intended. When a graphic is coherent, everything that makes up the graphic—the lines, points, curves, and colors—is compatible with its meaning (Kosslyn, 1989). Anything less causes confusion, inaccurate interpretation, and slowed-down comprehension.

The Proof

Perhaps the most famous example of what happens without coherence is the Stroop Effect, an oft-repeated experiment first conducted in the 1930s. Participants were asked to read the names of colors that were printed in a different color ink than the name denoted, so that the word "blue" might be displayed in red ink and the word "green" in purple ink.

The interesting finding was that it took subjects longer to read the words printed in a mismatching color than in a matching color. There are many theories as to why conflicting information slows down the brain's response time, but most important is the fact that when a visual and its meaning are not entirely aligned, it causes some form of cognitive interference. Here is another example.

Confusion with Pyramids

The pyramid shape is often fraught with problems for conveying meaning. Perhaps the most well-known example is shown in Figure 14.18, the U.S. Food Pyramid published in 1992. First, people complained that it was difficult to judge the relative size of the six bricks representing food groups in the pyramid.

But that was not the least of it. What brought the greatest criticism was the hierarchical interpretation of the pyramid, which placed the least healthy food group at the top and the healthiest foods toward the bottom. Because pyramids are understood according to an up-down metaphor, the visual logic of the diagram was confusing and easily misinterpreted (Perelman, 2011).

As a spatial metaphor, the top of a pyramid should represent the most important entity, rather than the least important. But the top of a pyramid is typically the smallest part. Thus, there are two factors to account for when using a pyramid: the relative size of each section and their hierarchical order (top to bottom). The failure in visual logic of the food pyramid caused confusion because it lacked semantic cohesion.

Confusion with Graphs

Unfortunately, it is not hard to find graphics that don't quite make sense. Another example is when negative values in a bar graph are displayed above the zero line. Again, this goes against the up-down metaphor people use to interpret columnar bar graphs. Figure 14.19 shows a before-and-after version of a bar graph illustrating historical increases and decreases in applications for a fictitious college. When the bars representing negative numbers extend upward (on the left), the visual logic is confusing. When the bars extend below the zero line (on the right), it is consistent with the metaphor we use to interpret negative numbers.

The bottom-line advice is to check that your visuals are cohesive and logical at every level of meaning. This is one of the most effective ways to ensure that your graphics are understood as intended so they facilitate sense-making.

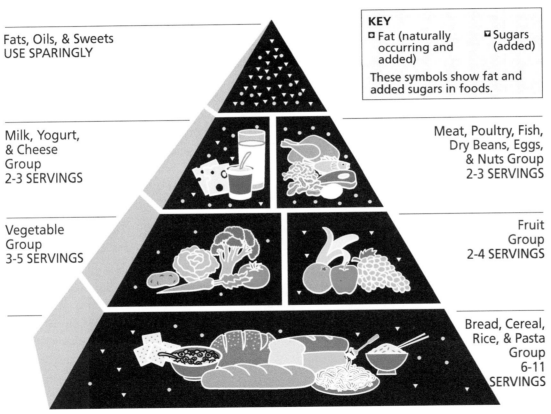

Food Guide Pyramid
A Guide to Daily Food Choices

KEY
- ◻ Fat (naturally occurring and added)
- ◹ Sugars (added)

These symbols show fat and added sugars in foods.

Fats, Oils, & Sweets
USE SPARINGLY

Milk, Yogurt, & Cheese Group
2-3 SERVINGS

Meat, Poultry, Fish, Dry Beans, Eggs, & Nuts Group
2-3 SERVINGS

Vegetable Group
3-5 SERVINGS

Fruit Group
2-4 SERVINGS

Bread, Cereal, Rice, & Pasta Group
6-11 SERVINGS

Source: U.S. Department of Agriculture/U.S. Department of Health and Human Services

FIGURE 14.18. *The food pyramid lacks coherence because the least healthy foods are placed at the top.*

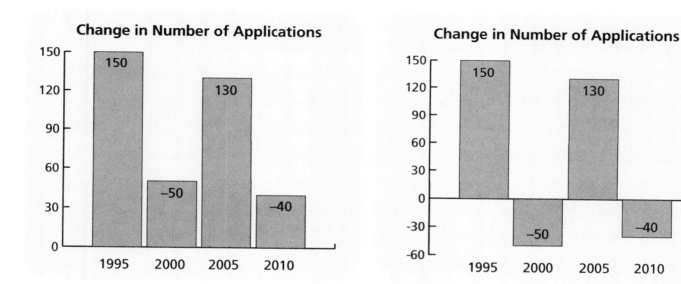

FIGURE 14.19. *Negative amounts represented above the zero line (shown on the left) are inconsistent with how we interpret negative numbers, whereas the graph on the right is compatible with its meaning.*

THE TAKEAWAYS

- To ensure proper interpretation, use conventional symbols that are familiar to your audience.

- To extend meaning, use visual metaphors to relate new content to familiar concepts.

- Use text tables, sequences, and layers to break content into small and meaningful chunks, so the audience is able to process the information without being overwhelmed.

- To avoid having your graphics misinterpreted, ensure that they are semantically coherent—every mark should be compatible with its meaning on every level of interpretation.

Tell Stories with Visuals

"Story is the language of experience."
— Lisa Cron

THE FRAMEWORK

THIS CHAPTER answers these questions:

- What is visual storytelling?
- How do I design a visual story?
- How can my visuals make a narrative most effective?

Did you ever sit through a bad movie or read a poorly written novel because you were compelled to find out what happened at the end? Stories keep us engaged because they spark our curiosity. We *must* find out how the protagonist fares and we can't stop watching, reading, or listening until we know. Stories are also captivating because they touch our emotions. If we feel empathy for the characters, we experience the pain of their struggles and the joy of their successes.

For generations, people have been using the allure of stories to pass on knowledge, skills, and wisdom within communities and cultures. Stories help us make sense of the experiences we have and to learn from the experiences of others. This prepares us for unexpected events that may occur in the future.

In this chapter, you will learn how to convey a narrative using a combination of images and words. You will see how to use visual language to bring stories to life.

VISUAL STORYTELLING

"A story is the narration of a sequence of events deliberately arranged for telling," wrote master cartoonist and writer Will Eisner (2008, p. 3). This concise explanation makes two important points. First, storytelling involves a sequence of events. In the case of visual storytelling, it is a sequence of images, usually accompanied by text. Second, this sequence of events is intentionally structured to tell a story. It has a beginning, a middle, and an end. In this chapter, we will look at several options for creating stories told in a sequence of static images.

Reading visual stories is not the norm for most adults, who spend nearly all of their reading time with the written word. In fact, visual stories are typically relegated to children's books and comic books. In light of this, do not be surprised if you must convince stakeholders that visual stories are indeed appropriate for adults. You can point to the increased popularity of graphic novels and the effectiveness of graphic textbooks for college students (see *Atlas Black: Management Guru* for an example).

Yet, even in this environment, a visual approach to storytelling is gaining acceptance in eLearning, training, and presentations as it becomes clear that a narrative format is a valuable medium for learning. See Figure 15.1 for a visual storytelling example from an eLearning course.

BENEFITS OF VISUAL STORYTELLING

Visual storytelling is an engaging way to present new information and to influence attitudes. It is an ideal approach to setting up scenarios that build problem-solving skills. Stories are more absorbing than plain facts and figures. Here are some other benefits of visual storytelling.

Visual Stories Chunk Information

Visual stories are often divided into panels—smaller segments on the screen. This provides the type of information chunking that makes it easier for people to learn. When stories are divided into panels or one action per screen, it slows down the pace of the information flow, which accommodates the capacity of working memory.

Visual Stories Provide a Common Understanding

When a person progresses through a story that is told in both visuals and text, it is similar to watching a movie. Each audience member sees the same pictures, providing a standardized basis for understanding the story.

In contrast, when reading a *written* story, readers may form mental pictures of the narrative that are unique to their own experiences. Without viewing visuals, it's possible that a story could produce many individualized interpretations, which is appropriate for literature, but not for most instances of learning. Visual stories, therefore, may help you communicate a consistent message among varied audience members.

FIGURE 15.1. *Visual storytelling is a compelling way to present new information and to establish problem-solving scenarios. Design by d'Vinci Interactive.*

Visual Stories Evoke Emotions

A strategic way to connect with an audience is to elicit their emotions. As a story unfolds, a person's feelings may range from fear, anger, or disgust to joy, surprise, or amusement. Evoking empathetic emotions is particularly valuable when it comes to persuasion. That is why presenting a narrative or anecdote is often more powerful than only presenting statistics.

Although both words and images evoke feelings, pictures are able to represent emotions in a concrete way. As shown in Figure 15.2, pictures convey a character's emotional state through facial expressions, gestures, and pose (Feng & Halloran, 2012).

FIGURE 15.2. *Visuals convey emotions through facial expressions, gestures, and pose.*

Visual Stories Arouse Curiosity

Why do people become hooked on stories and want to keep reading or watching until the conclusion? It may be associated with the brain chemical dopamine, which contributes to human curiosity and compels people to want to learn more (Weinschenk, 2011). This curiosity can keep a person glued to a story, regardless of what else is going on.

Intriguing visuals can have a similar effect. They, too, can pique a learner's curiosity and create anticipation. Imagine how an unusual or mysterious photograph might motivate a learner to think: "What's going on? I need to find out" (Figure 15.3). This type of curiosity can heighten someone's motivation to discover what happens next, all the while he or she is processing important instructional points.

FIGURE 15.3. *Visuals can create suspense or intrigue in a story.*

WHAT VISUAL STORIES CAN CONVEY

Unlike other graphic formats, visual stories are designed for a narrative framework. One straightforward approach for designing a story structure is to create a timeline in three parts: set up a problem, elaborate on the problem, and resolve the problem (Ware, 2008). This type of sequence is a comfortable and familiar approach to storytelling. With a structure in place, a visual storytelling format is a powerful channel for communication. The visual format is rich with ways to express ideas, emotions, and events. Through a visual narrative, you can do all of the following (McCloud, 2006):

- Portray the physical features of the characters;
- Convey emotions through body language; expressions of the eyes, mouth, and hands; and pictorial devices (for example, little hearts between two people falling in love);
- Tell what the characters are saying and thinking;
- Show action through body position and motion lines;
- Depict scenes and the objects that make up the scenes;
- Depart from physical reality by representing imaginary worlds and beings;
- Imply action or words that are taking place off-screen; and
- Show hidden actions that only the reader, not the other characters, can see.

You can also use visual stories to communicate about many different types of topics because the content is wrapped in the story package. A visual story is as likely to be effective for teaching how to fix a machine as it is for persuading an audience to adopt a healthy lifestyle. Stories provide creative opportunities and solutions in most subject areas.

VISUAL STORY FORMATS FOR LEARNING

One of the first considerations when visualizing a story is to decide on the style of images that will be most beneficial. What type of pictures will hold people's interest? What image treatment will make the story most meaningful? There are several types of illustrated and photographic options that allow for a creative and effective design.

Realistic Illustrations

Realistic drawings are usually rendered by a professional illustrator, many of whom work on a freelance basis. By realistic, I mean that the characters and objects have a strong resemblance to what they represent, even if the story takes place in a fantastic universe. Realistic illustrations are an excellent format for instruction because hand-drawn graphics have visual appeal. See Figure 15.4 for an example of this approach.

Cartoon Illustrations

Cartoon characters are simpler than realistic illustrations and often have exaggerated features. The effect is often humorous or amusing, as in Figure 15.5. Although some audience groups may consider a cartoon approach too juvenile for their tastes, many adult learners seem to enjoy these illustrations and accept them as a conventional approach to instruction. The best approach is to test cartoons on your audience first to find out their reaction.

Stock Photo Characters

Another image style for visual storytelling is to use photographed eLearning characters like those shown in Figure 15.6. These stock photo cutouts come in assorted poses that express varied gestures and emotions suitable for storytelling. You can show the characters interacting with each other to convey the story and can purchase backgrounds to fit the environment you need. Look for a good selection of diverse models from which to choose, allowing you to make your stories inclusive.

Custom Photos

If your story and content require custom characters or a unique setting, you can also arrange your own photo shoot. When possible, use a model with acting experience to more easily convey the events and emotions you are seeking to express. Also, using an experienced photographer who understands lighting will provide a high-quality product. If you want to create your own cutout characters, shoot the model against a solid-color wall or screen.

Photo Album Effect

A casual effect for a visual story is to make the images appear as though they are part of a photo album. To achieve this, place a thick white border around the photographs—a leftover convention of how photographs used to be developed. Another is to place the images in a slightly angled or overlapping position, which gives the sense that the photos were placed somewhat randomly. You can add captions to the bottom of the photos to support a narrated story, as in the custom photographs shown in Figure 15.7.

FIGURE 15.4. *Example of realistic illustrations with an imaginary character in instructional materials for adult learners. Illustration by Robert Schoolcraft.*

Sexual Harassment in the Workplace

Ted was a successful sales manager who led his team to record years, but he had one glaring problem.

He frequently made jokes and comments of a sexual nature to the female members of his team.

Martha, a new employee, immediately reported his behaviors to HR in an email. She stated his actions were indicative of sexual harassment.

Not all unwanted behaviors, however, are considered sexual harrassment. Learn more.

FIGURE 15.5. *Cartoon illustrations are drawn with simplistic features.*

FIGURE 15.6. *eLearning characters use one model in varied poses. Cutout person courtesy of the eLearning Brothers.*

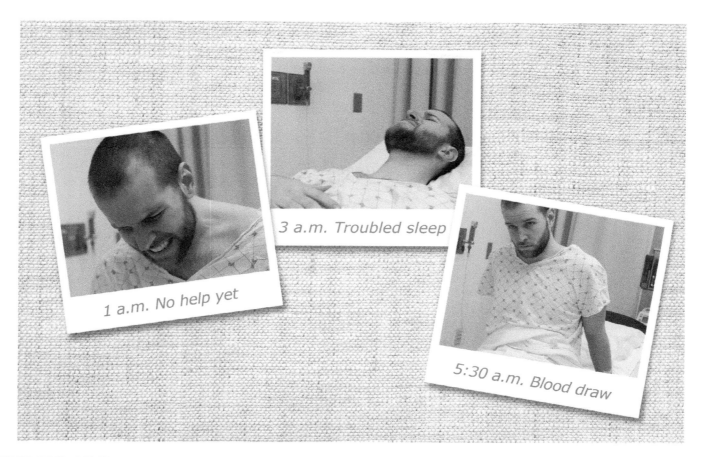

FIGURE 15.7. *Screen from a custom photo shoot using captions to enhance the storyline.*

Photo Essay Technique

When images can carry most of the information, you may want to tell a story with a photo essay. This is a journalistic style for arranging a series of photographs in a narrative sequence. Imagine how powerful a photo essay might be for educating about a social problem or a scientific issue or for following an event over time. Use this treatment to describe content that benefits from strong images, to persuade, to show evidence, or to have a potent impact.

In the photo essay, it is conventional to place captions below each image or to use audio narration. This helps readers grasp the key points. It is also helpful to set up the essay with an establishing shot and then move closer to the subject. When photos are the main content, use varied imagery to capture action and emotions. The photo essay is under-used in instruction, making it an attractive way to capture an audience's attention.

THE VISUAL LANGUAGE OF STORIES

Although graphic novels, narrative tales, and even cave paintings use sequential imagery, you are probably most familiar with the comic format because many visual techniques derive from this style. As noted previously, the comic format uses a mix of images and words displayed in a sequence of panels that separate a story into meaningful units. This format works as well with photographs of people as it does with illustrations. Each panel or frame usually represents a moment in time, but it can also represent different views or places where the action is happening simultaneously.

In the comic format, each character's speech is typically displayed within a word balloon, although the balloon is not a requirement. This approach pulls from a rich tradition of visual language. Some of the main visual language categories of the comic format are explained next. Take advantage of them.

Panels

Although you can tell a story in full-screen images, you may find that panels are the best approach, as they allow you to display more key events of the story. There is a great deal of freedom in the content you can display in a panel. You can show a setting, characters, objects, or symbols. For example, to set up the location of a scene, you might show tall buildings and a busy city street in the first frame. Or when discussing how the mind works, you might choose a text caption and show a brain with gears. You don't always need to show a literal representation.

Continuity. During design, consider how the images and text you select for each panel determine the continuity and meaning of the story. A quick change from panel to panel can be disorienting, such as placing characters in a completely different environment with no mention of why the setting has changed.

FIGURE 15.8. *A quiet panel with a silhouette slows down the pace of a story. Illustrations courtesy of DIY eLearning.*

Pacing. Panels can also help you pace the story. To build tension prior to a turning point or for a pregnant pause before a punch line at the end, comic artists may insert a quiet panel that shows a character in silhouette with silence or just a few words. See the example in Figure 15.8. This slows the pace down.

RESOURCE: PANEL COMPOSITION

For more ideas on improving the composition of your panels, search online for *Wally Wood's 22 Panels That Always Work!!* Written for comic artists as a spoof, it has become a classic reference for ways to make scenes with lengthy dialog more interesting.

Gutters

The gutter is the white area between the borders of the panels that provides a space in the story sequence. Some comic creators put a great deal of emphasis on the importance of the gutter. A narrow gutter moves the story along at a faster pace than a wide gutter. A very wide gutter might be interpreted as a transition to another scene.

Word or Speech Balloons

Word balloons are another visual language convention in the comic tradition that can be used with any type of character—illustrated or photographed. The word balloon is a graphical representation of speech, consisting of a shape for the text and a tail that points to the speaker.

There are numerous variations in the shapes and line types you can use for speech balloons. When appropriate, allow the speech balloon to augment what the character is saying or feeling. A speech balloon rendered with a jagged line will express the intensity of a character who is yelling. A speech balloon drawn with a dotted line expresses the hush of a whisper. Unusual speech balloon shapes can express various moods and sounds. See some examples in Figure 15.9.

If word balloons aren't appropriate for your content or audience, simply place the text near the character with a line pointing from the text to the speaker. Some refer to this as an *open word balloon*.

Thought Balloons

Thought balloons look like clouds with text, where the bubbles lead to the person who is thinking. Their ethereal appearance aptly represents a character's inner world. Use these to add another level of depth to the story, revealing the private world that the reader, but not the other characters, knows about.

Captions

Captions are a narrative device usually displayed in boxes at the top or bottom of a panel. They represent the voice of someone telling a story, such as an omniscient narrator or the protagonist. Captions convey story information that cannot be expressed by a character. You can narrate an entire story in captions, with the characters acting out the events. Figure 15.10 shows an example

FIGURE 15.9. *You can make word balloons expressive of the storyline by modifying the line type and shape.*

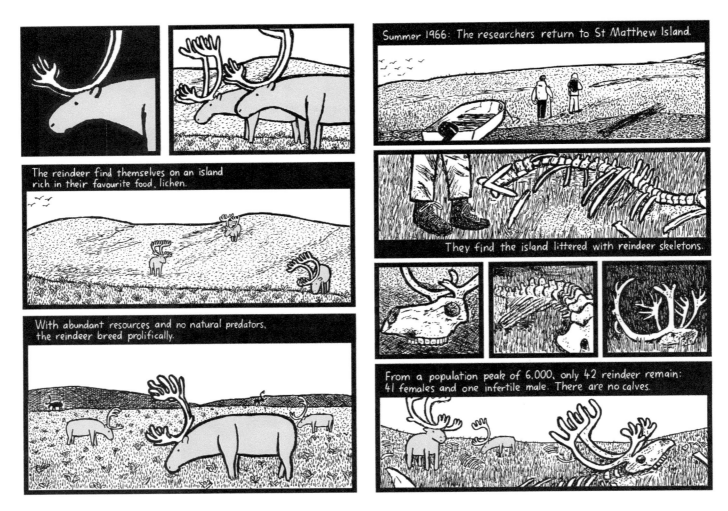

FIGURE 15.10. *Example of an illustrated story narrated in captions. Illustrations by Stuart McMillen from the book* St. Matthew Island.

of an illustrated story that is narrated in this way. Or you can mix captions in with a story that uses speaking characters, as a way to carry the narrative forward. You can create captions in any shape, size, or color, but in comic books they are often drawn in yellow rectangles.

Pictorial Devices

In the world of comics, pictorial devices are a form of visual language that amplifies an emotion or action, adding energy to static images. Here are a few pictorial conventions from the comic format that may enhance your storytelling endeavors.

Action or motion lines. Action lines deserve special attention because of their value for enhancing visual stories. They symbolize dynamic movement and yet can be drawn in a simple way, shown in Figure 15.11. When a character is running, a few straight lines behind the person indicate speed. When a character throws a ball in the air, a few curved lines indicate the path that the ball traveled. The length and shape of the lines also add to the meaning. Short lines indicate greater speed than long lines; wavy lines indicate an irregular movement, such as floating.

Quiver lines. Quiver lines are a special type of action line that indicate back and forth movement, such as shaking or surprise. The short lines are drawn close to the outline of a shape. As with so many visual indicators, context is everything. Quiver lines around a person hugging himself in the snow indicates shivering, and quiver lines around an old truck on a bumpy road represent the truck's vibrations.

So many more. Listing all the pictorial devices employed in comics and graphic novels could fill pages. Some of these marks have been used for decades, and others are created or modified to meet an illustrator's need in the moment. See Figures 15.12 and 15.13 for a collection of familiar pictorial devices you might wish to use in visual storytelling. This list was partially gleaned from the satirical book, *The Lexicon of Comicana*, where you can find a humorous look at pictorial devices.

Sound Effects

Sound effects are words that mimic a sound, such as *Crash, Boom,* and *Pow,* rendered in expressive lettering. You could call this the visualization of onomatopoeia. Sound effects enhance an image by providing an imaginary audio channel, which adds another dimension to the visual. Although sound effects may be difficult to justify in a serious instructional piece, they can add excitement and fun to lighter topics.

FIGURE 15.11. *Action lines and quiver lines represent different types of movement.*

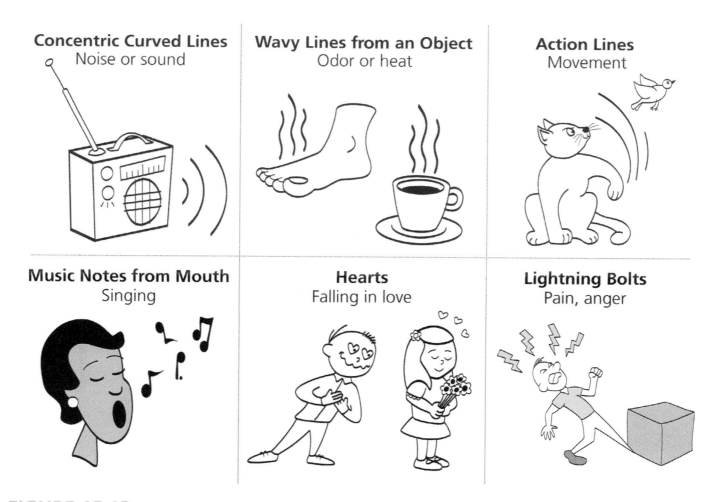

FIGURE 15.12. *Some well-known pictorial devices for storytelling that amplify actions and emotions. Illustrations by Kevin Thorn, NuggetHead Studioz.*

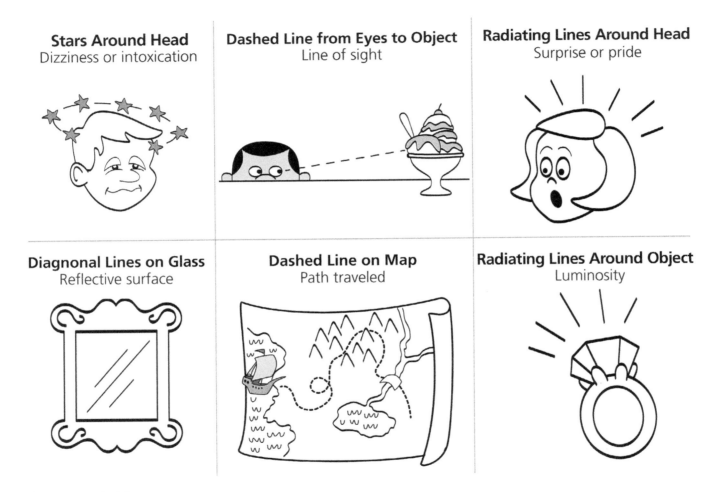

FIGURE 15.13. *More pictorial devices for storytelling that amplify actions and emotions. Illustrations by Kevin Thorn, NuggetHead Studioz.*

DESIGNING THE VISUAL STORY

Similar to how comic books span many pages, a visual story in an eLearning format spans many screens. The layout must work to keep the narrative flowing, and the images and text must express the intended message of the script. Here are some design considerations that will need your attention.

Panel Layout

In Western languages, people read from left to right and top to bottom. This is also the pattern readers follow in visual stories. Your panel layout, therefore, should support eye movements that flow left to right first and top to bottom second. One way to ensure that a reader's eye moves left to right first is to use panels of varying widths staggered in each row and a wider gutter between rows than between panels. This can stop readers from making the mistake of reading top to bottom first, because it emphasizes a horizontal flow (see Figure 15.14).

Placing Word Balloons

Word balloons should also encourage left to right reading. Consistently place them so that any conversation between two people starts with the balloon on the left. Any other pattern will cause confusion. This can be tricky in some panels. When you can't make the balloon placement work in this way, use a few panels that show only one person speaking until the correct rhythm picks up again.

Another guideline is to leave sufficient space for one or more word balloons in a panel. Ensure that the characters and objects are placed so that the text will fit comfortably in a point size that is legible. Also check that the balloon is not hiding a person, object, or scenery that is important to the meaning of the story.

Image Detail

If you are using one image per screen or slide, there is usually sufficient room for detail. But if you are using four or five panels to a screen, you will need to decide what details to include and what to omit. As a general rule, include what is most important to the message you want to convey in each panel. Omit extraneous details that obscure the focal point. At times, you may want to use panels with nothing but an empty background when there is a lot of text in the panel or to focus on the characters alone.

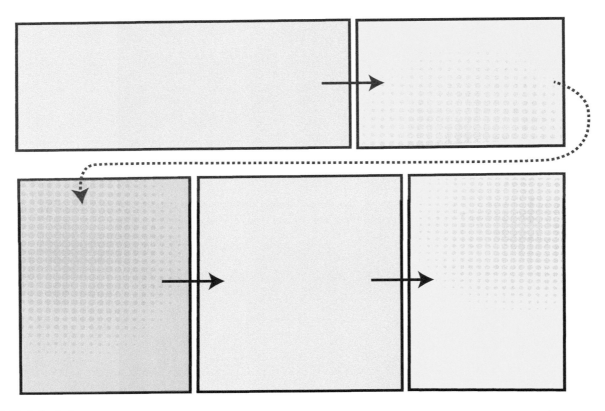

FIGURE 15.14. *Varying the size of panels in each row helps readers move from left to right before top to bottom.*

Comic Typefaces

Although you can use a standard typeface for the text inside speech balloons, you may want to select a typeface designed for the comic format. These look more like the hand lettering that readers associate with comics. Although the aesthetics of comic typeface designs is debated, it will appeal to some readers because it adds authenticity to the look and feel of the visuals. See the Resources box for places to find comic typefaces.

If your final product will be compressed, as is done with many authoring tools for eLearning, you may need to use a larger point size than usual. Always check that the text is legible when compressed and displayed in a browser.

RESOURCES: COMIC TYPEFACES

Where to purchase professional comic typefaces:

- blambot.com
- comicraft.com

Where to find free comic typefaces:

- fontsquirrel.com
- dafont.com

Text and Image Balance

In visual storytelling, text and image rely on each other, so they must be well-integrated and balanced. In most cases, you won't want a word balloon with text to fill up a small panel (unless you are showing someone droning on, that is). The solution is to increase the size of the panel to gain a sense of balance or to separate the text between two panels if the balloon becomes too unwieldy.

Another visual aspect to consider during design is the angle of the image or "camera." This is what we'll explore next.

CAMERA SHOTS AND ANGLES

If you were making a film, would you use the same point of view for each shot or would you vary it depending on the meaning or emotion of the story? Most likely you would do the latter, showing the scene from a distance to provide context and then showing a character close up, to convey his or her emotions. You can avoid a monotonous approach to storytelling by borrowing camera techniques from film. If you consider that every panel represents one moment in a scene, imagine yourself behind the camera for each frame. This is one way to make your story dynamic.

Camera Shots

Camera shots refer to the scale of what is shown in the frame. Even though you are using static graphics, you can translate camera shots from film and photography to convey images in ways that help you express the meaning of a story. Here are some conventional shots to consider. Remember to choose a shot that allows room for text, too. You can see the composition of each shot in Figure 15.15.

Extreme Close-Up

Close-Up

Medium Shot

Long Shot

FIGURE 15.15. *You can borrow camera shots from film to make a visual narrative more powerful.*

FIGURE 15.16. *A bird's-eye view creates a striking overview of a scene. Illustration by Robert Schoolcraft.*

- **Extreme Close-Up (ECU).** A very tight shot that shows a very narrow field of view. For example, it only shows the character's eyes or mouth.

- **Close-Up (CU).** A tight shot, but the view is pulled back a little so that the frame is cropped at a character's head and shoulders.

- **Medium Shot (MS).** The camera has a wider and longer field of view. If a character is in the scene, he or she is shown from the waist up. Close-ups and medium shots are typically the most common shots for telling a story, at least in the comic format.

- **Long Shot (LS) or Wide Shot (WS).** These terms are often used synonymously. The view often shows the full body of a character in his or her surroundings. It is often used as an establishing shot to provide context at the start of a scene.

- **Two Shot.** This shot shows two people in the frame.

You may be thinking that camera shots are easy for illustrators to accomplish, but what if you are using stock photo cutouts or stock cartoons? You can also make these work. For a long shot, resize the characters so that they appear small in a larger environment. For a close-up, drag the characters so they are large and crop them so that only the head and shoulders are showing.

Camera Angles

Whereas the shot defines what will be in the frame, the angle refers to the vantage point or view through which a reader sees it. An unusual vantage point can evoke a mood and add an original touch. It is another way to approach the visual language of storytelling.

Camera angles are difficult to replicate when using stock photos and illustrations, which are usually shot at eye level. But you can work with camera angles if you are creating custom illustrations or photographs. For example, you might want to show Main Street from a high-level view as an establishing shot for a story that takes place in a small town. What follows is a description of what you can achieve with various camera angles:

- **Eye-Level Shot.** The eye-level view depicts everything from the perspective of the other characters. This is how you normally see the world, so this vantage point is familiar. This angle is the most common one for storytelling.

- **Worm's-Eye View.** You can make characters appear important or ominous by showing them from a worm's-eye view, which is below eye level. Worm's-eye often distorts the size of a character, making him or her look larger. You most likely need an illustrator or a custom photo shoot to create graphics from this angle.

- **Bird's-Eye View.** The high-level vantage point has the opposite effect of the worms-eye view, by showing a scene from above eye level. This point of view provides an overview of a scene, which is good for an establishing shot. It can also make characters seem small, weak, or less important. See Figure 15.16 for a bird's-eye angle used as a closing shot to a visual story.

- **Tilted.** Depicting a scene from an angle that is tilted to the vertical lines of the frame makes the panel dramatic and dynamic. Use this technique to add emphasis and variety when it adds meaning to the story and corresponds with its emotional tone.

THE **TAKEAWAYS**

- Visual stories are effective because they present content in small chunks, promote a common understanding, elicit emotions, and hold interest.

- Visual stories are appropriate for many types of content, including skill development, knowledge transfer, and changing attitudes.

- Some important decisions to make regarding visual story design include the format (photographs or illustrations), layout, typography, the camera shot, and the camera angle.

- Take advantage of the rich visual language of telling stories with pictures by using elements, such as panels, speech balloons, pictorial devices, and sound effects.

16

Make Numbers Interesting

"Data and visualization don't always have to be just about the cold, hard facts."
— Nathan Yau

THE FRAMEWORK

THIS CHAPTER answers these questions:

- Why don't my numbers line up evenly?
- How can I make statistics visually appealing?
- When should I use a graph versus a table?
- What are the best practices for designing with numbers?

Do you need to communicate financial data, research statistics, or other types of quantitative information but find it difficult to make it engaging? You've probably discovered that many audiences shut down when they see screens filled with statistics or data. That's because the display of numerical facts can easily become meaningless. It is too easy for numbers to be seen as abstractions.

In this chapter, you will see that there are many ways to make numbers relevant and meaningful. You will see how to liven up the design of statistics and to present data so they are comprehensible. You will find solutions for taking the boredom out of numbers.

TYPOGRAPHY OF NUMBERS

Numerals are an exceptional case in typography, so this is a good place to begin. How you work with numerals is often different from how you work with text. For example, did you ever try to line up a list of numbers only to end up with an unruly column? The design gods were not working against you. If the numerals didn't align properly, you were probably using a typeface that uses proportional spacing.

Although they may be beautifully designed, proportionately spaced characters will not line up perfectly in a tabular format because the characters vary in width. For aligning numbers in columns, use a *monospaced* typeface instead. These are also known as *tabular figures*. (*Note*: If you find the terminology in this topic unfamiliar, please read Chapter 6, Working with Type, first.)

What Is a Monospaced Typeface?

All of the letter and number figures of a monospaced typeface have the same width. Use them any time it is important for numbers and letters to take the same amount of horizontal space on the screen or slide, such as for displaying data tables or demonstrating programming code. Figure 16.1 shows how a proportional typeface compares with a monospaced typeface in columns of numbers.

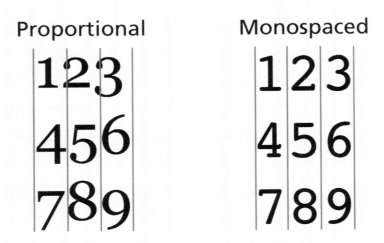

FIGURE 16.1. *The symbols of proportional fonts have varied widths. Monospaced fonts have the same fixed width and are best for aligning columns and for programming code.*

Avoid using a monospaced typeface for body text because it is more difficult to read when compared to proportionately spaced letters. If you want to simulate typewriter text or create an off-beat look, however, you have permission to go with monospaced.

Which Typefaces Are Monospaced?

Both the Windows and Mac operating systems come with several monospaced typefaces. Most likely, you can find one or more of these on your computer:

- Windows: Consolas, Courier, Courier New, Lucida Sans Unicode
- Mac: American Typewriter, Andale Mono, Courier, Courier New, Lucida Console, Monaco, Menlo

Lining and Oldstyle Figures

One other useful thing to know about number typography is that there are two basic styles of numerals: oldstyle and lining.

Oldstyle figures. These numerals have an x-height with characteristics similar to their typeface. That is, some numerals have ascenders that extend beyond the x-height and some numerals have descenders that extend below the baseline. Oldstyle figures blend well with running text, such as when using quantities and addresses.

Lining figures. These numerals sit on the baseline and their height is usually the same as the capital letters. Lining figures are a modern version of numerals and many typefaces default to lining figures. Although they sit on the baseline, lining figures do not always integrate well with text because they are tall. In this case, you can set them at a smaller point size.

Both oldstyle and lining figures can be designed with proportionally spaced or monospaced numbers. Compare the differences between oldstyle and lining numerals in Figure 16.2.

THINKING ABOUT NUMBERS

For design purposes, we can organize quantitative information into two categories: the first is statistical facts, and the second is raw data. Statistical facts refer to simple statements that present a summary or interpretation of data, such as the average salary of instructional designers worldwide for a specific year. A statistical fact tells how much or how many.

Datasets, on the other hand, refer to a larger collection of information gathered for the purpose of analysis and measurement, such as the salaries of instructional designers in the past decade by country. Each category of quantitative information has its own visual design challenges and opportunities.

First and foremost, we must accommodate how the brain deals with numbers to be effective at communicating statistics and data. Here are some ways that human cognition affects the way people understand and use numbers.

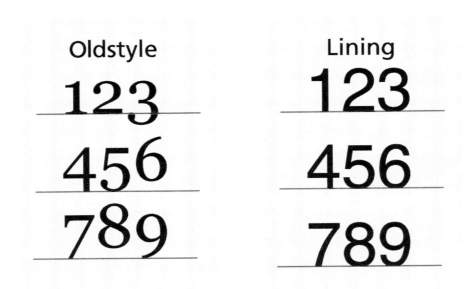

FIGURE 16.2. *Unlike oldstyle figures, lining figures sit on the baseline.*

Approximate Number Sense

People have an approximate, rather than an exact, number sense. This means that audience members may not remember a specific statistic for long. Rather, they will remember it in a way that is meaningful to them. For example, in a presentation about local real estate values, a person is more likely to remember which neighborhoods have the highest price increases, rather than remembering the exact percentage of the increase.

Phenomena Are Interesting

John Tukey, a well-known statistician, argues that people are more interested in events and experiences than in numbers. "Much of what we want to know about the world is naturally expressed as phenomena, as potentially interesting things that can be described in non-numerical words" (1990, p. 330). The phenomena derived from the numbers are of most interest to people.

Practically speaking, this means that the figures you present should support a meaningful and relevant fact, event, or trend. Look for the underlying concept or story that will make your statistics relevant to the audience. Then design with that message in mind.

Spatial Metaphors Are a Reference

You'll also find that people use spatial metaphors to understand visualized data. For example, when a vertical column in a bar graph is taller than the others, viewers know this indicates an increase in quantity. Not only have we learned to read bar graphs, but using height to represent an increase in quantity is analogical to tangible items stacked up high. Readers use their experience with space as a reference to understand many types of visualizations.

Familiarity Is Good

People respond to what seems familiar. When learning a new mathematical skill, people are more likely to understand examples when you explain them using familiar objects or scenarios. For instance, when explaining mathematical averages to college students, it would be more effective to demonstrate the average annual cost that students pay for college textbooks than the average annual costs of running a large government. In addition to using familiar examples, people readily respond to and understand analogies when teaching mathematical concepts (Willingham, 2009). Now let's look at some compelling approaches for designing statistical facts.

DESIGN OF STATISTICAL FACTS

When you need to portray a few statistics rather than large datasets, there are several treatments that are more effective than placing the number facts in a bullet list. First, determine the purpose of the communication. Then consider whether some of the ideas presented in this chapter can help your message. The options for presenting numerical facts discussed in subsequent pages include ways to:

- Single out and emphasize a specific number,
- Use numbers to tell a story,
- Combine the figure with a familiar shape symbol,
- Transform a numerical fact into a metaphor, and
- Make the statistic concrete.

Single Out the Numeral

One simple yet visually appealing approach for presenting one or a few statistics is to make each statistic seem exceptional. Set the numeral alone in a very large point size while using a smaller point size for the accompanying text. See the example in Figure 16.3.

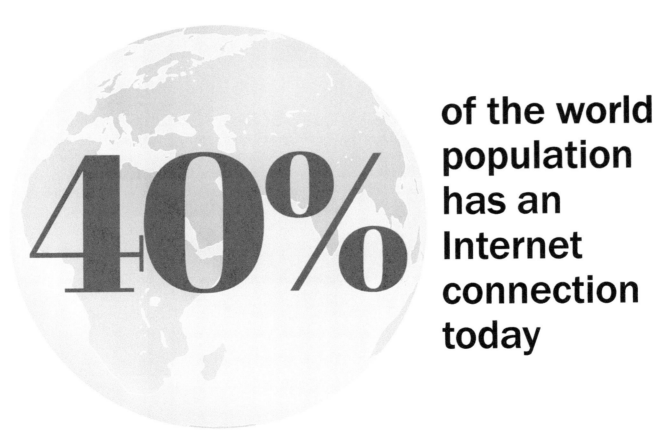

FIGURE 16.3. *Emphasize the number through contrasting size, color, and typeface.*

You can find this type of solution in publications that single out important statistics, such as annual business reports and college viewbooks. In presentation slides, you may choose to present one statistic at a time or a few on a screen, revealed progressively. In eLearning, one statistic per screen could become a slow form of torture if the user is required to repeatedly click "next." So beware of this potential problem.

You can also single out a statistical fact by using a bold, impressive typeface in a contrasting color to make the numeral more prominent, as demonstrated in Figure 16.3. Other options for showing that the number is important are to outline the number or to place a drop shadow behind it.

Use Numbers to Tell a Story

What do designers mean when they say statistics can tell a story? To understand this, it helps to think like a journalist. Effective journalists know that behind every piece of statistical information, there is something that will give it meaning and relevance to the audience. A narrative that uses the data to make a point, to profile a person, or to uncover trends can make numbers come alive. It also provides a design direction for adding visual interest. If you do research and interview subject-matter experts to probe beyond the facts, let the story inform your visual design.

Here is an example. According to statistics provided by the PEW Charitable Trusts, 23,000 people die every year in the United States from infections caused by antibiotic-resistant bacteria. Although the statistic alone is shocking, what is its relevance? The underlying message is that there are too few drugs available to meet current and anticipated patient needs for antibiotic-resistant drugs. Notice in Figure 16.4 that projecting the story behind the numbers makes a difference in the design treatment. The story expressed through your choice of visuals helps to draw the audience into your content.

Use Symbols to Convey Meaning

When you combine statistics with symbols, you're adding a second channel to your message. In addition to communicating the numerical fact, you're conveying its broader meaning. The triangle-shaped symbol indicates a warning on road signs and in computer error messages. As shown in Figure 16.5, delivering a statistic on this symbol signals a potential hazard—associating the data with a problem that needs to be tackled.

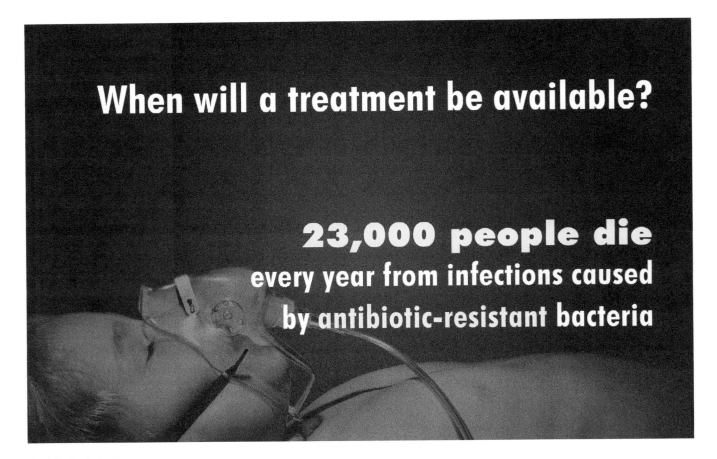

FIGURE 16.4. *Use a visual to express the story behind the numbers.*

FIGURE 16.5. *Represent a statistic with a compatible symbol.*

Create a Metaphor

Because analogies work to improve understanding, consider whether your statistics can be transformed into a visual metaphor. Metaphors work like cognitive shortcuts. You've probably seen examples of metaphors representing numbers. For example, in fundraising drives, charities use a thermometer to indicate how close they are to reaching their fundraising goal. The graphic in Figure 16.6 shows how to use a gauge metaphor to represent a statistic.

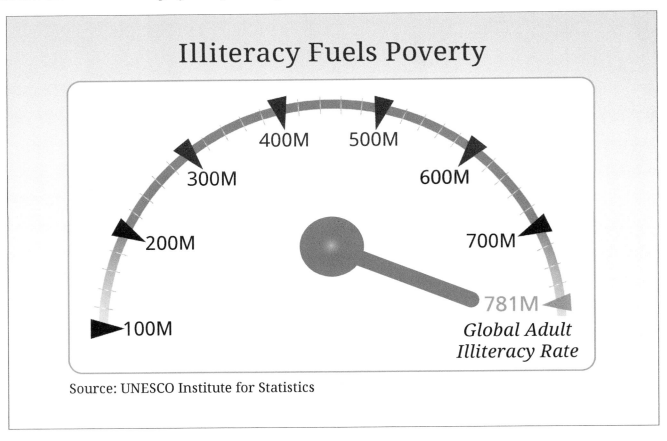

FIGURE 16.6. *Representing a statistic with a metaphor. Graphic courtesy of Get My Graphic.*

Make Numbers Concrete

The capacity to learn about the world through our senses is basic to human understanding. Whenever you can transform statistics or data from something abstract to something tangible, you make it easier to comprehend and easier to remember. And probably because of this, it makes numbers more appealing.

This is easy to accomplish when you want to visualize percentages. See the example in Figure 16.7. All you need is 100 similar shapes. Color the corresponding number of shapes to show what the percentage represents.

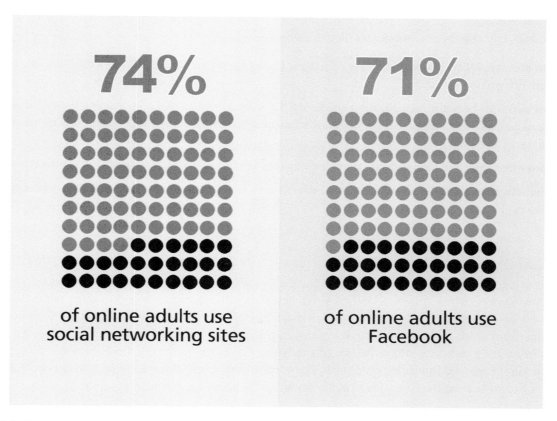

FIGURE 16.7. *A simple technique for making percentages concrete.*

VISUALIZING DATA

As you saw, there are often straightforward solutions for displaying simple statistics with flair. Displaying data is a bit more complex. The essential purpose of data visualization is to provide people with a cognitive aid for understanding information. A picture of the data, such as a graph, enables an audience to see relationships, correlations, and trends. Visualization allows viewers to glean insights and to discover patterns in the data that would not be visible as raw numbers.

Benefits of Visualizing

Here are some additional benefits of representing data in a visual format:

- **Adds to memorability.** The visualization of statistics and data provides an audience with a tangible representation of it, which increases memorability.

- **Increases comprehension.** Visualization speeds up the comprehension of data because the components of a graph or chart are encoded with meaning. The length of a bar in a bar chart represents a value, as does the number of icons repeated in a pictograph.

- **Structures information.** Visualization provides structure and order to data, making it easier to perceive and apprehend.

- **Sustains attention.** Visuals capture attention more so than lists of numbers. An aesthetically pleasing graph invites a viewer to explore.

Types of Graphs

One of the easiest ways to visualize data is through graphs. They are familiar to adult learners and can often be understood with little effort. As Stephen Few wrote, "Because of their visual nature, graphs represent the overall shape of the data" (2013, p. 48).

If you are working with data, you should know which graph format to select and how to design it. The most common format for making comparisons is the bar graph, although a pictograph is also useful. The line graph is effective for depicting trends over time. For representing parts of a whole, people generally use pie charts—although these are not as accurate as you might think. These four graph types are shown in Figure 16.8. There are numerous other graph formats, of course. You can learn more about other types of graphs from the books listed in the Books on Visualization Resource.

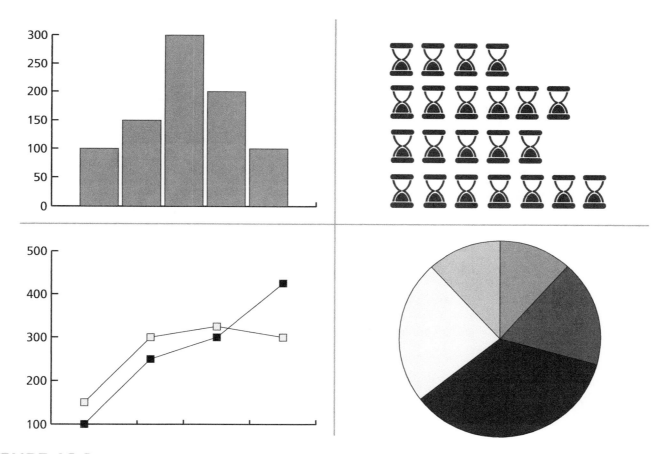

FIGURE 16.8. *Four common types of graphs for visualizing data: bar graph, pictograph, line graph, and pie chart.*

Accommodate Perception

Choose a graph type based on what you want the viewer to comprehend. Consider that we understand graphs because meaning is encoded in the graph's visual properties. We know that the angle of a line sloping downward means a decrease in quantity and an upward slope means an increase. The direction of the slope is a visual property that represents the meaning of the data.

RESOURCES: BOOKS ON VISUALIZATION

- *The Functional Art: An Introduction to Information Graphics and Visualization* by Alberto Cairo

- *Show Me the Numbers* by Stephen Few

- *Visualize This: The Flowing Data Guide to Design, Visualization, and Statistics* by Nathan Yau

- *Data Points: Visualization That Means Something* by Nathan Yau

- *The Wall Street Journal Guide to Information Graphics* by Donna Wong

Yet not all graphs are equally effective at conveying information, because we are able to perceive variations in some visual features more easily than others. That is why it is smart to accommodate perception in your choices and your designs. Figure 16.9 shows the results of research done by Cleveland and McGill (1984), demonstrating which graphical forms lead to the most accurate judgments. According to the authors, more accurate judgments result in a greater likelihood of the viewer seeing patterns and extracting correct information.

For example, viewers can detect varying positions on a common scale with little effort. That is why it is relatively easy to make comparisons using a bar graph. Another perceptual task that can lead to accurate judgments is line direction. Thus, it is fairly easy to determine the direction of a trend in a line graph.

Then there are features that are more difficult to correctly perceive, such as judging the size of an area or volume. The human brain is not very good at comparing areas, which explains why it is often difficult to accurately compare the size of wedges in a pie graph. Avoid these graphs when an audience needs to make accurate comparisons.

Parts of a Graph

In order to engage in the visual design of a graph, it is helpful to know its parts. In his book, *Data Points*, author Nathan Yau organizes the parts of a graph into four categories, described below (Yau, 2013):

- **Visual cues.** These are the features of the graphic that map back to the data, such as the position of a point on a grid, the length of lines, and the colors of symbols.

- **Coordinate system.** The coordinate system is the structured space in which the elements are placed. Line graphs and bar graphs use the x- and y- (Cartesian) coordinate system. Pie charts use a circular or polar coordinate system, where the elements are placed by radius and angle.

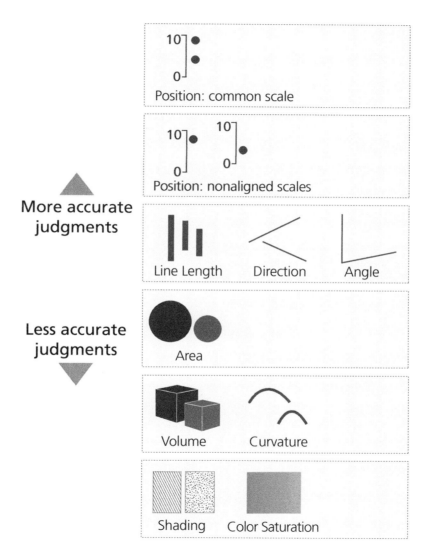

FIGURE 16.9. *A continuum of graphical forms that lead to the most and the least reliable judgments in graphs. Perceptual accuracy of features in the same box are equivalent. Based on Cleveland and McGill, 1984.*

■ **Scale.** Scale refers to the intervals in your coordinate system that are marked on the x-axis and y-axis in the Cartesian system. The scale typically starts at zero.

■ **Context.** Context includes anything that will increase a viewer's understanding of the information. This includes a descriptive graph title, labels on the elements, and arrows and callouts to point out key information.

Let's examine each graph type in more detail.

MAKING COMPARISONS WITH BAR GRAPHS

When your main purpose is for the viewer to compare values, use a bar graph or a pictograph. As you know, bar graphs consist of a series of bars laid out on a grid or scale along a common baseline. The height or length of each bar is measured along this scale, so the intervals of the scale are important to consider. The bars can be placed vertically or horizontally. For time series data represented on a vertical or columnar bar graph, label the units of time on the horizontal x-axis and the value of the quantity along the vertical y-axis. Do the reverse for a horizontal bar graph.

Bar graphs are effective at showing specific values in a series, such as over time, as shown in Figure 16.10 on the left. And they are also suitable for topics that are not related to time, such as for comparing commodities, prices, or behaviors, shown in Figure 16.10 on the right.

Grouped Bar Graph

Use a grouped bar graph when you need to compare two or more variables in a category. To create this type of graph, place the related bars next to each other on a common baseline, as shown in Figure 16.11. Apply the grouping principle by placing the corresponding bars close together while leaving sufficient space between groups.

Recall from Cleveland and McGill's research that people are adept at accurately perceiving the differences in line length on a common scale, making bar graphs easy to interpret. Here are some guidelines for designing bar graphs:

■ Use the same color for bars that represent the same data, as this encourages comparison.

■ To give one piece of data prominence, use a contrasting color or color saturation for that bar.

■ Place the bars below the baseline when displaying negative numbers.

■ 3-D bar charts can make graphs harder to read because the depth cues that show the third dimension may be distracting.

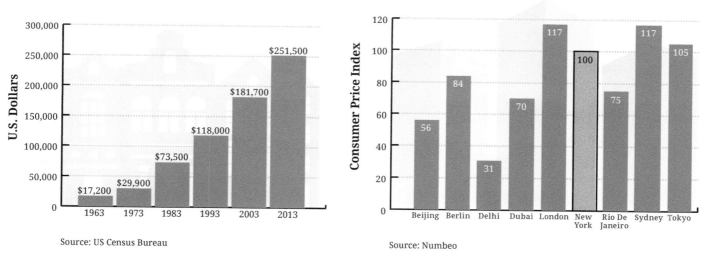

FIGURE 16.10. *Use bar graphs for comparing and contrasting specific values.*

Stacked Bar Graph

Stacked bar graphs are similar to traditional bar graphs, but the bars are divided into independent variables or subgroups. You can see in Figure 16.12 that each subgroup shows its relative contribution to the whole entity. Use this type of graph when it is important to show the relationship of the subgroup to the total or when the total sum of the subgroups in each category is important. Be aware that viewers may have difficulty interpreting stacked bar graphs. Although it is easy to see the total of all subgroups in one category, it is difficult to compare subgroups across different categories.

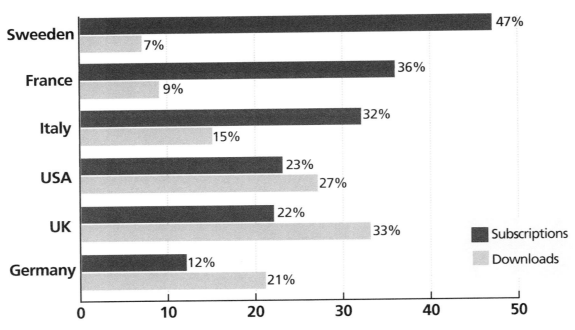

DIGITAL MUSIC TRENDS: STREAMING VERSUS DOWNLOADS

Percentage of Internet users buying subscriptions versus downloading music in selected countries.

Source: Ipsos Media CT

FIGURE 16.11. *Grouped bar graphs allow for comparison of more than one variable in a category.*

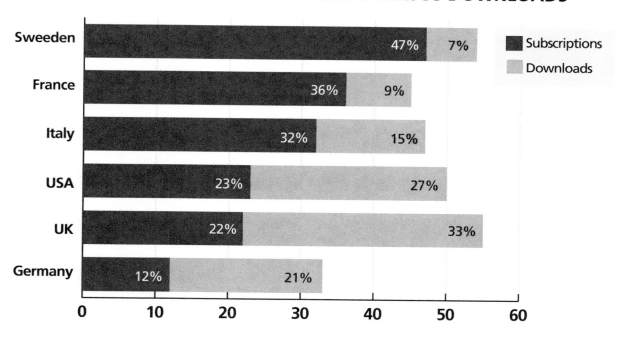

DIGITAL MUSIC TRENDS: STREAMING VERSUS DOWNLOADS

Percent of Internet users buying subscriptions versus downloading music in selected countries.

Source: Ipsos Media CT

FIGURE 16.12. *Use a stacked bar graph to show a part-to-whole relationship and to illustrate the total sum of the subgroups.*

MAKING COMPARISONS WITH PICTOGRAPHS

The pictograph looks like a horizontal bar graph, but it uses simple illustrations instead of a bar. Rather than using a scale, each picture represents a quantity. Figure 16.13 shows how a pictograph can grab attention and make data easier to understand.

To create a pictograph, determine the quantity that each picture will represent. Then select a simple, yet recognizable graphic that communicates something about the data. Use a graduation cap or a diploma if presenting data about high school

FIGURE 16.13. *Pictographs make quantities concrete.*

graduation rates, for example. Then repeat the picture until it equals the appropriate value. Here are some guidelines for designing pictographs:

- Choose an appropriate value for the icon so it will not need to be repeated too many times.

- Select an image that will work if you only need to show a fraction of the icon in order to make the number accurate.

- Vertically align the icons to help the viewer make comparisons.

- Label each row with the value it represents.

- Include a key near the graph.

FINDING TRENDS

When you want to communicate how a quantity progressively changes over time, a line graph is the format of choice. Line graphs depict the rise and fall of one or more continuous data sets. This format is more effective than a bar graph at conveying information when there are many data points to display. It also presents a way for the audience to see trends rather than just individual values. With line graphs, viewers can see what precedes and follows phenomena and what patterns emerge from the data.

Line Graphs Connect the Dots

Line graphs make use of data points plotted as x- and y- coordinates that are then connected with a line. The direction of the line drawn between the points demonstrates the changes in quantity, which is assumed to be along a continuous scale. If the audience needs to compare several datasets, place two or three line graphs on one scale, as shown in Figure 16.14. Here are some guidelines for designing line graphs:

- When placing multiple lines in the graph, use different colors or line types, particularly if the lines cross each other.

- To emphasize key data, make one line thicker and darker or brighter.

- To point out a particular data point, make it larger than the others or place a labeled arrow directed at the point.

- Use a callout with additional information to add key content to the graph.

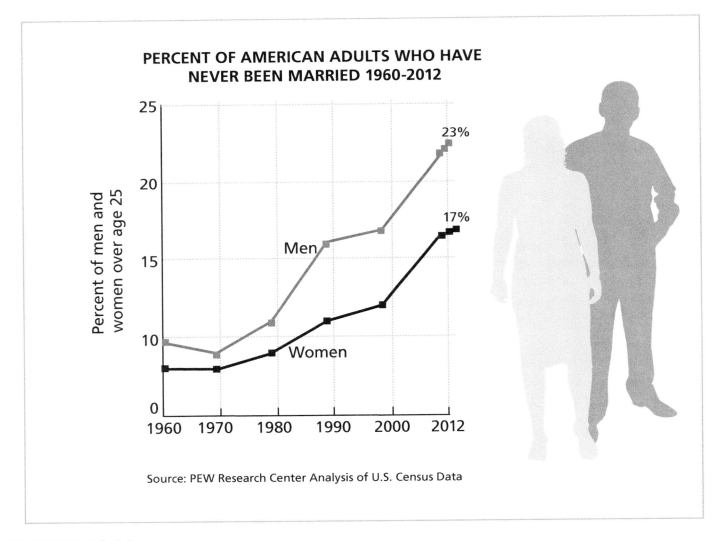

FIGURE 16.14. *Line graphs show the movement of numerical data.*

SHOWING PARTS TO WHOLES

A key purpose of the circle graph, known as the pie chart, is to show the size of each part as a percentage of the whole in order to make comparisons between wedges. You may recall that it is difficult for viewers to make precise judgments when it comes to assessing area and judging angles (Cleveland & McGill, 1984). This means viewers cannot accurately infer the area of a pie chart's wedge nor be able to compare and judge one wedge to another with any precision. If you want viewers to make accurate comparisons, do not use a pie chart. Instead, consider replacing the pie chart with a bar chart when it will provide more meaning.

Pie Charts Have Limited Value

Does a pie chart have any usefulness? To be honest, not that much. Many data visualization experts are quick to say that they don't use pie charts. But if you are in love with these graphs, here is a suggestion. Use a pie chart with no more than two or three wedges to convey an impression. In this way, the pie chart is less of a cognitive aid and more of a technique for adding visual impact, as shown in Figure 16.15. Essentially, use a pie chart to convey relative amounts or a sense of the numbers. Find another graph form to precisely visualize data.

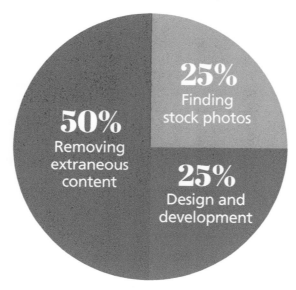

How Instructional Designers Spend Their Time

FIGURE 16.15. *Pie charts have limited value and are best used to convey an impression.*

Here are a few tips for designing pie charts, just in case you are a rebel:

- Because each wedge represents a part of the whole, the percentages must add up to 100 percent.
- Do not use too many wedges, as this can become confusing.
- For emphasis, use a bright color or pattern to make a wedge prominent.
- Place the most important wedge in the 12 o'clock position, when possible.
- Place the percentage value on each wedge or directly next to it.

RESOURCES: VISUALIZATION TOOLS

These applications enable you to create different types of graphs.

- Adobe Illustrator
- Google Spreadsheets
- Many Eyes
- Microsoft Excel
- Microsoft PowerPoint
- OmniGraffle
- Tableau

GRAPH DESIGN GUIDELINES

Many online and desktop tools exist for creating graphs, from spreadsheet applications to special programming languages designed for visualizations. I recommend trying a few of the applications listed in Resources: Visualization Tools. If you have previous experience creating graphs, you may now have an improved design sensibility for making them more effective. Here is a summary of guidelines for graph design:

- **Avoid 3-D.** Adding a third dimension to a graph—depth—has a certain appeal, but it may make it more difficult to extract information from the graph. The third dimension rarely adds meaning.
- **Emphasize key data.** Use contrasts in hue, brightness, or line thickness to emphasize the data that is most important.

- **Annotation.** If supplemental information will improve understanding, add it in the form of callouts, arrows, and additional labels.
- **Provide context.** Use descriptive titles. Label the axes, units, and graph elements.

▪ **Readability and legibility.** Make labels clear and place them in a consistent position. If you place a label at the end of a horizontal bar, then place all labels in that same location.

▪ **Scale.** Use a grid so readers have a reference. Ensure that the grid intervals are equal in size. The size you choose will affect how the data appears, so use a measurement that will accurately reflect the data. Whenever possible, start the scale at zero, which most people expect.

▪ **Establish a visual hierarchy.** Create a hierarchy so that the foreground elements are noticed more than the background. A gray grid will recede into the background, but will still be visible for reference, allowing the foreground elements to have the focus.

DATA TABLES

A table does not magically transform data into a visualization, nor does it have the aesthetic appeal of a well-made graph. But the data table can be quite remarkable. It takes unmanageable data and compresses it into an organized structure of rows and columns. It turns raw numbers into something meaningful that people can read and use. Data tables, therefore, should have a place in your repertoire of number display formats.

Uses for Data Tables

The quantitative values in a table are encoded as text, not as a visual element like those in graphs. Use data tables when the audience needs to:

▪ Get at accurate information quickly,

▪ Look up exact values in a small dataset,

▪ Compare figures in different rows and columns, and

▪ See the totals at the end of each row or column.

Tables may not provide the meaning that a reader derives from graphs, but when designed correctly, they have their strengths, as shown in Figure 16.16.

Table Design Guidelines

A person's ability to quickly make use of table data is influenced by his or her familiarity with the tabular format, the complexity of the data, and how well the table design matches its purpose. An effective design allows people to clearly see the values as

Five-Year Trend of Average Reported Salaries
for Learning Experience Designers in Selected Countries

Country	2010	2011	2012	2013	2014
Australia	$75,159	$87,570	$90,268	$99,293	$94,665
Canada	$74,799	$76,395	$75,615	$79,846	$79,153
India	$36,580	$36,969	$33,664	$30,854	$33,743
United Kingdom	$74,559	$76,559	$72,778	$76,315	$70,871
United States	$79,221	$79,961	$78,937	$78,984	$78,932

Source: The eLearning Guild Research

FIGURE 16.16. *A well-designed data table provides quick access to specific values.*

they scan the table and understand how the numbers relate to each other. Here are some guidelines that will make a table ready for use:

Know the Purpose

- **Match the design with the purpose.** The more familiar users are with a table grid, the faster they can search it to extract the data. Meet the expectations of the audience by sticking to the conventions they expect, as defined by the purpose of the table. For example, a table in an eLearning course might be displayed to make a quick point. A table as a performance support aid for looking up values will have more detail.

- **Order data to match the purpose.** Structure and arrange the data to facilitate how it will be used. If the purpose of a table is to find the populations in major cities, then organize the data alphabetically by city. If the purpose is to show the annual decrease in electronics prices, then arrange the data by time.

Improve Readability

- **Remove clutter.** To enable quick scanning, focus on the most important data and remove all extraneous information. Also, avoid clutter around the body of the table.

- **Use sufficient white space.** Use white space between rows and columns, around headings, titles, labels, and explanations. White space makes a table easier to read.

- **Make effective use of the grid.** Use the table grid to guide the eye in the appropriate direction and to improve readability. If you want to draw the eyes horizontally across the rows, avoid vertical column lines or keep them subdued. Use a quiet color behind the data in the direction the data should be read (horizontal for rows, vertical for columns).

- **Highlight the most important data.** Consider highlighting specific values to emphasize your message by drawing a box around the data or highlighting it in a contrasting color.

- **Write clear headings.** Table headings can present design problems. Consider breaking up a long table heading into two or three lines or include heading details in a footnote. Avoid abbreviations and acronyms that readers won't understand.

Clarify the Numbers

- **Round the numbers in most cases.** Populating a table with rounded integers makes it easier to read and to spot trends. Although this may not be appropriate for data presented to experts, whole numbers are sufficient for novices and lay people.

▨ **Perform computations for users.** When possible, don't ask users to perform arithmetic computations or mental transformations with the data. Instead, do this for them by providing summary information in an additional row or column, such as totals and averages. This facilitates quicker comprehension and interpretation.

▨ **Make it easy to compare numbers.** Side-by-side comparisons seem to be easier to make than above-below comparisons. Also, the eye can run down a column rather quickly, but many people need to use their fingers as a guide to read across rows.

Use Typographic Principles

▨ **Create a visual hierarchy.** Use typography to create emphasis and to guide the reader's eye. Make headings larger or in boldface for emphasis.

▨ **Use a monospaced typeface for alignment.** Alignment makes a table easier to read. Align all numbers, commas, and decimal points in columns by using a monospaced typeface.

THE TAKEAWAYS

▨ Use a monospaced typeface to evenly line up numbers and letters.

▨ When presenting a few statistical facts, add impact by making the numeral big and bold, telling a story with numbers, integrating the statistic with a meaningful symbol, using a metaphor to improve understanding, and visualizing the statistic to make it concrete.

▨ To show differences in quantitative information, rely on the features of line length and location on a grid.

▨ Use a bar graph or pictograph to help viewers make comparisons and a line graph to show trends.

▨ Use a data table when the audience needs to look up or compare specific values.

REFERENCES

Alter, A., and Oppenheimer, D. "Predicting Short-term Stock Fluctuations by Using Processing Fluency." *Proceedings of the National Academy of Sciences*, 2006, *103*(24), 9369–9372.

Beard, Christina. *Critiqued: Inside the Minds of 23 Leaders in Design*. San Francisco, CA: Peachpit Press, 2013.

Bowers, J. *Introduction to Graphic Design Methodologies and Processes: Understanding Theory and Applications*. Hoboken, NJ: John Wiley & Sons, 2011.

Brumberger, Eva. "The Rhetoric of Typography." *Technical Communication*, 2003, *50*(2) 206–223.

Caputo, T. *Visual Storytelling: The Art and Technique*. New York, NY: Watson-Guptill, 2002.

Cairo, Alberto. *The Functional Art: An Introduction to Information Graphics and Visualization*. Berkeley, CA: New Riders, 2013.

Clark, R. C., and Lyons, C. *Graphics for Learning: Proven Guidelines for Planning, Designing, and Evaluating Visuals in Training Materials*. San Francisco, CA: Pfeiffer, 2010.

Cleveland, W., and McGill, R. "Graphical Perception: Theory, Experimentation and Application to the Development of Graphical Methods." *Journal of the American Statistical Association*, *79*(387), 1984, 531–554.

Cowan, N. "The Magical Number Four in Short-Term Memory: A Reconsideration of Mental Storage Capacity." *Behavioral and Brain Sciences*, 2001, *24(1)*, 87–114.

DeCarlo, D., and Santella, A. "Stylization and Abstraction of Photographs." *Siggraph: Proceedings of the 29th Annual Conference on Computer Graphics and Interactive Techniques*, 2002, 769–776.

DiMarco, J. *Digital Design for Print and Web: An Introduction to Theory, Principles, and Techniques*. Hoboken, NJ: John Wiley & Sons, 2010.

Eitel, A. "How a Picture Facilitates the Process of Learning from Text: Evidence for Scaffolding." *Learning and Instruction*, 2013, *28*, 48–63.

Eisner, Will. *Graphic Storytelling and Visual Narrative*. New York, NY: W.W. Norton & Company, 2008.

Eppler, M. "A Comparison Between Concept Maps, Mind Maps, Conceptual Diagrams, and Visual Metaphors as Complementary Tools for Knowledge Construction and Sharing." *Information Visualization*, 2006, *5*, 202–210.

Few, S. *Show Me the Numbers: Designing Tables and Graphs to Enlighten*. Burlingame, CA: Analytics Press, 2013.

Feng, D., and Halloran, K. "Representing Emotive Meaning in Visual Images: A Social Semiotic Approach. *Journal of Pragmatics*, 2012, *44*, 2067–2084.

Frank, O., and Gilovich, T. "The Dark Side of Self- and Social Perception: Black Uniforms and Aggression in Professional Sports." *Journal of Personality and Social Psychology*, 1988, *54*(1), 74–85.

Galer, M. *Photography Foundations for Art and Design* (4th ed.). Burlington, MA: Focal Press, 2007.

Ginns, P. "Integrating Information: A Meta-Analysis of the Spatial Contiguity and Temporal Contiguity Effects." *Learning and Instruction*, 2006, *16*, 511–525.

Goodrich, K. "What's Up? Exploring Upper and Lower Visual Field Advertising Effects." *Journal of Advertising Research*, 2010, *50*, 91–106.

Healey, C. "Choosing Effective Colors for Data Visualization." *IEEE Visualization '96 Proceedings*, 1996, 263–270.

Hegarty, M., and Canham, M. "Effects of Knowledge and Display Design on Comprehension of Complex Graphics." *Learning and Instruction*, 2010, *20*(2), 155–166.

Hockley, Wiliam E., and Bancroft, Tyler. "Extensions of the Picture Superiority Effect in Associative Recognition." *Canadian Journal of Experimental Psychology*, 2011, *65*(4), 236–244.

Itten, Johannes. *The Art of Color: The Subjective Experience and Objective Rationale of Color*. Hoboken, NJ: John Wiley & Sons, 1997.

Jamet, E., Gavota, M., and Quaireau, C. "Attention Guiding in Multimedia Learning." *Learning and Instruction*, 2008, *18*, 135–145.

Joseph, J.H., and Dwyer, F. "The Effects of Prior Knowledge, Presentation Mode and Visual Realism on Student Achievement." *The Journal of Experimental Education*, 1984, *52*(2), 110–121.

Kaya, N., & Epps, H. "Relationship Between Color and Emotion: A Study of College Students." *College Student Journal*, 2004, *38*, 396–405.

Kosslyn, S. "Understanding Charts and Graphs." *Applied Cognitive Psychology*, 1989, *3*, 185–226.

Kosslyn, S. *Elements of Graph Design*. Cranbury, NJ, W.H: Freeman Publishers, 1994.

Kulhavy, R., Stock, W., and Kealy, W. "How Geographic Maps Increase Recall of Instructional Text." *Educational Technology Research and Development*, 1993, *41*(4), 47–62.

Larkin, J., and Simon, H. "Why a Diagram Is (Sometimes) Worth Ten Thousand Words." *Cognitive Science*, 1987, *11*, 65–69.

Laufer, D. *Dialogues with Creative Legends and Aha Moments in a Designer's Career*. San Francisco: New Riders, 2012.

Levie, W. "Research on Pictures: A Guide to the Literature." In D. Willows & H. Houghton (Eds.), *The Psychology of Illustration: Vol. 2, Basic Research*. New York, NY: Springer-Verlag, 1987.

Lin, Y., Yeh, C., and Wei, C. "How Will the Use of Graphics Affect Visual Aesthetics? A User-Centered Approach for Web Page Design." *International Journal of Human-Computer Studies*, 2013, *71*(3), 217–227.

Mangan, J. "Cultural Conventions of Pictorial Representation: Iconic Literacy and Education." *Educational Communication & Technology*, 1978, *26*(3), 245–267.

Marmor, M., and Ravin, J. *The Artist's Eyes*. New York, NY: Abrams Books, 2009.

Mayer, R.E. "Comprehension of Graphics in Texts: An Overview." *Learning and Instruction*, 1993, *3*(3), 239–245.

Mayer, R.E. *Multimedia Learning* (2nd ed.). New York, NY: Cambridge University Press, 2009.

Mayer, R.E., and Moreno, R. "Nine Ways to Reduce Cognitive Load in Multimedia Learning." *Educational Psychologist*, 2003, *38*(1), 43–52.

McCloud, S. *Making Comics: Storytelling Secrets of Comics, Manga and Graphic Novels*. New York, NY: Harpers, 2006.

Meggs, P., and Purvis, A. *Meggs' History of Graphic Design*. Hoboken, NJ: John Wiley & Sons, 2011.

Michas, I., and Berry, D. "Learning a Procedural Task: Effectiveness of Multimedia Presentations." *Applied Cognitive Psychology*, 2000, *14*(6), 555–575.

Norman, D. *The Design of Everyday Things* (rev. ed.). New York, NY: Basic Books, 2013.

Ozcelik, E., Karakus, T., Kursun, E., and Cagiltay, K. "An Eye-Tracking Study of How Color Coding Affects Multimedia Learning." *Computers & Education*, 2009, *53*(2), 445–453.

Ozcelik, E., Arslan-Ari, I., and Cagiltay, K. "Why Does Signaling Enhance Multimedia Learning? Evidence from Eye Movements." *Computers in Human Behavior*, 2010, *26*, 110–117.

Paivio, A. *Mental Representations: A Dual-Coding Approach*. New York, NY: Oxford University Press, 1986.

Paivio, A. "Dual Coding Theory and Education." Draft chapter for the conference on "Pathways to Literacy Achievement for High Poverty Children," The University of Michigan School of Education, 2006, September–October.

Palmer, S., and Rock, I. "Rethinking Perceptual Organization: The Role of Uniform Connectedness." *Psychonomic Bulletin & Review*, 1994, *1*(1), 29–55.

Perelman, A. "The Pyramid Scheme: Visual Metaphors and the USDA's Pyramid Food Guides." *Design Issues*, 2011, *27*(3), 60–71.

Pett, D., and Wilson, T. "Color Research and Its Application to the Design of Instructional Materials." *Educational Technology Research and Development*, 1996, *44*(3), 19–35.

Pham, M., Cohen, J., Pracejus, J., and Hughes, D. "Affect Monitoring and the Primacy of Feelings in Judgment." *Journal of Consumer Research*, 2001, *28*(2), 167–188.

Phillips, B. "Thinking into It: Consumer Interpretation of Complex Advertising Images." *The Journal of Advertising*, 1997, *26*(2), 77–87.

Pieters, F., and Wedel, M. "Attention Capture and Transfer by Elements of Advertisements." *Journal of Marketing*, 2004, *68*(2), 36–50.

Plass, J., Heidig, S., Hayward, E., Homer, B., and Um, E. "Emotional Design in Multimedia Learning: Effects of Shape and Color on Affect and Learning." *Learning and Instruction*, 2014, *29*, 128–140.

Poulin, Richard. *The Language of Graphic Design: An Illustrated Handbook for Understanding Fundamental Design Principles*. Beverly, MA: Rockport Publishers, 2011.

Prabu, D. "News Concreteness and Visual-Verbal Association: Do News Pictures Narrow the Recall Gap Between Concrete and Abstract News?" *Human Communication Research*, 1998, *25*(2), 180–201.

Reber, R., and Schwarz, N. "Effects of Perceptual Fluency on Judgments of Truth." *Consciousness and Cognition*, 1999, *8*, 338–342.

Salzt, I. *Typography Essentials: 100 Design Principles for Working with Type*. Beverly, MA: Rockport Publishers, 2011.

Scheiter, K., Gerjets, P., Huk, T., Imhof, B., and Kammerer, Y. "The Effects of Realism in Learning with Dynamic Visualizations." *Learning and Instruction*, 2009, *19*, 481–494.

Schnotz W., and Bannert, M. "Construction and Interference in Learning from Multiple Representation." *Learning and Instruction*, 2003, *13*(2), 141–156.

Schwarz, N. "Feelings as Information: Implications for Affective Influences on Information Processing." In L. Martin and G. Clore (Eds.), *Theories of Mood and Cognition: A User's Guidebook*. New York, NY: Psychology Press, 2001.

Song, H., and Schwarz, N. "If It's Hard to Read, It's Hard to Do: Processing Fluency Affects Effort Prediction and Motivation." *Psychological Science*, 2008, *19*, 986–988.

Smerecnik, C., Mesters, I., Kesels, L.T.E., Ruiter, R.A., De Vries, N.K., and De Vries, H. "Understanding the Positive Effects of Graphical Risk Information on Comprehension: Measuring Attention Directed to Written, Tabular, and Graphical Risk Information." *Risk Analysis*, 2010, *30*(9).

Snowden R., and Thompson, P. *Basic Vision: An Introduction to Visual Perception*. New York, NY: Oxford University Press, 2012.

Stoops, J., and Samuelson, J. *Design Dialogue*. Worcester, MA: Davis Publications, 1990.

Tabbers H., Martens, R., and van Merriënboer J. "Multimedia Instructions and Cognitive Load Theory: Effects of Modality and Cueing." *British Journal of Educational Psychology*, 2004, *74*(1), 71–81.

Taylor, C., Clifford, A., and Franklin, A. "Color Preferences Are Not Universal." *Journal of Experimental Psychology: General*, 2013, *142*(4), 1015–1027.

Tselentis, J. *The Graphic Designer's Electronic-Media Manual: How to Apply Visual Design Principles to Engage Users on Desktop, Tablet, and Mobile Websites*. Beverly, MA: Rockport Publishers, 2012.

Tucker, J. "Psychology of Color." *Target Marketing*, 1987, *10*(7), 40–49.

Tukey, John. "Data-Based Graphics: Visual Display in the Decades to Come." *Statistical Science*, 1990, *5*(3), 327–339.

Tversky, B., Morrison, J., and Betrancourt, M. "Animation: Can It Facilitate?" *International Journal of Human-Computer Studies*, 2002, *57*, 247–262.

Tversky, B. "Visualizing Thought." *Topics in Cognitive Science*, 2011, *3*(3), 499–535.

Um, E., Plass, J., Hayward, E., and Homer, D. "Emotional Design in Multimedia Learning." *Journal of Educational Psychology*, 2012, *104*(2), 485–498.

Valdez, P., and Mehrabian, Albert M. "Effects of Color on Emotions." *Journal of Experimental Psychology: General*, 1994, *123*(4), 394–409.

Vekiri, I. "What Is the Value of Graphical Displays in Learning?" *Educational Psychology Review*, 2002, *14*(3), 261–312.

Walker, Mort. *The Lexicon of Comicana*. Lincoln, NE: iUniverse.com, 2000.

Ware, C. *Visual Thinking*. Waltham, MA: Morgan Kaufmann, 2008.

Ware, C. *Information Visualization*. Waltham, MA: Morgan Kaufmann, 2012.

Weinschenk, S. *100 Things Every Designer Needs to Know About People*. Berkeley, CA: New Riders, 2011.

White, Alex. *The Elements of Graphic Design*. New York: Skyhorse Publishing, Inc., 2011.

Whitehouse, A., Maybery, M., and Durkin, K. "The Development of the Picture-Superiority Effect." *British Journal of Developmental Psychology*, 2006, *24*(4), 767–773.

Williams, R. *The Non-Designer's Presentation Book: Principles for Effective Presentation Design*. San Francisco, CA: Peachpit Press, 2009.

Willingham, D. "Is It True That Some People Just Can't Do Math?" *American Educator*, 2009–2010, Winter, 14–19.

Winn, W. "Learning from Maps and Diagrams." *Educational Psychology Review*, 1991, *3*(3), 211–247.

Wigan, M. *The Visual Dictionary of Illustration*. New York, NY: Fairchild Books, 2009.

Yau, Nathan. *Data Points: Visualization That Means Something*. Hoboken, NJ: John Wiley & Sons, 2013.

Zang, L., and Lin, W. *Selective Visual Attention: Computational Models and Applications*. Hoboken, NJ: Wiley-IEEE Press, 2013.

ABOUT THE AUTHOR

Connie Malamed consults, writes, and speaks in the fields of online learning, visual communication, and information design through her company, Connie Malamed Consulting. She has more than twenty years of experience designing learning and visual solutions for nonprofit organizations, higher education, government, and business.

She is the author of *Visual Language for Designers,* the writer behind the popular website, theelearningcoach.com, and the creator of Instructional Design Guru, a mobile reference app for instructional design. Malamed is fascinated with the intersection of cognitive psychology and visual communication. With degrees in art education and instructional design, she energetically pursues ways to improve instructional and information graphics.

Index

Page references followed by *fig* indicate an illustrated figure; followed by *t* indicate a table.